Praise for *Trans Yout*

"*Trans Youth Stories* is absolutely incredible. I devoured it, beginning to end. The pieces made me smile, cry, laugh out loud, and feel my heart practically bursting inside my chest with pride and admiration for these young people generously sharing their deeply personal art and stories with us. I think this work is exactly what is needed to further understanding and support for young trans and gender-nonconforming people."
—Theresa Thorn, co-host of the *One Bad Mother* podcast and author of
It Feels Good to Be Yourself: A Book About Gender Identity

"Each voice in *Trans Youth Stories* uniquely and eloquently conveys the trans youth experience. And that experience is not solely one of crisis and transition—there are many ways to be trans, and this book is about listening to trans youth, honoring their experiences, and uplifting their knowledge. A must-read!"
—Kathie Moehlig, Founder, TransFamily Support Services

"*Trans Youth Stories* makes an important addition to the literature on trans and non-binary youth experiences. Each theme centres trans voices from start to end and is commented on by trans scholars who offer thoughtful reflections on possible ways forward to better support and accompany young people on their journey as growing human beings. *Trans Youth Stories* should be included in all school curricula as it provides powerful material to discuss issues related to gender identity and gender expression in various contexts."
—Annie Pullen Sansfaçon, Professor and Canada Research Chair on Transgender Children and their Families, School of Social Work, Université de Montréal

"*Trans Youth Stories* is an illuminating window into the diverse lives of our trans and gender creative youth. They share outstanding stories of self-discovery, bravery, and resilience as they deal with navigating gender journeys, discrimination, mental health difficulties, families, and school life. Family members, care providers, teachers, and youth should read *Trans Youth Stories* to understand the lived experiences of our trans and gender creative kids."
—Dr. Charles Ho, MD, Child & Adolescent Psychiatrist, BC Children's Hospital Gender Clinic

"The collection of stories, poems, and artwork in *Trans Youth Stories* provides the reader with insight into the maelstrom of ups and downs, fears and triumphs, and self-reflections and affirmations that is the lived experience of many trans youth. The contributing authors and artists have generously shared their deeply personal, witty, insightful, and sometimes dead-silly, thoughts and musings, and the reader will hopefully get a sense of the vast panoply of identities and the hard-fought resilience that have emerged as these youth come to be the person they see inside."
—Daniel L. Metzger, MD, Pediatric Endocrinologist, BC Children's Hospital
Clinical Professor, University of British Columbia

"Voice matters. In a world that too often silences, sensationalises and simplifies trans youth experiences, *Trans Youth Stories* is a vital tonic. A vibrant collection that powerfully shares the everyday moments, feelings, and challenges of being and becoming trans, with guiding questions and resources to find out more. Dive into the diversity and enjoy this open dialogue with the experiences of trans youth in their own words."
—EJ Renold, Professor of Childhood Studies, Cardiff University

"Beguiling, provoking, unsettling, generative, this book takes us into the becoming of trans youth. Their words and art are connected through commentary to scholarship in trans studies, histories, literatures and practice to illuminating effect. An invaluable resource for all those working with, caring for and about trans youth and issues—and for anyone interested in the exuberant, gender-troubling creativity and insight with which trans youth invent themselves. In their own words: a unique, a wonderful thing ... a work of art."
—Dr. Sara Bragg, Lecturer and Programme Leader in the Sociology of Education, UCL Institute of Education

"This book uniquely combines the experience of trans youth with the understanding of adult researchers. 'Strength is not ignoring the hurt, it's softening into it and living through it,' Riley writes. Trans youth will see their experience of transphobia and resilience mirrored in the book, and adult allies will find context and explanation. A stunning resource."
—barbara findlay QC

"It is so incredibly important that trans youth tell their own stories and are able to see themselves reflected—this book is an absolutely gorgeous and inspiring example of just how resilient and beautiful our young people are. Our young people are the future, and it's certainly looking bright."
—Fox and Owl, My Genderation

"This book is exactly what the world needs right now. We've heard from doctors, we've heard from parents, we've heard from teachers. It's time we hand over the mic to trans kids themselves. And this book does that so beautifully. It's a tome full of inspiring resilience and determination. It's a perfect 'it gets better' collection."
—Justin Tindall, MPH, Director, Programs and Operations, It Gets Better Project

"In creating a narrative that goes beyond 'those of tragedy or triumph,' *Trans Youth Stories* has filled a glaring gap in the catalogue of writings about transgender and other gender diverse young people. Highlighting many of the unique gender-related experiences of these amazing kids, the book also demonstrates that our trans youth have complex and full lives beyond their own gender journeys. In so doing, they help to inform the reader's appreciation for the unique gender of all young people."
—Joel Baum, MS, Senior Director, Professional Development, Gender Spectrum

"*Trans Youth Stories* is a powerful tool that challenges preconceived notions by providing a space for trans youth to be themselves. These stories inform and uplift. In other words, they show trans youth as more than their oppression. *Trans Youth Stories* reshapes the stories we believe to be true by sharing the stories we live to tell."
—Trans Student Educational Resources (TSER)

"This book's publication is timely. Gender diverse young people including those who are trans and non-binary now feature frequently in the media. Their medical care, which is vital for many of them, is undergoing intense scrutiny through Court hearings and major reviews. So far, the voices of these young people themselves have scarcely featured in the debates. This fine book will help to redress that imbalance."
—Gender Identity Research & Education Society (GIRES)

Trans Youth Stories

Trans Youth Stories

An Intergenerational Dialogue after the "Trans Tipping Point"

Edited by Dr. Lindsay Herriot and Kate Fry

WOMEN'S PRESS

Toronto | Vancouver

Trans Youth Stories: An Intergenerational Dialogue after the "Trans Tipping Point"
Edited by Dr. Lindsay Herriot and Kate Fry

First published in 2021 by
Women's Press, an imprint of CSP Books Inc.
425 Adelaide Street West, Suite 200
Toronto, Ontario
M5V 3C1

www.womenspress.ca

Library and Archives Canada Cataloguing in Publication

Title: Trans youth stories : an intergenerational dialogue after the "trans tipping point" / edited
    by Dr. Lindsay Herriot and Kate Fry.
Names: Herriot, Lindsay, editor. | Fry, Kate, editor.
Description: Includes bibliographical references.
Identifiers: Canadiana (print) 20210227257 | Canadiana (ebook) 20210227311 | ISBN
    9780889616257 (softcover) | ISBN 9780889616264 (PDF) | ISBN 9780889616271 (EPUB)
Subjects: LCSH: Transgender people's writings, Canadian. | LCSH: Youths' writings, Canadian.
    | LCSH: Transgender youth—Canada—Juvenile literature. | LCSH: Transgender people—
    Canada—Juvenile literature. | CSH: Canadian literature (English)—21st century.
Classification: LCC PS8235.T45 T73 2021 | DDC jC810.8/092830971—dc23

Cover image by Astrid Neilson-Miller and Asa O'Connor-Jaeckel
Cover design by Em Dash
Page layout by S4Carlisle Publishing Services

21 22 23 24 25   5 4 3 2 1

Printed and bound in Ontario, Canada

Canadä

Dedication

To trans youth: past, present, and future

Table of Contents

Acknowledgements

Trans Youth Stories was at one point named after a project titled the Trans Tipping Point (TTP), now called the Gender Generations Project (GGP). It is an intergenerational community that serves trans youth. Mentors are the heart of the GGP, and without their generosity in relationship building and workshop programming, the GGP simply would not exist. We are grateful to the following mentors for their love and expertise over the years: Akira Imai, Al Cusack, Alexa McDaniel, Arran Liddel, Astrid Carter, Charlie/Henrietta Dubét, Chase Willier, Christopher Wolff, Cole Devoy, Dani Cooper, Gavin Somers, Jo Cuffe, Jo Nazatul, Julian Paquette, Kai Taddei, Kat Palmateer, Kori Doty, Laurie Feehan, Rose Cotton, Sabrina Symington, Serena Bhandar, Ziggy Schutz, Sophia Rawl, Tash McAdam, and Will Weigler. In addition to the mentors, Morgane Oger and Dr. Lee Airton served as unifying, energizing, and inspiring keynote speakers who gave us all new ways to think about trans activism, resistance, and resilience.

If the mentors are the GGP's heart, then its volunteers are surely its backbone. Many of the following individuals, couples, and families opened their homes and billeted youth and mentors and then rolled up their sleeves to run the kitchen. Behind the scenes they gave rides and swept floors, took out the garbage, and set up tables. We are so grateful to Arran Liddel and Gen Walsh; Ashling Ligate and Beckham Ronaghan; Astri Jack and Ainsley Kling; Chava Nagalia; Darcy Allder and Heather Zeh-Allder; David Tillson; Glynne and Suzie Evans; Jordan Watters; Katrina McGee and David, Sol, and Rosa Bodrug; Kelly Legge/Persi Flage; Lindsay Cavanaugh; Whitney Walsh; Macaulay Mauro; Morgan Brooks; Nickie and Tyler Lewis; Robin Stevenson and Cheryl May; Roe and Corrie Campbell; Sean Brown; Shahriar Khan; and Zinnia Clark and Tyler Schaus.

The GGP gratefully acknowledges and appreciates the monetary and in-kind donations of the following organizations who took a chance on a fledgling research project and whose material contributions made the magic happen: the British Columbia Teachers' Federation (BCTF); the British Columbia Ministry of Children and Family Development (MCFD); Community Cabbage; the Centre for Outreach Education (CORE) at Uvic; Vanya McDonell, Thomas King, and the team at the Fairfield Gonzales Community Association; UVic's Legacy and Legacy Maltwood art galleries; Jason Venkaya and Oregano's Pizza; PFLAG Victoria; Power to Be; the Tegan and Sara Foundation; Tessa McLoughlin and the team at KWENCH; Trans Care BC; Vancouver City Savings Credit Union; the Vancouver Island Public Interest Research Group (VIPIRG); the Victoria Foundation; and the Victoria Pride Society.

Finally, we are grateful to Lizzie Di Giacomo, Katie Yantzi, the blind reviewers, and the team at Canadian Scholars Press who took a chance on this new type of text and generously and graciously guided it through to fruition.

KATE:

I would like to first thank my former roommates at Bisley House: Haneen Ghebari, Dana Johnson, Bonnie Wearmouth, and Amy Bader. They were not only hugely supportive during GGP's first year but were also patient in putting up with my antics and generously opening their home to house-visiting mentors. I'm appreciative of the support of my parents, Jake Fry and Dr. Beth Seaton. I feel lucky to have grown up in a household that was accepting of LGBTQ+ people well before I was born. My participation in this project was informed by the fantastic friends I've made throughout my life: Jae Levy, Kara Stanton, Kelly McLeod, Katie Hughes, Avery Burrow, Ciara Gordon, Evan Wendel, and Gina Hay. I am constantly learning what community means from you. Last but certainly not least, huge thanks to Dr. Lindsay Herriot, who has been an incredible mentor to me and without whom I would never have had the opportunity to work on this extraordinary project.

LINDSAY:

First and foremost, I'm appreciative of Lauren M., who shared the challenges and magic of gender transition with me so many years ago. Wishing that this book had existed when you were a little girl, or even when you were socially and medically transitioning as an adult, was in many ways the inspiration for this project. I am also grateful to long-time mentor Dr. Alan Sears, whose peerless example of how to build mentoring relationships informed the structure, process, research design, and community-building of the GGP.

Working with co-founder and co-conspirator Kate Fry for all these years has been a dream come true. Not many people would turn a casual coffee conversation into a multi-year, fly-by-the-seat-of-your-pants adventure, but that's Kate. Thank you, Kate, for your friendship, spontaneity, inventiveness, and quick wit. Likewise, considerable gratitude is owed to jack-of-all-trades Tash McAdam, who served as a founding mentor, volunteer, managing editor, and problem solver extraordinaire. Your meticulous organizational skills and logistical wizardry are legendary. Thank you also to my colleagues Dr. Lee Airton, Don Cochrane, and Dr. Kathy Sanford for believing in this unconventional approach to participatory action research from its inception.

Every editor should be blessed by dear ones such as Amy Ashmore, Dr. James Grayson, Alison Zacharias, Caitlin Mooney, Dr. Paula Dubois, and Dr. Rod Knight, who provided levity and cheerleading throughout. Furthermore, my folks, Blaine Lewis and Leone Wilkinson, took their usual enthusiastic encouragement of me to new levels by running errands, coordinating the pizza parties and barbecues, and being on grandparent duty so I could do this work. I was also lucky to be surrounded by a smattering of supportive siblings, such as my sister, Dr. Lara Hiseler; godsisters Bekah Sears and Dr. Dusty Johnstone; brothers Sean Lewis, Seth Bryant, and Andrew Manderson; brother-in-law Rob Hiseler; and sisters-in-law Ana Manderson and Jody Reimer, who offered wisdom and mirth throughout.

On the home front, I am continually appreciative of my children, Finnegan and Corbin, who were so patient while I did this work. May the world you grow up in be filled with lots of joyful gender identities and expressions. Finally, I cherish the incalculable emotional and practical contributions of my long-suffering and good-humored spouse, Ryan. I am grateful to you most of all.

Trans Tipping Point Logo

By Dylan Ariawan, age 18, and Elliot Kahn, age 10

The Trans Tipping Point logo was conceptually created within a day and started with the yin yang design of two elements. We specifically chose the transgender and non-binary flags to represent the organization because most of the participants identify in the transgender and non-binary spectrum. The community focuses more on the experience of gender than sexuality, so it is a safe space for all to relate to each other.

Introduction

By Dr. Lindsay Herriot and Kate Fry

Welcome.

This book began as a conversation, and we hope it will spark many more. Standing in front of the Vancouver Skytrain one otherwise ordinary morning, we (Lindsay and Kate) lamented how we seemed to only come across two narratives of young, transgender life in the mainstream: those of tragedy or triumph. We knew from our trans friends and family that there were so many more complex, messy, and nuanced stories of young trans life and wished more of these multidimensional stories were more widespread. Saddened, we wondered: if that lack of diversity was uncomfortable to us as cisgender, bisexual/lesbian women, how might it feel for our trans siblings and especially for trans youth?

The Transgender Tipping Point (TTP), now called the Gender Generations Project (GGP), was born out of that conversation and out of a need for many more conversations and representations of what young trans life might look and feel and be like. Recognizing how cis adults tend to do most of the talking about trans youth, we wondered how we might use our cis adult privilege to centre trans youth instead. The goal was not to "give" trans youth a voice—they already have one—but rather to harness our privilege to amplify those voices.

Hosted by the University of Victoria and the Fairfield Gonzales Community Association on unceded Lekwungen-speaking territories in Victoria, British Columbia, Canada, we coordinated three weekend-long writing retreats for trans youth, ages ten to eighteen, from across the country. A team of all-trans adult mentors—ranging from emerging to established artists, authors, activists, and academics—applied to come and teach, while Kate and Lindsay tended to tender hearts and washed dishes.[1] The result of these retreats is this book, which is a humble addition to the growing body of work by and for trans youth.

This collection presents a spectrum of life experiences from trans youth under the age of eighteen. Their stories are told in art, poetry, fiction, memoir, letters, and essays. Some of the stories might feel heavy, while others are light-hearted or even a bit silly. Some of them might introduce you to ideas you've never thought about before, while others might feel all too relatable. Some probably do all of the above! At the beginning of each chapter, we ask questions that will help you reflect on the stories and draw connections to your own life, regardless of your own gender identity or expression. We also open each chapter with a list of books we love, curated by genre, so that readers of all ages and abilities can "choose their own adventure" in learning more about the themes from each section.

Each chapter concludes with a response by an adult scholar in transgender studies, offering tips and advice for what readers can do next. Nearly all of the adult scholars are also trans themselves, and half of them served as a mentor or volunteer during the retreats, which means they knew and worked with the very youth whose work they responded to. The adult responses do not evaluate or correct what the youth expressed but instead offer research-based context and commentary from beginning and experienced scholars. Structuring the book in this way centres youth voices and expertise in an intergenerational dialogue of what it might mean to be a young trans person today.

Not every reader will see their own experiences reflected back to them in this volume. Although the authors embody ethnic, geographic, and gender diversity, the same identities that are already privileged (that is, white, masculine, able-bodied, etc.) are similarly overrepresented here. Furthermore, our youth participant pool reflects our location in coastal British Columbia. Had the GGP developed in a different province, then the youth authors would have surely come from similarly nearby geography. Thankfully, this is not the final word on young trans life, either in Canada or elsewhere. *Trans Youth Stories* is instead a modest first step in broadening existing narratives of young, trans realities in a single volume. It is a sample of some, but certainly not all, or even most, of the stories about what it might be like to grow up trans.[2] We're optimistic that this is the beginning of many more published works by trans youth and invite readers to start dreaming up, drafting, and diversifying version 2.0. For a more detailed account of how this book came to be, please see the concluding methodology chapter at the end of this volume.

Enjoy.

ABOUT THE GENDER GENERATIONS PROJECT

The GGP began as a one-year writing project that grew into an ongoing intentional, intersectional, and intergenerational collective. Centring all trans, non-binary, Two-Spirit, and otherwise non-cisgender youth in the fullness of all of their identities, we welcome mentors, volunteers, and their loved ones to build gender joy. Headquartered on unceded Lekwungen-speaking territories in Victoria, British Columbia, we offer free services, programming, volunteering, and paid work opportunities year-round. One hundred per cent of the royalties from this book go to support the GGP. Please visit gendergeneration.org for more information.

THE CASE FOR A YOUTH-AUTHORED SCHOLARLY ANTHOLOGY

The caring professions[3] have a long history of academic writing about children and youth. Our data often takes the form of observations, interviews, photovoice, focus groups, and youth-created drawings, and is communicated through adult-authored manuscripts. This work has contributed to the expanding knowledge base about children and youth, and how the caring professions might better engage with them.

Often absent from all of these methods, including participatory action research, are pieces of research that are written by youth themselves. Taking the maxim "nothing about us without us" from disability studies to heart, as well as Article 12 from the UN Convention on the Rights of the Child's statement that "children have the right to freely express their views on all matters and decisions that affect them, and to have those views taken into account at all levels of society" (UNHRCRC, ratified in 1989), this book partially fills that gap. We are hopeful that the scholarly world in particular will benefit from including a youth-authored volume among its ranks to complement the more traditional methods of research reporting. From a methodological perspective, a youth-authored book powerfully changes research *about* youth to research *with and by* youth.

To avoid romanticizing youth voices, our book includes adult perspectives as responses to the youth writing at the conclusion of each thematic section. This intergenerational dialogue links the youth's work to the scholarly literature in the field and offers crucial academic and practical interpretations. Rather than an authoritative evaluation of the youth's work, the scholarly responses summarize, contextualize, and extend each thematic section. These seven responses could easily constitute a book on their own, but to assemble them separately would miss the point of this methodological approach, namely that adults use their power and privilege to amplify and engage with youth telling their own stories. The responses, therefore, are literally at the periphery of each section, with the youth-created writing occupying the centre. This reasoning is also why we have included the methodology section at the end rather than the beginning of this volume; we needed the youth's expertise of their own lives to take centre stage.

In addition to the content-specific research about the various domains of youth trans life in the volume, our book is presented as a methodological roadmap for how youth-centred and youth-authored contributions can add to the growing field of participatory action research. We look forward to seeing many more youth-authored collections about a host of lived experiences and identities becoming post-secondary textbooks and mainstream volumes.

NOTES

1. An in-depth description of our process and methodology is in the Appendix at the end of this volume.
2. The Books We Love lists at the beginning of each chapter were curated with this gap in mind. Texts were selected to spotlight stories that were sadly underrepresented in our own book, particularly those from Two-Spirit and BIPOC trans women, girls, and femmes.
3. Can include, but are not limited to: child and youth care, counselling, education, health sciences, medicine, nursing, occupational therapy, psychology, social work, speech therapy, etc.

CHAPTER ONE

Childhood Cultures

KEY THEMES

- Gender roles in children's media
- Gender in play/playing with gender
- Adult and internalized expectations of children's gender expressions

CRITICAL QUESTIONS

- How did you understand gender as a child? Do you have specific childhood memories of learning about or playing with gender? For example, do you remember any games or toys you were told you should or shouldn't play/play with because of your gender?
- How does children's media currently portray the gender binary? If you could make changes to the way gender is represented in one piece of children's media, what might they be?
- How do adults shape, reinforce, and disrupt dominant gender roles?

BOOKS WE LOVE

Picture Books

Bone, J., Bone, L., & Docampo, V. (2014). *Not every princess*. Washington: Magination.

Ismail, Yasmeen. (2016). *I'm a girl!*. London: Bloomsbury. *Also available in French*

Pitman, G. E., & Tobacco, V. (2020). *My Maddy*. Washington: Magination Press.

Stevenson, R. (2021). *Pride puppy!* Victoria: Orca Books.

Walton, J., & MacPherson, D. (2016). *Introducing Teddy: A gentle story about gender and friendship*. New York: Bloomsbury.

YA and Graphic Novels

Gino, A. (2019). *George*. New York: Scholastic Press. *Also available in French*

G, M., & Zuckerberg, J. R. (2019). *A quick & easy guide to queer & trans identities*. Portland: Limerence Press.

John-Barker, M., & Scheele, J. (2020). *Gender: An illustrated guide*. London: Icon Books.

Nicholson, H. (2016). *Love beyond body, space and time: An Indigenous LGBT sci-fi anthology*. Winnipeg, MB: Bedside Press.

Ryle, R. (2019). *She/he/they/me: For the sisters, misters, and binary resisters.* Naperville, IL: Sourcebooks Inc.

General Audience

Ehrensaft, D. (2017). *The gender creative child: Pathways for nurturing and supporting children who live outside gender boxes.* New York: The Experiment.

Gill-Peterson, J. (2018). *Histories of the transgender child.* Minneapolis: University of Minnesota Press.

Gosset, R., Stanley, E., & Burton, J. (2017). *Trap door: Trans cultural production and the politics of visibility.* Boston: MIT Press.

Meadow, T. (2018). *Trans kids: Being gendered in the 21st century.* Oakland, CA: University of California Press.

Travers, A. (2019). *The trans generation: How trans kids (and their parents) are creating a gender revolution.* New York: New York University Press.

Memoirs/First Person Narratives

Bird, J. (2019). *Sorted: Growing up, coming out, and finding my place (a transgender memoir).* New York: Tiller Press.

Dawson, K. (2018). *Gender games: The problem with men and women from someone who has been both.* London: Two Roads.

Johnson, G. M. (2020). *All boys aren't blue: A memoir-manifesto.* New York: Farrar, Straus, and Giroux.

Kobabe, M. (2020). *Gender queer: A memoir.* Portland: Oni-Lion Forge Publishing Group.

Proulx-Turner, S. (2008). *She walks for days inside a thousand eyes: A two-spirit story.* Winnipeg, MB: Turnstone Press.

The Blue Fairy

By Ajam, age 14, and Owen Miller, age 16

and the mauve ones
are boys,

and the white ones
are girls,

and the blue ones
are just little
sillies who are not
sure what they are.

-Peter Pan
J.M.Barrie

Mixed-Up

By Asa O'Connor-Jaeckel, age 13

Have you seen
Those children's toys?
The ones at kids' sections
In libraries
Or in daycares.
The ones with three cubes
On a vertical pole
That you can spin around.

On each side of the cube
Is the head, body or feet
Of a cartoon animal.
If you spin the cubes in
Different directions
You can get a mixed-up body
Of an animal.
The lines will match up
But the rest won't fit.
That's how it feels sometimes.
Somebody spun my cubes
And I'm all mixed up.
But the rest of me isn't on
Those cubes.

Pink Herrings

By Christopher, age 17

The doctor's office feels perfectly square
A cubic terrarium for one anomaly
When he leans forward and says to me,
"Surely there must've been signs."

I say, "Surely there must've been, sir,
But when I was an infant, I didn't know how to speak."
Funny how infants can be—
And between all the gibberish and crying
(Though maybe I cried because I was so misaligned)
It was difficult to distinguish the babbling from the prophecy.

"Surely there must've been signs, sir,
When I clambered from the crib to the playground
And built a new identity out of sand and mismatched Legos.
Surely it was obvious: boy now, boy then.
But I was also a velociraptor
And a dragon tamer
And a space captain.

"Surely there must've been signs,
But when I wasn't out hunting outlaws
I was having tea parties with the plush cavalier
In an empire of rosy sheets and dollhouse furniture
Painting butterflies, humming lullabies
Not knowing that signs cancel out signs.

"Sir, I'm sure there were signs
Lost amongst these pink herrings
And I'll dig up each one if that's what it takes
But what better sign than me sitting here now?
And I can't help but wonder what difference it makes."

Avatars

By Lupus, age 14

This piece is dedicated to all those who could not be freed from their cage, and for the people strong enough to break through.

Have you ever heard of the video games *The Sims 4* or *IMVU* (*I Am Virtual You*)? Well, they are both avatar games—games in which you create your own character. The best thing about these games is that your character can be anything … in the binary world of Male and Female. Do you ever see those *Game of War* advertisements with the blond lady that has big breasts? What about *GTA* (*Grand Theft Auto*) games, where all the young guys have six-packs or eight-packs and huge muscles? I'm not saying that it's wrong for every character (male or female) to have Barbie/Ken figures. It's just unrealistic.

Personally, I don't mind the gender binary in some of these games. I find fake virtual males with lots of muscles kind of attractive. At least they are somewhat achievable and realistic for real humans. (Everybody is different; don't feel bad if you don't have big bulky muscles.) On the other hand, in every single game I've seen with female avatars, all the avatars have big butts and breasts and teeny-tiny waists. I probably don't like that idea because I'm not attracted to females, although it could also be my view of a reflection of what society thinks women should look like. Whatever it is, I don't approve.

In contrast, in the game *The Sims 4* you can create your own virtual characters that can range from fat to skinny, buff to bony, etc. However, the game still stays within the gender binary. I don't think that many game developers actually know what the term *non-binary* means, but the game still gives all types of clothing for both sexes/genders. I know clothes aren't the only thing that contributes to a non-binary individual, but it's a pretty great option to have a variety of clothing to choose from. When designing a character, you can adjust their size, shape, and every little detail of every little thing about them. That leaves you with your own personally designed character, fit to your taste. (God, I sound like I'm writing a game review.)

I really love these games because I get to create a "me" that I like. This character is the person I see in the mirror. This character is what I hope to someday be. To be truthful, I'm already halfway there. I have been most of my life, because on the inside, I already am that avatar.

Be It Not Black and White

By Ajam, age 14

Childhood and Cultural Representations

By Christopher Wolff

The poems, stories, and artworks of the trans and non-binary youth in this first chapter represent the poignant insights these youth have about their own experiences with the rigid binary of gender that is enforced upon all of us before we can even name it. I will continue the challenge in their works by discussing the shifting notions about gender and the gender binary they are responding to, and how their work connects with increasing, more nuanced trans visibility and representation in art and media, including film and TV, video games, and literature, as well as how cis stereotypes of gender continue to limit the full spectrum of expression of the experience of being trans and non-binary.

When friends of mine had their first child, they told me the question they got the most (before and after the birth) was: "Is it a boy or a girl?" My friends refused to answer this question, and also pointed out how it didn't really matter, and every time, the person who was asking got quite upset. It seems that people *have* to know your gender, even if you aren't born yet, and there are only the two options: male or female.

The pieces in the first chapter of this book show that this is not true. The youth of the Gender Generations Project (GGP), for whom I have served as a trans adult mentor in the workshops leading up to the writing of this book, know that. I have talked with them about the fact that the gender binary, while seeming impervious, is extremely limiting in describing our own realities. These youth know that, instead, gender has many flavours, some in-between, some entirely outside of the female–male spectrum. And they also know that, even in the year 2021, when transgender and non-binary and Two-Spirit people have become much more visible, a lot of folks still try by all means to keep the outdated model of the gender binary alive.

CHALLENGING THE GENDER BINARY

Take Ajam's beautiful painting "Be It Not Black and White." The painting's title works with another equally artificial binary—black/white—and juxtaposes that (racially charged) binary with the colors that are most symbolic of the gender binary: pink (femininity) and blue (masculinity). Notions of certain traits associated with gender are directly corresponding to how children should dress and behave; how they should *be*. Modern advertising has only reinforced that with waves of pink princesses and blue superheroes, and little boys certainly can't wear pink, much less a dress. That is how it (mostly) still works in our cisnormative world, a world that assumes that "people normally or naturally remain in the gender they were assigned at birth" (Barker & Scheele, 2016). Ajam's literal blurring of these gendered lines, by letting the pink and blue fade in different shades, bringing grey areas to the forefront, emphasizes that those boundaries are not as clean-cut as they seem to be. Having certain colours for certain genders and gendered traits is much more arbitrary, as a look at history shows: only a hundred years ago, Western society deemed it the other way around, with pink being the boy colour and blue the girl colour (Feinberg, 1996, p. 106). This is a reminder for us that attitudes about gender roles and their accessories change, and also that these changes and attitudes have imposed rigid hierarchies on people by associating their gender with a cultural normative standard of existence. Western societies in particular have also enforced gender normativity as part of colonization, whereas Indigenous cultures often were and are much more fluid and varied when it comes to gender expression (Driskill et al., 2011a, p. 34). Only recently have these histories been unearthed and reclaimed, undermining the white, Western notion of fixed genders and corresponding traits. The term *Two-Spirit* is as an important counterbalance to non-Western, non-white gender and sexual expression, giving voice and visibility to identities from different Indigenous cultures that continue to be oppressed and erased (for more on Two-Spirit identities, please see Driskill et al., *Queer Indigenous Studies* and *Sovereign Erotics* [both 2011] as well as Whitehead [2020], *Love After the End*).

Art has often presented and worked with shifting notions of gender, especially when the culture at large was still struggling with processing these changes. Encouraging youth to work creatively—to work with the knowledge they have about themselves—is something parents, educators, and other allies can and should do. Through writing, drawing, painting, making music, etc., youth can find their voice and express what they feel more easily. As an adult mentor who has witnessed the youth of the GGP creating stories and images for this book, it is astonishing, beautiful, and spectacular to see how they all have blossomed through being creative together. Research by Karkou and Glasman (2004), Houbolt (2010), Bungay and Vella-Burrows (2013), and others supports that impression: personal development in youth is strongly fostered by being able to create art.

TRANS AND NON-BINARY IMAGES IN THE MEDIA

We are always hoping to find ourselves in others, especially as young people—to find a connection between us and our fellow humans. A big part of establishing that connection is through our culture, and the images our culture chooses as representative for us. Until recently, trans folks had a hard time seeing anybody like themselves in popular culture. And if we did, it was cisgender people's ideas of who we are. Trans people have been portrayed as villains, freaks, and victims, making others shudder, pity, and objectify us, as the 2020 documentary *Disclosure* so painfully reveals. We have been exotic objects to be gawked at and made fun of. Characters written by cisgender authors choosing an "outlandish" topic. Roles played by cisgender actors looking for a "challenging" part. Documentaries made by cisgender filmmakers showing only the most exploitative moments of our struggles. These kinds of portrayals have really hurt us, because they have reinforced negative stereotypes about transgender folks and made us into caricatures instead of real people, as the GLAAD report *Victims or Villains: Examining Ten Years of Transgender Images on Television* (2012) and other research (Phillips, 2006) has found.

Not to mention that, oftentimes, these portrayals have conflated gender and sexuality (Erickson-Schroth, 2014, p. 554), as if the experiences of all people in the LGBTQ+ community are the same. Particularly for young trans and non-binary people, these viewing experiences are depressing and hurtful, leaving them wondering if society will ever accept them as themselves.

Thankfully these stereotypes are beginning to vanish. Take Hollywood, the dream machine responsible for many of our ideas about how others live and what they look like. Slowly but steadily, transgender representation is making inroads, especially in TV. Actors like Laverne Cox (*Orange Is the New Black*) and Leo Sheng (*the L Word: Generation Q*) are having great success and are tearing down walls that have made trans performers invisible until now. Directors like Lana and Lilly Wachowski and TV producers like Janet Mock are creating nuanced, complex roles for trans actors in groundbreaking shows like *Sense8* (2015) and *Pose* (2018). "The characters become more iconic because the people representing them are also transgender. It takes the story from a place of purely make-believe a[nd] repositions it as a radical act i[n] telling narratives that are nontraditional, but extremely important to hear" (Conrad, 2015, p. 10). While actors and celebrities are mostly part of the adult world, their visibility reaches all generations of trans people, influencing how youth experience a sense of which bodies are considered beautiful and "normal." We will therefore need trans actors of all sizes, shapes, and looks (particularly BIPOC trans and non-binary actors) to reach the same status cisgender adults currently hold in media culture—certainly not an easy task considering Hollywood's continued investment in cisnormative beauty standards. There is much work left to be done. For example, there is the continued practice of casting of cis actors in trans roles (e.g., Matt Bomer in the 2018 film *Anything*, or Scarlett Johannson's attempted casting as a trans man), which Hollywood still deems perfectly acceptable. No major American studio film has ever featured a transgender actor in a transgender role.[1] As Conrad writes, "There absolutely needs to be a reenvisioning of acting standards when it comes to transness and the portrayal of trans bodies; particularly that standard needs to be centered on the plethora of trans experiences as dictated by actual trans people. It's inadequate to position ... cisgender interpretations of transness as the epitome of transgender experience" (2015, p. 13). Hopefully the public outcry from trans people and their allies will soon make the practice of casting cis actors in trans roles obsolete, and we will see more trans actors hired for complex, interesting, and positive portrayals of people like ourselves.

Documentaries like *The Death and Life of Marsha P. Johnson* (2017)[2] are also unearthing the significant contributions and legacies of trans women of colour in the rise of the gay rights movement. And some reality TV shows have exposed a wide audience to the reality of the trans experience, such as *I Am Cait* (2015–2016), depicting Caitlyn Jenner's post-transition life (and also featuring trans activist and performer Kate Bornstein), and *I Am Jazz* (2015–2018), featuring transgender teenager Jazz Jennings. Through these out trans celebrities, both trans and cis audiences gain an understanding of the multiple realities of life as a transgender person. Whereas cis viewers can build on their empathy and respect for fellow humans who are less different from them than they might think, for young people just starting their journey of transition, these past and current public figures give them a sense of pride in their history and hope for a happy life as a visible trans person. As Barbra Penne notes, "Transgender youth look to such figures to know that they, too, can live fulfilling, successful lives" (2016, p. 7). This is equally applicable to non-binary folks, who are seeing slower gains in representation onscreen, although actors like Asia Kate Dillon, who played the first non-binary character on the show *Billions*, and *Pose*'s Indya Moore have helped increase the visibility of non-binary folks on TV, giving non-binary youth hope that they too will find acceptance as themselves in the world.

REPRESENTATION AND (TRANS)GENDER STEREOTYPES IN VIDEO GAMES

Besides movies and TV shows, video games are another large part of youths' daily entertainment, and Lupus's piece "Avatars" takes a closer look at this part of pop culture. Lupus points out the gender stereotyping that is a part of most video games: avatars that are essentially caricatures of human bodies. Yet Lupus also makes the important point that these caricatures are what we've been conditioned to see as beautiful when they write, "I find fake, virtual males with lots of muscles kind of attractive." It is a big part of why those images continue to have a hold on us, and it is also the reason why many folks who are transitioning strive very hard to reach those "ideal" bodies. For example, there is a whole online culture on YouTube dedicated to trans men trying to get lean and bulky, with filmed workouts, testosterone-boosting nutrition tips, and, for both trans men and women, the photographic journey from pre-hormones to years on testosterone or estrogen plus top surgery and bottom surgery results (O'Neill, 2014). The "shirtless hot trans guy" has already reached internet fame, considering the flood of such images on social media (Raun & Keegan, 2017) have specifically taken a closer look at trans male selfie culture, even prompting their own Buzzfeed list (Talusan, 2016). The pressure to conform to an image of a man that is physically desirable—with a full beard and shredded torso—is crushingly high. And here we come to Lupus's main point, a statement on what, in the end, makes these video games so important nonetheless, especially for trans folks: "I really love these games because I get to create a 'me' that I like. This character is the person I see in the mirror. This character is what I hope to someday be."

Adrienne Shaw (2009) and Elizaveta Friesem (Shaw & Friesem, 2016) and others posit that being able to choose a game character that you envision yourself as is an important form of escapism for trans people, especially before being able to transition. "For transgender people, the ability to finally express yourself, as yourself, in a new and wonderful world is such a gift. It's only temporary, but it helps us and I like to believe that it gets us through our offline struggles a little easier" (Veritas, 2016). The possibility of playing a character that matches your gender means a safe space and option to express your gender identity, which might not otherwise (yet) be possible. That is why popular culture and its representational images are so important and play a significant role in young trans people's mental well-being.

The same stereotypes that reinforce the gender binary also create unrealistic expectations of what the preferred gender of a trans person should look like. Lupus mentions *The Sims 4*, where you can pick individual body size, clothing, and other details for your character, yet there is only the option to choose a male or female gender. Rarely is there space in video games for non-binary, agender, or genderfluid avatars that people who identify as such could look to for representation. "I can create an avatar that looks pretty much like me, but they will always be misgendered ... and called either 'she' or 'he.' I get misgendered almost constantly in the real world; I'd love the ability to escape that drudgery in my hobby of choice ..." (Morse-Noland, 2017). While there is slow progress on out trans characters in video games, they seldom cross the line of the gender binary, mostly presenting as cis male or female.[3] Challenging cisgender game creators to do better, giving trans game creators the chance to work in the industry, and striving to transcend the gender binary in games (and other forms of entertainment) will have to be on our collective agenda for some time. This includes giving non-white gamers the opportunity to participate in the development of characters and games, challenging the same white, Western, cis beauty standards that are still so prevalent in the entertainment industry.

"MIXED UP": CISGENDER STEREOTYPES OF GENDER AND THE TRANS EXPERIENCE

Asa's poem "Mixed Up" uses a common child's toy to reflect on the literal clumsy awkwardness of the gender binary. The toy allows children to match up images to form the body of an animal, but the final creation can consist of the feet of one cartoon creature and the head of another. The dots may be connected, but the animal looks like it is stitched together all wrong: "The lines will match up / But the rest won't fit." While the toy depicts cartoon animals, it is easy to see why Asa chose it as a metaphor for human bodies. The gender binary is supposedly clear-cut and obvious, but the poem illuminates how artificial and arbitrary the binary model is. While the outward appearance of a person's body might "line up" to the binary model of gender (and even that is often not true, in the case of people who are intersex), their inner sense of their gender doesn't align. And while hormones and surgery are helpful for many people wanting to match their inner and outer gender identity, a good deal of trans folks are living in between or completely outside of the binary and don't subscribe to it.

Christopher's poem "Pink Herrings" also deals with cis-stereotypical ideas about transgender people. In this case these stereotypes are voiced by a medical practitioner questioning the speaker's sense of his gender by asking for childhood "signs" that the speaker is indeed a boy. In a detailed and clever response, the poem points out how questionable and irrelevant these signs are. Looking for "proof" that someone is "really" trans relies on a culturally constructed idea of what a cis boy is, in opposition to a cis girl, and that a transgender person must exhibit "typical" behaviour of the gender they are. But if a child is both gender conforming and nonconforming, what does that make them? The speaker says that, as a child, he was "hunting outlaws," something that it is assumed boys do, but also "having tea parties," which our culture has decided is a feminine activity. "Signs cancel out signs," showing that these signs are ultimately meaningless in determining someone's gender. Christopher's poem is an excellent way of supporting self-determination when it comes to gender identity: only you yourself can truly know your gender, and it is possible and valid that your gender identity evolves.

The poem also sets up a trans youth versus a cis adult person who thinks they know better than the youth, therefore continuing the problematic process of adults making decisions for (their) children, starting with assigning them a gender at birth, although, as the poet points out, "I didn't know how to speak." How can one express how they feel about their gender if they cannot use language yet? Or, once they can, if they do not know the words to express how they feel? Christopher repeatedly chooses words like *anomaly*, *misaligned*, and *mismatched* to highlight how the youth in the poem is caught in a world ruled by a cisnormative gender binary, where being trans or non-binary can make one feel like an alien, because that binary makes absolutely no sense.

While more cis people are becoming aware of the existence of trans folks, non-binary people often struggle for recognition and acceptance of who they are. Misgendering and lack of understanding is a lot more common for non-binary people, as cis people are reluctant to rediscover the use of singular "they" pronouns (in use since the 16th century; see Airton, 2020) or to even entertain the thought that a person might not feel as though they are either male or female.[4] Having to deal with a world that wants to separate everything with a male–female binary creates the feeling of invisibility and invalidity for young people who do not feel like either. Educating yourself about gender identities outside or in between the binary and respecting non-binary folks' pronouns and gender expression—in short, "allowing people to choose *not* to choose" (Town, 2017, p. 106)—is a crucial task for allies as well as trans people who use he or she pronouns. Unfortunately, denying the validity of non-binary genders is something that the trans community also sometimes struggles with. "Many trans youth feel astounding pressure to prove we can fit into pre-existing gender categories in our society and to prove we can live up to the standard of a 'real' man or woman, even among other trans youth" (Erickson-Schroth, 2014, p. 456). Not policing other people's genders is something that not only cis but trans folks need to work on: there is no one right way to express male or female gender, and passing as one or the other is not mandatory for a trans person.

THE "TRANS STORY" IN LITERATURE

Literature is another powerful cultural expression that children and youth look to when searching for trans representation, and it is sometimes surprising where that representation can be found. Ajam and Owen's illustration features a fairy from J.M. Barrie's *Peter Pan*: the blue fairies, as stated in the original text, are "not sure what [gender] they are," neither boys nor girls. Finding a line in a classic literary work that is explicitly trans-positive is a gift that can mean the world to a questioning child. Luckily, trans children and youth do not need to hunt quite as hard for that representation anymore. There has been a veritable boom in literature when it comes to transgender protagonists. The majority of these, however, are still written by cisgender authors, with only a few trans writers having published books that centre trans children and youth. Similar to representation in film and TV, non-binary characters are still fairly rare in literature, and more stories about non-binary people, especially in books for children and youth, are needed to balance this inequity and to give youth positive examples of non-binary lives and experiences.

Jackson Radish's comment on trans young adult literature that "there's still not that much out there [and] a lot of the stuff that's out there is not actually very good" (Erickson-Schroth, 2014, p. 448) unfortunately rings mostly true. Among other YA novels like April Daniels's *Dreadnought* (2017) or Elliot Wake's *Bad Boy* (2016) that were published in the last few years, Meredith Russo's *If I Was Your Girl* (2016) found the most widespread recognition, being widely recommended as a "Teen Read" and receiving a Stonewall Book Award. However, stories like the one told in *If I Was Your Girl* still revolve around the same stereotypes that are often used by cis authors writing about transgender characters. The protagonist, Amanda, tries to blend in with the cis world through medical transition (she is post-op and stealth throughout the book). She has a desire to hide the fact that she is trans, because she believes or fears that being trans makes her undesirable as a friend, family member, and romantic partner. In short, being as close as possible to cisgender is the ideal. For many young trans readers who harbour similar fears, it can be depressing to find those sentiments verified in such a widely read book and may make them question if they themselves are worthy of love and acceptance as they are. In some ways, the novel even follows the so-called "acceptance narrative" as summarized in Robert Bittner's work (2017)—though told by and centred around a transgender teenage girl, the focus is on cisgender characters and the question of whether they will accept Amanda because of her trans identity. Russo acknowledges in an afterword that she "cleaved to stereotypes and bent rules to make Amanda's [transness] as unchallenging to normative assumptions as possible" (2016, p. 276) in order to reach a wide audience.

In fact, YA novels like Cris Beam's *I Am J* (2011) that Radish praised in the 2014 edition of *Trans Bodies, Trans Selves* now feel outdated. Stories like Beam's focus on the character's suffering pre-transition, with an in-depth explanation of the medical aspects of transition directed at readers who have little or no knowledge about being trans, i.e., who are cis (although the author mentions in the afterword that her point of view is that of a cis parent of a trans child). Titles like *I Am J* repeat much of the knowledge that trans youth already have, and make the case that medical transition is what being trans is all about and is needed in order to be happy in your body. Finding the same kind of story and information when you are looking for someone like yourself can be frustrating. It is therefore the hope of the youth from Trans Tipping Point, as well as mine, that this book with their stories will bring more non-stereotypical trans and non-binary stories into the mainstream. In addition to the stories in this book, the "Books We Love" sections at the end of each chapter provide an excellent sample of additional works presenting realistic and nuanced portrayals of young trans and non-binary protagonists.

In comparison, literature for adults has seen a veritable explosion of transgender authors publishing in various genres. Vancouver-based Arsenal Pulp Press alone has published a number of trans and non-binary authors, among them multimedia artists Vivek Shraya, Ivan Coyote, Rae Spoon, and Kai Cheng Thom. Publishing houses like Topside Press are exclusively bringing out stories by trans authors. There is a growing number of books that resist the medicalization and normalization of gender and successfully present alternatives to the all-pervasive gender binary. Novels like Imogen Binnie's *Nevada* (2013) tell the story of trans and questioning young adults, not shying away from flawed characters and demonstrating that being trans is just one aspect of the protagonist's journey.

Trans activist Jennifer Finney Boylan's hope that we will go "from a single, simple narrative to a series of messier ones" (Town 2017, p. 110) is equally valid for YA literature about trans and non-binary youth, and indeed for the stories assembled in this book. The experience of being a trans adult mentor with the GGP was particularly positive and validating for both the youth and me. Since everyone in the workshops—including facilitators and youth attendees—was trans, no one had to feel like the "token trans," allowing everyone to be their full, beautiful, creative selves and write about their own stories. Hopefully there will be many more stories that represent the multitude of our life experiences, where being trans or non-binary is just one part of us, not the whole. Where trans authors can write trans characters that are complex, without being pressured to write only positive figures because of the "burden of representation" (Erickson-Schroth, 2014, p. 564) that demands all trans people be perfect in order to be accepted. Furthermore, "there is an empty space within publishing for more literature with genderqueer, inter-sex, and gender variant content in which characters, like so many real youth, do not necessarily identify with a specific binary gender" (Bittner, 2017, p. 69).

So what can you do as a cis, trans, or non-binary ally to trans and non-binary youth to help increase accurate representation in the surrounding culture? You can, for example:

✓ **Ask non-gendered questions about babies.** When you know that a baby is arriving, you can ask all sorts of questions (When is the due date? Do you have a chosen name? Is their room all decorated? How are you feeling?) instead of "Is it a boy or a girl?" You can also give cards, gifts, and balloons that don't say "boy" or "girl" and aren't pink or blue.

✓ **Check in with how *you* view gender and the gender binary in your own life.** Are certain tasks, jobs, or traits associated with a man in your head? Or a woman? Why not examine those thoughts, and ask yourself where they come from and if it really has to be that way? Try practising using neutral or no pronouns for describing people and animals (for example, "That person dropped *their* ice cream cone" or "That dog in the park was chasing *their* tail") and see how it changes your perspective!

✓ **Practising pronouns.** Everyone makes mistakes when they're learning new pronouns and especially when they're learning how to use nonbinary pronouns like they/them for the first time. The learning curve can take time, just like when someone changes their name after getting married or divorced. When someone reminds you that you've used the wrong name or pronoun, they're not saying you're a bad person or that you don't care about trans people, and you definitely shouldn't beat yourself up about it. Just gracefully apologize, use the correct name or pronoun, and move on.

✓ **Support trans authors and stories by buying our books, music, films, and other creations.** For a lot of us, our art is our only source of income, so you are also directly supporting our livelihood! Make sure to pay attention to our work itself and not just the fact that we are trans, though—not everything in our art will be about that, and we most certainly do not want to be reduced to it as artists.

✓ **Advocate for change.** There are lots of little ways to make big institutions more welcoming. Let's use the library as an example. You could ask your local library to purchase books by trans authors (like the ones recommended in this book!). Most libraries will take purchase suggestions from their patrons, and it might be a great conversation starter to inquire as to how the library (a public space after all) can become a more inclusive place. Does it have an all-genders washroom? Do they accept chosen names on library cards? Are they putting on trans-centred events? These questions and more are great ways to advocate for trans and non-binary folks.

NOTES

1. The Academy Award winner for Best Foreign Film in 2018 was given to *A Fantastic Woman (Una mujer fantástica,* Chile, 2017), with trans actress Daniela Vega playing the lead.

2. However, the director of this movie, a white cis man, has been accused of plagiarizing archival footage discovered by activist Reina Gossett, a trans woman of colour, from her short film *Happy Birthday, Marsha.*

3. A few recent video games feature, either explicitly or implicitly, non-binary characters, e.g., Cirava Hermod from *Hiveswap* and *Hiveswap Friendship Simulator: Volume 2* or Alex Cyprin from *Astoria: Fate's Kiss.*

4. For more scholarship and practical tools around the singular *they,* please see the Pronoun Specific Resources at the end of this book.

REFERENCES

Airton, L. (2020). *Gender: Your guide: A gender-friendly primer on what to know, what to say, and what to do in the new gender culture.* Avon: Adams Media.

Barker, M., & Scheele, J. (2016). *Queer: A graphic history.* London: Icon Books.

Binnie, I. (2013) *Nevada.* New York: Topside Press.

Bittner, R. (2017). *Theorizing trans readership: Examining ways of reading trans themed young adult literature* (Unpublished manuscript, Simon Fraser University, Vancouver, Canada).

Bungay, H., & Vella-Burrows, T. (2013). The effects of participating in creative activities on the health and well-being of children and young people: A rapid review of the literature. *Perspectives in Public Health, 133*(1), 44–52.

Conrad, A. (2015). *Towards a truer representation: Transphobic casting politics and the cis-gaze in film* (Summer Research, 239. University of Puget Sound, Tacoma, WA).

Driskill, Q., Finley, C., Gilley, B. J., & Morgensen, S. L. (Eds.). (2011a). *Queer Indigenous studies: Critical interventions in theory, politics, and literature*. Tucson: University of Arizona Press.

Driskill, Q., Justice, D. H., Miranda, D. A., & Tatonetti, L. (2011b). *Sovereign erotics: A collection of two-spirit literature*. Tucson: University of Arizona Press.

Erickson-Schroth, L., ed. (2014). *Trans bodies, trans selves: A resource for the transgender community*. New York: Oxford University Press.

Feinberg, L. (1996). *Transgender warriors: Making History from Joan of Arc to Dennis Rodman*. Boston: Beacon Press.

GLAAD. (2012). *Victims or villains: Examining ten years of transgender images on television*. Retrieved from https://www.glaad.org/publications/victims-or-villains-examining-ten-years-transgender-images-television.

Houbolt, S. (2010). Youth arts: Creativity and art as a vehicle for youth development. *Youth Studies Australia, 29*(4), 46–52.

Karkou, V., & Glasman, J. (2004). Arts, education and society: The role of the arts in promoting the emotional wellbeing and social inclusion of young people. *Support for Learning, 19*(2), 57–65.

Morse-Noland, N. (2017). *Why games need more non-binary character options*. Last modified August 31, 2017. Retrieved from https://www.themarysue.com/games-need-nonbinary-character-options/.

O'Neill, M. G. (2014). Transgender youth and YouTube videos: Self-representation and five identifiable trans youth narratives. In C. Pullen (Ed.), *Queer youth and media cultures* (pp. 34–45). London: Palgrave Macmillan.

Penne, B. (2017). *Transgender role models and pioneers*. New York: Rosen Publishing.

Phillips, J. (2006). *Transgender on screen*. New York: Palgrave Macmillan.

Raun, T., & Keegan, C. (2017). Nothing to hide: Selfies, sex and the visibility dilemma in trans male online cultures. In P. G. Nixon & I. K. Düsterhöft (Eds.), *Sex in the digital age* (pp. 89–100). London: Routledge.

Russo, M. (2016). *If I was your girl*. New York: Flatiron Books.

Shaw, A. (2009). Putting the gay in games: Cultural production and GLBT content in video games. *Games and Culture, 4*(3), 228–253.

Shaw, A., & Friesem, E. (2016). Where is the queerness in games? Types of lesbian, gay, bisexual, transgender, and queer content in digital games. *International Journal of Communication, 10*: 3877–3889.

Talusan, M. (2016, February 3). *26 trans guys who are way too hot to handle*. Retrieved from https://www.buzzfeed.com/meredithtalusan/26-trans-guys-who-will-make-you-thirsty?utm_term=.elwx6pKBRN#.jmbGqV0nPy.

Town, C. J. (2017). *LGBTQ young adult fiction: A critical survey, 1970s–2010s*. Jefferson, NC: McFarland.

Veritas, C. (2016, February 11). *Video games allow transgender people to be themselves*. HuffPost. Last modified February 11, 2017. Retrieved from https://www.huffingtonpost.com/charlize-veritas/transgender-people-video-games_b_9205330.html.

Whitehead, J. (2020). *Love after the end: An anthology of Two-Spirit & Indigiqueer speculative fiction*. Vancouver: Arsenal Pulp Press.

CHAPTER TWO

Families

KEY THEMES

- Parental expectations of children's gender expressions and identities
- Family rejection, disappointment, tolerance, acceptance, and affirmation
- Relationships between gender roles and family roles

CRITICAL QUESTIONS

- What expectations does your family have of you or other family members based on gender? Are there certain responsibilities women in your family have that men do not, or vice versa?
- In what ways do the pieces in this chapter highlight the importance of family affirmation for transgender youth?
- Can you think of other areas in which family acceptance is important for you? For example, is it important in such areas of life as choosing friends, what or where you'll study, or what types of paid and unpaid work you should do?

BOOKS WE LOVE

Picture Books

Adeyoha, K., Adeyoha, A., & McGillis, H. (2017). *47,000 beads*. Toronto: Flamingo Rampant.

Adeyoha, A., & Williams, A. (2015). *The zero dads club*. Toronto: Flamingo Rampant.

Labelle, S. (2020). *My dad thinks I'm a boy?!* London: Jessica Kingsley Publishers. **Also available in French*

Love, J. (2018). *Julián is a mermaid*. London: Walker Books. **Also available in French*

Lukoff, K., & Juanita, K. (2019). *When Aidan became a brother*. New York: Lee and Low Books.

YA and Graphic Novels

Belge, K., & Bieschke, M. (2019). *Queer: The ultimate LGBTQ guide for teens*. Minneapolis: Zest Books.

Barker, M. J., & Scheele, J. (2016). *Queer: A graphic history*. London: Icon Books.

Deaver, M. (2019). *I wish you all the best.* New York: Push.

McAdam, T. (2020). *Blood sport.* Victoria: Orca Books.

Schmatz, P. (2015). *Lizard radio.* Somerville, MA: Candlewick Press.

General Audience

Brill, S. A., & Kenney, L. (2016). *The transgender teen: A handbook for parents and professionals supporting transgender and non-binary teens.* Jersey City, NJ: Cleis Press.

Eriksen, T. (2017). *Unconditional: A guide to loving and supporting your LGBTQ child.* Coral Gables, FL: Mango Publishing Group.

Feinberg, L. (1996). *Trans warriors: Making history from Joan of Arc to Dennis Rodman.* Boston: Beacon Press.

Miller, L., & Elin, L. (2020). *Families in transition: A resource guide for families of transgender youth* (2nd ed.). Toronto: Central Toronto Youth Services Publications. *Also available in French*

Nealy, E. C. (2017). *Transgender children and youth: Cultivating Pride and joy with families in transition.* New York: WW Norton.

Memoirs/First Person Narratives

Faludi, S. (2017). *In the dark room.* New York: HarperCollins Publishers. *Also available in French*

Jetté Knox, A. (2019). *Love lives here: A story of thriving in a transgender family.* Toronto: Penguin Canada.

Little Thunder, B. (2016). *One bead at a time.* Toronto: Ianna Publications.

Lohman, E., & Lohman, S. (2018). *Raising Rosie: Our story of parenting an intersex child.* London: Jessica Kingsley Publishers.

Talusan, M. (2020). *Fairest: A memoir.* New York: Viking.

Family

By Ajam, age 14

As Long As I'm Healthy

By Max, age 13

Do you want a boy or a girl?
I don't care
as long as it's healthy
Then I was born
A little girl
They were happy
But later in life
I realize
I'm not a girl
but a boy
I stop eating regularly
I don't get enough sleep
I hate myself
Why can't I be normal?
Eventually,
I muster the courage to tell them
They had a boy
not a girl
They ignore it
What happened to
not caring
As long as I'm healthy?

Daddy's Little Girl

By Danny Charles, age 17

The doctor painted me pink when I wanted to be blue.

My dad wanted me to be the princess for Halloween. He would dress me in pink fluffy dresses when I wanted to be a cool boy ninja.
He would give me the sparkly pink wand when I wanted the cool nunchucks or a big sword.

When I told him I wanted to transition to be a boy, the dread on his face seemed like he lost his little girl, like his little girl just vanished right in front of him, like his little girl just died in his arms.

I kept saying, "I'm sorry," realizing now I shouldn't have been sorry.

I remember I used to be your whole world, but then you left without saying goodbye.

I never wanted to be a princess,
I never liked the big fluffy dresses,
I never liked the wand,
I never liked being ladylike.

I'm showing everyone I can be a better man than he will ever be.

Never be sorry for who you are; everyone in the LGBTQ2+ community will be standing behind you and will hold you up when you can't hold yourself up.

Be Strong Like Windows

By Samuel Busch, age 17

I got glass stuck in my shoes
I got glass stuck in my teeth
Trying to speak is like cracking down on crime, my every rebellious thought an offence
to a patriarch more ingrained in western culture than the shards in my gums
And even in your own home you'd expect without tracking the glass inside, you could
walk bare or sock footed with no need to tread lightly, but no.
The eggshells, landmines or whatever analogy you like stalks you to sanctuary.

However feminist you proclaim or may be, my kind is still included in those you are
meant to advocate for
I am all boy
Not yet man
If you look for man, blink once, blink twice
You will miss him looking for the misogynist your father is.

(And I had to explain what misogyny was to you)

You don't hear about my victories
because you shook your head when people asked who this young man with you was
when they said "he"
when they say "he"

you get frustrated that people see me as male with a costume change and a haircut
'cause that's how fragile these social constructions are

you didn't hear about when I got through going to the bathroom for the first time
or when I called the doctor after two years walking barefoot on broken glass with both
of us digging our heels in
crushed pieces, making sand with the relational friction and societal tension.

I'd always laugh to myself when I saw trans guys' bios that said "self-made man"
but it makes sense now.
I did this myself, every stitch, every goddamn rhinestone
I trained my voice down
I did the research
I made the composition of language that aligns with my inner feelings
I did the work
I did some work, though work was not needed and I was enough,

the world required me to look male enough
and I achieve that most days

but this is my body and this is my life
the only one to carry me through sweet and strife
The only one I get to be held in by my boy, partner or wife

I'd like to be happy in it.
just as you hope for yourself.
It's not easy being this transparent about my emotions
but it's necessary for me to survive.
To be all cellophane and windowpanes
all clear wrap and cleaned glass

I will be made crystal under pressure.
I am precious.

Mommy

By Ask Spirest, age 18

1. "I love you and forgive you, even after stealing $20 you originally gifted me for my birthday cake two years ago, because you wanted a book about dragons."

2. "If you let anyone lick your nipples, even if you're just playing pretend at being Mommy, your nipples will turn dark and everyone will know what you have done."

3. "Don't stick pencils in your hole down there! Ever! Or anything else like a finger! Husbands only."

4. "If I had a gay son? Well I wouldn't. He wouldn't be my good son. I'll raise him as the Bible tells me to, then tell him to leave when he's old enough."

5. "Put on more clothes, it's cold outside!"

6. "Take off that tight fabric around your chest! You'll hurt yourself! Are these men's underwear?"

7. "God doesn't make mistakes."

8. "Are you a demon?"

9. "The Bible says: 'Boys wear boys' clothes, girls wear girls' clothes, and homosexuals will be punished eternally.' Why are you doing this to yourself? Do you want to face eternal flames forever?"

10. "If you leave me, I will die. You are the reason why I stayed when I had cancer."

11. "I cried for a week when you left."

12. "It's been over a year. Why won't you come home?"

13. "Where are you?"

14. "I'll always love you and respect you, anything you need, just let me know."

You Always Wanted a Girl

By Asa O'Connor-Jaeckel, age 13

Do her hair and
Understand her
Rarely have to
Reprimand her
Thoughtful child
Caring child
Sparkly, pink
Dress-wearing child

You always wanted a girl

And then your
Very first glimpse
Of me
The labia on
The ultrasound
Screen
The sign that
For you, clearly
Spoke
The news for which
You'd dared not
Hope

You always wanted a girl

After the birth
Amid the stress
The surgeries
The five-month
Mess
The one thing you
Could no doubt
Say
The one thing that
Had gone
Your way

Was that you had
Got your wish

You always wanted a girl

I know that you
Would want no
Other
I know you
Mean it when
You say
That you are the
Luckiest
Mother
I know all this
With my whole heart
I know
As well
There was once
That part

That always wanted a girl

T

By Samuel Busch, age 17

Every evening I make tea for my mother and I
It's one of my favourite habits.
To take out her cup and all that this ocean blue clay and glaze represent
and fill it with sweet, spicy, or herbal nectar, nay, ambrosia
And as all family relationships go, there are some nights you're just not up for serving
the god of your life their sacrifice,
My peace offering of Peppermint or Bengal Spice.

Every evening, as I walk into the kitchen from my abyss of a room in the basement,
I walk one of two ways:
A comfortable strut, as one does in their comfy clothes,
Or my slithery slink, hoping my presence she does not know
The meaning of these walks indicates something quite important.
Whether or not I am in the mood to make tea for my equally tired mother
A choice of one or the other, it does not matter
The footsteps would trip up the trap and a voice would ring out—
"Are you making tea?!?!"
"No, mom,
I'm not."
And I feel this cold.
Like every muscle lost it's circulation and the memory of the last ten years being her
child flashes before me reminding me of the handful of temper tantrums and dirty
blonde hair from seeing if scissors to my scalp would somehow make me feel better

The weight of being a good kid to her every single night for the rest of my life falls on
my shoulders
And when I say "nope," that does not mean I'm just not doing it yet,
That means that I do not want to.

Because I am tired of hearing the name you love in ears that bleed when they hear HB
Mama, when I look like a man, I'll still make you tea
H Busch
Like my love wasn't enough;
But I hope that you'll be beside me
when the Testosterone starts to change my sex from an F to an M
And when they ask who the boy at your side is, maybe one day you'll be as proud to call me
your son
as I am every night I deliver your tea.

Prejudice Candle

By Yakusinn DeBoer, age 18

The world probably won't stay dumb forever, and **transphobia** is ticking down quite slowly. So why watch it burn away slowly when you can torch it straight from the bottom with your own hands? That's exactly what this scratch board and digital piece is, except these hands are represented by a large fire-breathing dragon.

The Complexities of Family Rejection

By Kyle Shaughnessy

There is a slide I use in half-day workshops with parents and caregivers of trans youth that shows an illustration of a youth sitting on the curb outside the family home, bags packed, head in hands, with caregivers off in the distance calling out from the front door, "This will definitely be for the best" (Slap Upside the Head, 2013). It makes my stomach drop every time I see it up on the projector screen, and I feel it is pretty aptly placed for us to enter into a discussion around the risks of family rejection for our young people. But the one thing about this image is that, while painfully and shamefully common, not all instances of family rejection are as cut and dried as caregivers ejecting their young ones from the family home and on to the streets. The writing shared by Max, Danny, Samuel, Ask, and Asa, as well as the beautiful artwork by Yakusinn, is a testament to this.

Woven alongside reflections on best practice in supporting gender diverse youth, and in response to the personal and insightful creative work of six participants, this essay seeks to draw attention to the practical opportunities we have as supportive adults to foster and recognize resiliency in the young people we seek to serve, particularly when this resiliency is not being nurtured in their home environment.

Within all of the stories and artwork in this chapter is a consistent experience of rejection by parents and caregivers. Rejection through dismissal and denial, rejection through neglecting and ignoring, rejection through invalidating and undermining, rejection through threatening and coercion. For instance, we have Max's family, who claims to accept and love him unconditionally, yet continuously invalidates his experience by refusing to acknowledge his risk of sharing his authentic self. Then there is Ask's mother, who uses religion as a scolding mechanism and guilt as a control tactic, preventing him from flourishing in a way that challenges her comfort and ideas around gender. And then there are Danny and Asa, whose parents' affection and adoration seems unfairly invested in their child's performance of cisnormative femininity. We have Samuel's family, who consistently vacillate between overt disapproval and avoidance of their child's evolving gender identity and expression. Finally there is Yakusinn, who not only recognizes this rejection but illustrates action to counter it once and for all.

MacNamara (2014) interviewed fifty trans people on their experiences of family acceptance and support and found that those studied had defined family acceptance by the absence of the extreme forms of abuse and ostracism that transgender people can often face in society. This idea of support being a lack of abuse has set our communities up to accept treatment from our families that is still much less than what is required to instill feelings of efficacy, security, and connection. So, these seemingly more subtle forms of rejection, like the neglect and invalidation experienced by Max, Danny, Samuel, and Asa, are in some ways slipping under the radar that has become attuned to the visual of the young person sitting on the curb, physically ejected from the family home.

Some trans youth may respond to these various harms as frogs in a pot of water being incrementally heated to a boiling point, constantly adapting and readapting to an increasing amount of shame, invalidation, and violence, and at the same time, witnessing their own coping strategies become more and more self-harming over time. This is evident in Max's declining health and wellbeing:

I stop eating regularly
I don't get enough sleep
I hate myself
Why can't I be normal?

Some trans youth may respond by fantasizing about another trans-utopian life, outside and away from the family, where they see themselves landing when it is safe to go. We catch glimpses of this in Danny's visions and experiences of safety and inclusion in the LGBT community—"Everyone in the LGBTQ2+ community will be standing behind you and will hold you up when you can't hold yourself up"—and again in Samuel's commitment to moving toward his authentic trans embodiment:

I did this myself, every stitch, every goddamn rhinestone
I trained my voice down
I did the research
… I did the work

This is also abundantly clear in Yakusinn's dragon, ready to take on transphobia with one fiery breath.

Some trans youth may take it upon themselves to recognize the harm being done by such hateful and neglectful messages and attitudes, and make a choice to leave their family behind for their own well-being. Leaving one's family behind becomes more possible with age and access to resources. Yet, for young people like Ask, whose mother had to question, "It's been over a year. Why won't you come home?," this choice to leave is sometimes still pursued even in the absence of resources, from a place of necessity to find mental, emotional, spiritual, and physical safety. As is evident in the stories shared here, resiliency comes in all forms.

The support, encouragement, and unconditional love of parents, caregivers, and familial adults is what builds resiliency. Veale, Travers, and Saewyc (2017) report that having supportive family members can also act as a buffer for transgender youth from some of the negative health outcomes associated with minority stress, such as poor mental health. As anyone working with trans youth will tell you, lack of family support is the most common problem we work with and seek to remedy, or, at the very least, be a buffer against. Similar to a game of curling, we as supportive adults are furiously attempting to sweep away and smooth down any inconsistencies that would prevent young people from making it to the finish line. All the while, we are focusing on what innate qualities they already hold or are eager to develop that will help them be as resilient as possible for the life journey ahead.

A 2014 study of HIV positive gay men who experienced emotional neglect in early life found that the long-lasting mental health consequences of emotional neglect gave way to such issues as low self-esteem, suicidal tendencies, increased substance use, disordered eating, and risk-taking behaviours, such as unfavorable attitudes toward condom use (Klein, 2014). In the context of parenting transgender youth, neglect could be defined as proposing to love them unconditionally, while ignoring their requests for support in gender exploration, such as using new names or pronouns, or even entering into discussion around their feelings and experiences of gender.

This neglect is quite apparent in Samuel's piece, "Be Strong Like Windows:"

You don't hear about my victories
because you shook your head when people asked who this young man with you was
when they said "he"
... you get frustrated that people see me as male ...

Unfortunately, for parents uneasy with their child's gender diversity, the erasing and invalidating of young trans people's needs for emotional support does not stop them from existing and thriving on their own terms, as Samuel reminds us in the latter half of the piece: "This is my body and this is my life ... I'd like to be happy in it. ... I will be made crystal under pressure / I am precious."

Neglect also makes a very strong appearance in Max's writing:

I muster the courage to tell them
They had a boy
not a girl
They ignore it
What happened to
not caring
As long as I'm healthy?

Max is in a place where he has been questioning his own worth, yet found ways to stay present and assert himself. However, he's now left questioning why his parents' claims of unconditional love haven't materialized at a time when it is most needed. What Max has shared here, particularly around his suffering and mental health ("I hate myself / Why can't I be normal?") is a stark reminder of the absence of that support Veale et al. (2017) are referring to.

Perhaps Max's parents are not turning away because they feel hatred or overwhelming sadness over who their child is; perhaps this avoidance is simply coming from a place of uncertainty, or a worry that encouragement will only propel their child toward a life of difficulty. Maybe they are just "dumb," like Yakusinn muses about the rest of the world. This type of avoidance is quite common, and likely if they realized that their lack of communication or willingness to articulate their own insecurities (and therefore face them) is leaving Max stranded and making him susceptible to the aforementioned lasting consequences to his well-being, Max's parents would seek some type of support. However, we as a society are not quite there yet, including our social service sector that often has a hand in helping parents re-orient when headed down a harmful path.

This place of feeling lost, unprepared, or unskilled to do the support work we are being called on to do is not exclusive to parents and caregivers. It is not uncommon for service providers to assume that working with gender diverse youth is something that requires a unique skillset or a significant amount of training, and therefore feel the need to make a referral to a "gender specialist" when confronted with common adolescent issues in trans youth. This is not the case. The skills needed to guide transgender youth through anxiety attacks, struggles with housing, and relationships with peers are all consistent with the skills used with cisgender youth; the only difference is being able to apply a particular lens to the support being offered.

For instance, Danny could probably make use of the same grief and loss supports any young person of divorcing parents needs. And in moving out of his mother's house, Ask could have benefitted from the same supports available to other youth fleeing harmful living situations. Stoking the fire that is alive not only in Yakusinn's artwork but in their motivation to see transphobia "torch(ed)" would nurture their incredible resilience to a place of continued activism and advocacy, as it would in any driven youth. The added (not different) support skills come in when we show up with care and authenticity to discussions such as Danny's, relating the loss of his relationship with his father to his gender: "He lost his little girl … I remember I used to be your whole world, but then you left without saying goodbye / I never wanted to be a princess." While recognizing the real pain of transphobia and Danny's emotionally valid concern that he somehow caused his father to leave, we can also acknowledge it is not a deciding factor for a parent leaving (or being asked to leave) an unhappy partnership. When applying these skills to Ask's move out of his mother's home, as with any youth, we evaluate the safety of the new home (such as whether there is an adult present, particularly if the youth is quite young) and offer assistance with tenancy paperwork. The trans lens here can involve factoring in whether Ask's new roomies hold positive regard for trans people, or navigating legal names on tenancy forms in ways that are both comfortable for the youth and practical in terms of getting his urgent needs met.

Overall, applying your existing skillset to working with trans youth simply involves becoming familiar with common issues that trans youth face, and being able to consider how the specific needs of being gender diverse might play into each situation that arises. For instance, how might being trans play a specific role in making a referral to a detox facility? You will need to consider gender segregated spaces, legal name requirements on paperwork, etc. The same mindfulness techniques and coping strategies will be used with a trans youth having a panic attack; however, the event triggering the attack or the overall life stressors may be specific to misgendering, bullying, or having their gender status disclosed without consent. These situations are also an opportunity for trans youth advocates and skilled clinicians to work together, share knowledge around the nuances of working with trans youth, and practice tools for basic coping strategies.

Another major theme in the youth writing, which tends to arise in most work with trans youth, is parents' discomfort in using and experimenting with new names and pronouns. A quite blatant example is given by Samuel in "Be Strong Like Windows": "You shook your head when people asked who this young man with you was / when they said 'he.'" One would think that this particular issue of pronoun use might have resolved itself by now, as it becomes part of the common societal understandings of basic validation and respect toward trans individuals. However, respectful pronoun use still dominates most conversations with youth around what kinds of support are currently lacking. As any transgender youth advocate will tell you, using the pronouns that are most comfortable and reflective of a young trans person's identity supports their wellness and development (see also Wentling, 2015). It also honours and respects who they are.

While nearly all of the youth pieces make some mention of not being truly seen and respected by their parents, Samuel's writing consistently brings up his mom's unwillingness to recognize his gender identity by refusing to use his new name ("Because I am tired of hearing the name you love in ears that bleed when they hear HB"), or listen to his reflections on what it's like to venture into other gendered spaces ("you didn't hear about when I got through going to the bathroom for the first time").

In parent mentoring settings, the number one word that surfaces when parents either refuse or express discomfort at the prospect of using a new name or pronoun for their child is "awkward," closely followed by an expression of grief that this was not the name that was meaningfully chosen for them all those years ago. This awkwardness is easy to validate because it is true; it is awkward to begin calling someone or something by a new name, similar to the way we need to retrain our minds at the beginning of a new calendar year or when someone changes their last name after marriage. But, as with the formation of any new habit, it gets easier with practice. Parents are also not alone in their struggle with discomfort here; it is awkward for other supportive adults as well as peers and friends of youth who change their names and pronouns. Pronouns and names can be silly, awkward things, and using unfamiliar ones draws increased attention to this. Nonetheless, part of our role as adults is to bear the discomforts of the world, when doing so will enhance the quality of life for our young ones.

One of the ways youth advocates can help parents dip their toes into these unfamiliar waters is by asserting their own use of the child's new names and pronouns during any one-on-one interactions they have, and naming this time together as one where they are free to practice, struggle, make mistakes, and practice again. If parents are willing to challenge themselves, they will still make mistakes with these new names and pronouns dozens of times; why not get some of those out of the way in a supportive environment, where their child does not need to experience it? We must make a positive and humble connection with parents who are struggling and supportive. This is how our advocacy work can be most effective. When we take a combative stance with parents who are struggling, it puts them on the defence. This is a disservice to our young people.

So much of a parent's refusal or hesitation to validate their child's gender identity, including using a new name or pronoun or initiating conversations about their child's experience with gender, relates back to the aforementioned grief. Grief appears to have been a major experience for Danny's dad. "When I told him I wanted to transition to be a boy, the dread on his face seemed like he lost his little girl, like his little girl just vanished right in front of him, like his little girl just died in his arms." Asa seems to sense that this will be a barrier for their mom as well:

I know that you
Would want no
Other
I know you
Mean it when
You say
That you are the
Luckiest
Mother
I know all this
With my whole heart
I know
As well
There was once
That part

That always wanted a girl.

One thing that I have often seen noted by members of the trans community is an increased capacity for self-reflection and thoughtful awareness of one's self and impact on others. This is evident in Asa's thorough exploration of the role they've played in their family and what it meant for their mother to have a daughter. The deep reflection that Asa is engaged in as part of their gender journey is reassuring to witness, as well as the fact that they have at some point experienced the unconditional love of a parent, and likely will again, possibly after their mother accesses some additional support.

The idea of ambiguous loss is a common one to surface in conversations between parents and caregivers of transgender youth, or in therapeutic contexts that intend to support a parent through the feelings that may come up for them during their child's process of assuming a trans identity. Ambiguous loss is defined as a type of loss where closure is not apparent, and can be experienced when the loss of a loved one is psychological but not physical, or vice versa. Many parents of trans youth experience the disappearance of their child in the physical form they've always known but not the personality, or a disappearance in what they considered to be the essence of who their child is, although they are still physically present. In my professional practice, this is one of the most common hurdles that parents of trans youth describe in terms of being able to fully support, encourage, and be actively involved in their child's transition.

While the pain of ambiguous loss is one that can be alleviated with the support of a professional, this is also an area where peer support can play a major role. Ideally, these parents will not see this perceived loss as an end point, but a stop along the way to full support and loving participation, something that is only a temporary part of the process. Being able to spend time witnessing other parents' journeys and being witnessed themselves in a non-judgemental space can be instrumental in moving this process forward. Coolhart, Ritenour, and Grodzinski (2018) have studied the experiences of parents of trans youth going through ambiguous loss, and have identified reaching out for peer support as a major coping strategy along the path to full support. Luckily, connecting with other caregivers is something that parents regularly express a serious interest in, and the increasing number of in-person and online peer support groups can attest to this. A survey of parents of trans youth in British Columbia noted that 95 per cent of these parents would (71%) or might (24%) like to connect with other parents of trans youth for support (Buote, 2016). The desire to increase capacity to nurture and be involved in trans youth's lives is there.

Youth workers and gender diversity advocates are rarely equipped with the clinical skills required to tackle some of the larger traumas that threaten youth well-being, such as the abandonment that Danny writes about, when his father left "without saying goodbye." This is also evident in the ways that Ask's mother has used her relationship with religion to enforce shame and damning messages about sex and gender: "If you let anyone lick your nipples … your nipples will turn dark and everyone will know what you have done," and "the Bible says: 'Boys wear boys' clothes, girls wear girls' clothes, and homosexuals will be punished eternally.' Why are you doing this to yourself? Do you want to face eternal flames forever?" At times, advocates need to make a call between when a parent's lack of support can be addressed by increasing their knowledge of gender diversity, and when there may be a larger clinical issue at play. Due to unfamiliarity and harmful media representation, gender diversity can feel scandalous and distracting, and can act as an easy scapegoat for existing problematic dynamics within families such as abuse, codependency, narcissism, and more.

Examples of family dysfunction aren't always so apparent, and can commonly look like a parent who lets their public persona as the parent of a trans child take precedence over the best interests of their transgender child, or who is unwilling to afford their trans child a developmentally appropriate level of independence when accessing healthcare. Situations such as these require a trauma-informed lens beyond what can be offered through most peer support groups. In recent years there has been a significant increase in the number of opportunities for paid work as trans youth advocates within school systems, community centres, and youth programs. However, there also needs to be work done to improve the ability of clinicians and other family therapy professionals to meet and understand the nuanced needs of families with gender diverse youth.

The final theme in these deeply personal and artistic offerings that begs to be explored is the theme of resiliency. Youth involved in the GGP took a risk not only by getting involved, some of them travelling from across the country to participate, but in actively showing up to GGP events in ways that allowed them to be vulnerable in their writing process. The very existence of this project relies on youth resiliency. So, while much of the youths' writing on the topic of family is heartbreaking, the act of putting this heartbreak into words is evidence of that resiliency. These young people are supporting themselves and helping each other to thrive in the face of forces actively working against them.

Resiliency features in Max's ability to notice that the coping mechanisms he is using are harmful, and in making the decision to come out to his family as a way of intervening in his own declining wellness:

I stop eating regularly
I don't get enough sleep
I hate myself
Why can't I be normal?
Eventually,
I muster the courage to tell them

As well, Max's ability to identify that the rejection he is experiencing is not okay, and that he deserves connection and unconditional love, is reassuring, as the reader is able to envision him going on to both articulate his need for support and also seek it elsewhere in order to keep himself well. As is evident in the stories and artwork shared here, resiliency comes in all forms. Yakusinn's resiliency is on full display in their incredible artwork, "Prejudice Candle." They demonstrate not only hope in their statement that "the world probably won't stay dumb forever," but also extreme drive and action in how they see themselves dismantling current conditions through fire.

Danny's vision of himself and his commitment to becoming a better man than his absent father is displayed when he writes, "I'm showing everyone I can be the better man than he will ever be," and his exhortation to turn toward the love and support of the LGBTQ+ community who "will be standing behind and will hold you up when you can't hold yourself up" is moving to witness. A recent study of eighteen trans post-secondary students identified that an experience of kinship and connection to other trans students, including emotional support in stressful situations, was a major support to overall success (Nicolazzo et al. 2017). And, while formal research is lacking in terms of the role of peer connection and resiliency in trans youth communities, there seems to be an inherent knowledge amongst this group that your community will be there for you, as is evident in Danny's statement.

There is evidence of resistance in how Samuel writes of his relationship with his mother: "When I say 'nope,' that does not mean I'm just not doing it yet, / That means that I do not want to." However, there is also faith in possibility: "I hope that you'll be beside me … maybe one day you'll be … proud to call me / your son." Samuel's balancing of these two experiences of faith and resistance prompt curiosity and hope for those of us reading, that although there is much to resist right now, in terms of his mother's denial of his gender identity, there is the foundation of a loving relationship there that is expected to return at some point. And one only needs to get as far as the title of Sam's earlier piece to see how very committed he is to his own self-sufficiency and ability to thrive. Regardless of the support he receives, he is well aware that he has the strength required to live authentically: "I did this myself … I did the work … this is my body and this is my life … I'd like to be happy in it."

One of the most jarring pieces in this chapter is Ask's detailing of the comments he has had to endure from his mother over time. There is incredible power in Ask's writing as it moves through statements of religious condemnation, to comments inducing guilt, and then responses to Ask clearly having left home, such as "Are you a demon?," "If you leave me, I will die," and "Why won't you come home?" Ask recognizes the damage being done by his parent's behaviour, and makes a decision to remove himself for his own needs. This decision shows a phenomenal will to not only survive, but nurture those particular aspects of himself that are coming under attack. The end of the poem suggests that Ask's mother may have changed her perspective, which creates some hope, but it also contains an air of adult detachment and recognition of Ask's autonomy. When we consider the grim statistics such as those presented in research by Travers et al. (2012) of trans youth, which links parental rejection with poor mental health concerns and high rates of suicidality, one hopes that Ask's mother is now able to offer support. While parental rejection is a significant determining factor in poor health outcomes for transgender youth, a high level of parental support (Veale et al., 2015) is a predictor for positive health outcomes. It is for this reason that getting parents on-side is crucial; their support is one of the largest influences on transgender youth resiliency.

During the final writing and editing stages of this essay, I wanted to ensure that I had not misused the metaphor of the frog in the boiling water back in the second paragraph, when speaking about the possibility that trans youth may adapt to neglect and harm done by their families. Having done some research on its history, it seems I have applied the metaphor correctly; however, the idea that a frog will continuously adapt until it dies turns out to be an old myth. Experiments conducted in the last fifty years have shown that, typically, a frog will jump out of the pot once it becomes too unsafe to stay in the near-boiling water. This natural inclination toward self-preservation is evident as well in these young trans and non-binary people, many of whom who are living in unsupportive, harmful, or neglectful families and households. It is clear that their resiliency will take over, and that they can, will, and do recognize their incredible worth; they are aware that the problem does not lie with them, or even necessarily within their families, but within the violently limiting value systems being enacted and enforced by our society as a whole.

It is still very much on us, however, as service providers, family members, caregivers, educators, community leaders, and supportive adults in general, to nurture this resiliency that is so very obvious in these young people. What I hope can be taken away here is your consideration of the following, when supporting our young ones.

✓ **Make sure to care for yourself too**. It's okay to love your trans friend or family member and still feel unsure about the right thing to do. Gender is joyful, but it can also be confusing. When families and friends feel supported, they can better support a beloved trans youth. So find communities, either online or in person, of other supportive allies where you can make mistakes, ask awkward questions, grieve, rage, grow, and improve. Parents and Friends of Lesbians and Gays (PFLAG), the Family Acceptance Project (familyproject.sfsu.edu), and Gender Creative Kids (gendercreativekids.com) are great places to start. See the resources section of this book for a list of resources to help you find a community that's right for you or start your own.

✓ **Know when to keep it simple.** You don't have to be a world expert in gender to support a trans youth, and chances are they aren't an "expert" either. Start with empathy and nonjudgemental curiosity and let them take the lead. When you mess up, don't make it a big thing— just apologize and move on. Compassion and a willingness to try are much more important than knowing all the finer points of gender jargon.

✓ **Recognize that family rejection comes in many forms.** Just because a young trans person has a roof over their head does not mean that they are safe, and it does not mean that this roof is permanent or unconditional. Look closely and consider overall wellness and safety in the wider sense. It may not be safe or wise to urge youth to leave the family home, so having a clearer picture of what they're going through guides us in our work to help buffer them from the harms.

✓ **Honour chosen and original families.** Families are where we find belonging and kinship, are challenged to be and become our best selves, and are safe to come home to from the world (literally and figuratively). Families are where someone "gets" us at least some of the time. Families also grow and change over time, adding new members and losing others. Sometimes the ones we consider family aren't from our family of origin but are loved ones, friends, community members, and others with whom we cross paths and relate to along the way—a chosen family, or family of meaning. Our family of meaning doesn't have to replace our family of origin, but for some of us it will, and it's just as valid and valued as a family of origin. Families look however we need them to.

✓ **Know when and who to call for help.** No one expects you to know everything about how to support the trans youth in your life. It's okay to ask for outside support from educators, healthcare providers, and other affirming people and groups like counselors, social workers, youth groups, religious organizations, and so on. Some are listed in the resources section of this book. Listen to your heart, trust your gut, and ask for help when you need it.

REFERENCES

Buote, D. (2016). *C.A.L.L. out! Final evaluation*. Vancouver: Arbor Educational and Clinical Consulting Inc.

Coolhart, D., Ritenour, K., & Grodzinski, A. (2018). Experiences of ambiguous loss for parents of transgender male youth: A phenomenological exploration. *Contemporary Family Therapy, 40*(1), 28–41.

Klein, H. (2014). Early life emotional neglect and HIV risk taking among men using the Internet to find other men for unprotected sex. *Child Abuse & Neglect, 38*(3), 434–444.

MacNamara, J. (2014). *Appearance and acceptance: Toward a sociology of familial responses to gender* (Doctoral dissertation, State University of New York at Buffalo, Buffalo, NY). Available from ProQuest Dissertations Publishing. (Publication No. 3544643).

Nicolazzo, Z., Pitcher, E. N., Renn, K. A., & Woodford, M. (2017). An exploration of trans* kinship as a strategy for student success. *International Journal of Qualitative Studies in Education, 30*(3), 305–319.

Slap Upside the Head. (2013). Accessed August 22, 2013. Retrieved from http://www.slapupsidethehead.com/.

Travers, R., Bauer, G., Pyne, J., Bradley, K., Gale L, & Papadimitriou, M. (2012, October 2). *Impacts of strong parental support for trans youth: A report prepared for children's aid society of toronto and delisle youth services.* Trans PULSE Project. Retrieved from https://transpulseproject.ca/wp-content/uploads/2012/10/Impacts-of-Strong-Parental-Support-for-Trans-Youth-vFINAL.pdf.

Veale, J., Saewyc, E., Frohard-Dourlent, H., Dobson, S., Clark, B., & the Canadian Trans Youth Health Survey Research Group. (2015). *Being safe, being me: Results of the Canadian trans youth health survey.* Vancouver: Stigma and Resilience Among Vulnerable Youth Centre, School of Nursing, University of British Columbia.

Veale, J., Peter, T., Travers, R., & Saewyc, E. (2017). Enacted stigma, mental health, and protective factors among transgender youth in Canada. *Transgender Health, 2*(1), 207–216.

Wentling, T. (2015). Trans* disruptions: Pedagogical practices and pronoun recognition. *TSQ: Transgender Studies Quarterly, 2*(3), 469–476.

CHAPTER THREE

Bodies

KEY THEMES

- Metaphors for the gendered body
- Body acceptance and love
- Gender dysphoria and gender euphoria

CRITICAL QUESTIONS

- When do you feel most at home in your (gendered) body? What do you do to make you feel at home in your body?
- Are there ways of talking about trans or cis bodies that don't reinscribe the right/wrong body narrative? What might these be?
- How has the language that we use to talk about bodies been gendered? Do words like "tough" or "cute" mean different things when applied to different genders?

BOOKS WE LOVE

Picture Books

Lorenz, T. N. (2018). *Trans affirmation coloring book*. St. Paul, MN: Theo Nicole Lorenz.

Pessin-Whedbee, B., & Bardoff, N. (2016). *Who are you? The kid's guide to gender identity*. London: Jessica Kingsley Publishers.

Roher, M. (2016). *Is it a boy, girl, or both?* San Francisco: Wilgefortis Press.

Shraya, V., & Perera, R. (2017). *The boy & the bindi*. Vancouver: Arsenal Pulp Press.

Silverberg, C., & Smyth, F. (2013) *What makes a baby*. New York: Seven Stories Press.
  Also available in French

YA and Graphic Novels

Gonzales, M. C. (2018). *The gender wheel: A story about bodies and gender for every body*. San Francisco: Reflection Press.

Labelle, S. (2019). *Sex ed for everyone: Comics about relationships, identities and puberty*. Montréal: Serious Trans Vibes. *Also available in French*

Silverberg, C., & Smyth, F. (2015). *Sex is a funny word: A book about bodies, feelings, and YOU*. New York: Seven Stories Press. *Also available in French*

Simon, R. E., & Grigni, N. (2020). *The every body book: The LGBTQ+ inclusive guide for kids about sex, gender, bodies, and families.* London: Jessica Kingsley Publishers.

Vaid-Menon, A. (2020). *Beyond the gender binary.* New York: Penguin Workshop.

General Audience

Erickson-Schroth, L. (2014). *Trans bodies, trans selves: A resource for the transgender community.* Oxford: Oxford University Press.

Hunt, S. (2016). *An introduction to the health of Two-Spirit people: Historical, contemporary and emergent issues.* Prince George, BC: National Collaborating Centre for Aboriginal Health.

Sharman, Z. (Ed.). (2017). *The remedy: Queer and trans voices on health and health care.* Vancouver: Arsenal Pulp Press.

Tannehill, B. (2018). *Everything you ever wanted to know about trans (but were afraid to ask).* London: Jessica Kingsley Publishers.

Tolbert, T. C., & Trace, T. (Eds.). (2015). *Troubling the line: Trans and genderqueer poetry and poetics.* Callicoon, NY: Nightboat Books.

Memoirs/First Person Narratives

Chacoby, M., & Plummer, M. (2016). *A Two-Spirit journey: The autobiography of a lesbian Ojibwe-Cree elder.* Winnipeg, MB: University of Manitoba Press.

Hill, K. R. (2015). *Rethinking normal: A memoir in transition.* New York: Simon & Schuster.

Kergil, S. (2017). *Before I had words: On being a transgender young adult.* New York: Skyhorse Publishing.

Mock, J. (2014). *Redefining realness: My path to womanhood, identity, love & so much more.* New York: Atria Paperback.

Symington, S. (2018). *First year out: A transition story.* London: Singing Dragon.

Reflection

By Ajam, age 14

My Body

By Jaxon Steele, age 16

My relationship with my body has always been a complicated one.

It never felt quite right,
So I never treated it quite right.

It is bruised from too many risks taken,
      Battered from binding too tight,
            Scarred from when my own hand betrayed my skin.

My body feels like a prison:

      Hips too wide,
      Thighs too thick,
      Chest too large.

So I tried to starve
          them
             away.

Needless to say,
I did not succeed.

My body feels like a prison:

Whose bars did not shield me from abuse but
Merely watched as I shrank into myself.
As I retreated into the darkest corners of my mind to escape my waking nightmare.

My body feels like a prison:

      It does not
align
      with my mind.

It does not show people who I am.
It isn't me.
Just the vessel that must carry me through my life,
So I can alter it any way I please.

My body is starting to feel like less of a prison:

I'm now three and a half months on T.
My voice has dropped,
My face has changed,
And I'm starting to feel stronger.
I've learned to wear my blue like armour,
Even though sometimes its weight feels suffocating.

My body still doesn't feel quite like it was made for me,
But it feels just a little less alien.

And maybe,
Just maybe,
My body is finally starting to feel like home.

Hair Expression

By Tor Broughton, age 12

Flip back six years, I cut off around twelve inches of hair, leaving me with a bob. That was an insane moment for me. My hair has become a big part of my identity as a person and a significant part of my gender expression.

In the summer of 2016, I dyed my hair red and cut it into the haircut that my friends and I have now nicknamed the volcano. Yes, the top was red and in a faux-hawk and the sides were brown and buzzed. I did indeed look like a volcano. I also got references to murder scenes about the red. At the time, I got a lot of compliments on it and thought I looked incredible. As I look back on it, it might not have been the best choice …

Luckily, that isn't where my hair journey ended. I let the top grow out, cut out the red, and left my hair in a loose comb-over. We once again dyed the top, this time, blond. Buzzed the sides again and left them brown.

There were lots of side buzzes. Buzz, grow, buzz, grow, the same pattern. I can't handle having my sides longer than a pinky nail. It drives me insane. So I get them buzzed down the shortest they can be without being bald. I then repeat that habit every three weeks. Buzz, grow, buzz, grow.

I went between a lot of stages of my hair throughout the years. From super long hair down to my waist, to a bob cut, to some weird, emo-looking fringe haircut, to a faux-hawk, to where I am today, a loose comb over.

My hair represents a large part of me and my identity. For most of my life, I've used my hair as a form of expressing my gender, as well as my personality. As I began realizing my gender identity, I also began exploring different hairstyles and the two have now almost interlocked for me.

Because my hair is so closely bonded with me, I take pride in it. Even when I've made definite mistakes, such as the volcano. So when I'm teased or messed with because of my hair, it tends to hit deeper than it might for others. My hair is me, and that's who I am.

Strength

By Lupus, age 14

Do you know what it's like to be cast out by your own shadow?

What about to bully yourself, or try your best, but still get frustrated?

Do you ever wake up and hate yourself because you're not in the right body?

Do you ever cry yourself to sleep? Or pick your nails down to the blood and skin?

Do you know what it feels like to want to cut yourself into a thousand pieces,

So that maybe, just maybe, you can rearrange them to be the way you want them to be.

What is dysphoria? ... you all ask.

It's a blinding pain, one that will never stop challenging you.

You must spend every minute of every day trapped in a cage.

You must live with what you have until you are freed.

You must fight the urge to end it all, because you know deep down inside that your spark is very important and your life is your reward.

You will support the ones around you even though you don't get back what you wanted in return.

You won't be able to listen to your own advice.

You will feel *alone* ...

Although it may seem you have an army behind you, your ultimate battle is against yourself.

You must live from the heart, and not the mind that consumes and creates all the negative

thoughts that cause you to feel this way.

You must realize that no one can help you find yourself.

This is why we are all here on this planet.

This search for yourself, is where strength comes from.

If Dobby died a free elf, we should all die free too.

Be patient my friend, for your time will soon come.

Life Journey

By Maisie Bodrug, age 13

These two pieces represent the complexity of life and the confusion of puberty.

Dysphoria

By A.J. Gabriel, age 17

Is gender dysphoria kicking your ass right now? Yeah, me too. Here are some things I think about when I feel something isn't matching.

Little disclaimer: I have a tendency to cope with dysphoria through humor quite often. Something that has sprung from it is my ever-growing list of bizarre and just simply childish terms I use when referring to certain body parts. I hope that my awful innuendos are not too much to handle in this light read on coping with dysphoria.

I also cope with a hell of a lot of excessive self-love and self-congratulatory ideals. Sometimes it's hard to love yourself or to pretend you think you're deserving of self-love—but trust me, sometimes you're gonna be upset with yourself but that doesn't make you any less deserving of love.

BODY DYSPHORIA

- That body? It's on a cutie. That's you. Ur cute.
  - Love it. Are you missing parts or have ones you don't want? That's okay. Sometimes when you build furniture from a certain Nordic-themed store, they give you extra pieces that don't make sense, or they forget one or two. That's okay—it just is something that makes you, well, *you!*
- Boobs? On a guy? That's wild. Look at those squishy pillows! Heck yeah!
  - A boob? Two boobs!? WOW! That's pretty freaking wild, my pal!
  - Wait, are you missing boobs? Ah, heck, it be like that ... but hey, you can save your back and shoulders, so if you got removable boobies, that's okay!
  - If you got none, that's also okay!
  - Not everyone has boobs, and that's completely fine!
- Where's my dick?
  - Sometimes I get a weird feeling because I don't have the **ahem* pee-pee* that I wish I'd been born with. It's weird to have or not have the parts you wish you had, and honestly, it can be an intense dysphoric feeling sometimes.
    - If you are able to, I definitely recommend getting a packer or an STP (stand-to-pee) device if you are feeling the lack of a dong.
    - Even just stuffing a pair of balled-up socks in your pants can give you a little bulge and that makes it feel less awkward.
  - Be warned: I have had my packer fall out of my pant leg once, and that was horrifying, so be sure that everything is secured when you are wearing your devices!
  - Avoid embarrassing situations at all costs ... *like, oops, my no-no carrot took a tumble ... out of my pants ... oh well, that's just how it is sometimes, I guess.*
    - If you unfortunately are stuck with having said appendage, gaffs are great!
    - They even make ones with outlined labia on them, so that's pretty nifty too!

- Curvy? A boy with curves? You bet your bottom dollar that's what I am!
  - Bodies come in all shapes and sizes! Do you think we're gonna just let you hate it? Nah, *I love your body in the least creepy way possible* <3
  - I got myself a real thick, pudgy body, but that's just more of me to love!
  - Sometimes it feels a little odd to love yourself and to love your body, and that's okay!
  - Bodies suck sometimes, but that body hosts *a wonderful thing*.
    - (it's you)
    - (you're the wonderful thing)
    - (you are pretty cool)
  - Loving your own body is hard, and it doesn't make it any easier when you feel like it doesn't belong to you.
  - But that's the body you got as of now, and you are rocking it!

VOICE DYSPHORIA

- Is that my voice? Is that my voice?
  - I had really bad voice dysphoria when I first came out because my voice was kind of high-ish …
  - But do you know who else has a high-ish voice?
    - That's right.
    - Any person who has been socked in the nuts.
    - So that's okay.
  - And if your voice is a little low?
  - You know who has a real low voice?
    - Ladies with them real cool voices that when they talk leave all those around who hear them shaking in their boots.
  - You rock that voice, my pal.
- What if my voice was dramatically the opposite?
  - If you wanted a much lower voice, just imagine if it were ridiculously low …
    - Like, your voice on sulfur hexafluoride.
    - That's very deep and terrifying.
    - But what if that's how you got to sound all the time?
    - That's pretty wicked.
  - If you wanted a much higher voice, imagine if it were higher than Snoop Dogg on 4/20 …
    - Have you ever heard someone's voice on helium?
    - Imagine that, but even higher.
    - If you talked like that all the time, that would be pretty wild.
    - Think if you talked the way that one singer with that super high voice sang.
    - Again, that's pretty swanky.

- Sometimes talking is hard, some people don't talk at all, and that's pretty cool!
  - If your voice dysphoria is incredibly awful, take a minute to think about how there are people who don't or can't talk.
  - Imagine living in their situation if you aren't already.
  - Maybe learn to sign and expand your communication skills without having to hear the voice that you may dislike.
- I love the sound of [certain person]'s voice ... what if I sounded like that?
  - That would be weird.
  - Just to talk like, say, a friend or celebrity, even.
  - In the same tone.
  - Just like them.
  - All the time.
  - Wow.
- These vocal cords are made for screaming into the void
  - and that's just what they'll do.
  - Join me in a shout ...
    - AHHHHHHHHHHHHHHHHHH!
  - That was excellently refreshing. Thank you for joining me.

So those were my simple and strange ways that I get over my dysphoria. Yeah, some of them are quite silly, or ridiculous, but I find that if you can laugh at yourself, it won't bother you as much if other people laugh at you. I have been in some not-so-great situations in which people have used my dislike of myself against me to upset me, but now it's almost like I can make fun of myself too, in a way that doesn't make me upset anymore. It's hard to build resistance to rude people, but unfortunately, they aren't gonna disappear. I wish I could wave a wand and make people suck a lot less, but that's just how we are. Some of us are super great in some ways, and some of us are super terrible in other ways. We are all human, and this doesn't excuse us from our mistakes, but it doesn't mean we are irreparable. I believe in giving everyone kindness (I'm still working on giving it to everyone, but I hold a special place in my heart for nasty people. I want to kick my foot so far up their ass that they'll be pulling toes out of their teeth for years), and until someone proves they are not deserving of kindness, I will simply keep talking to them with kind words, and mild passive aggression :)

Disproportionate

By Samuel Busch, age 17

I feel disproportionate. The way a preteen is, like I was supposed to fill out this boy/femme body some time ago. My strange muscular thighs and semi-toned calves, full hips and short body. In short, I wish I would just be twinkie or otterish. Which is to say, tiny and thin or average height and stocky. But here I am, chunky hips, short legs and, so I've been told, a pretty face.

Several people have told me that I'm intimidating. Which makes no sense to a five-foot-two-inch tiny dude who was socialized female. Oh, and being told that my attractiveness is intimidating. Not only do I feel like a squishy little teddy bear. But the one that stays inside even after hibernation is over, saying, "Hey, yeah, I don't really want to come out right now. Like, I haven't shaved in a while."

Nobody cares what you look like; they're all thinking about themselves. "Yeah, okay, that sounds about right. I guess it's time, huh?"

Spring is here, and she's waiting for me to grow, to step out of this dark space or just open the curtains. Maybe I haven't been trying hard enough to get a bigger shoe size or sharper jawline or longer legs. Maybe she's just been waiting for me to see if I'd make the first move. She sits back, kissing two lips and inviting chrysanthemums to book and wine clubs or picnics on Sundays in the backyard. She spent weekends like me, wrapped up in snow-white blankets, suffocating under the cold, only to blossom and bloom from the pressure, and find I had new colours I didn't know of. We'd swaddle ourselves in each other, spring and fall, rebirth and death. Both new beginnings. Rain, showers, and seeds falling in sun. Cool sun. Not the boiling kind that forces us out of winter skins, but nurturing and soft.

I'll hold her. As little spoon as I am, I'll hold her. Growth, death, into new; scattering of seeds and all. She makes me pure again and reminds me small things are still whole, mustard seed still persists, tiny as it is, as minuscule, it's still whole and complete.

And so am I. I am whole; small, misshapen in ways, but inherently good.

The atom makes up almost everything. No, everything. And it's one of the smallest things we can fathom. I may see my body as unattractive and thus useless but it can lift my sister. It carries the dog's food from the car and helps my mom with everything she needs. It helps my dog up the stairs, my lumpy 11-year-old bear-sized lab, misshapen but perfect. The first love of my life, this fatty, cyst-covered furball.

So maybe my rolls and lumps are okay. If I can love him the way I do, people will love me too.

Butterflies

By Maisie Bodrug, age 13

We used to be ugly caterpillars
Sad at not being who we truly are
Stress eating until we are self-conscious of our weight

When the time comes, we hide in our delicate chrysalis
Away from the abuse of the outside world
Preparing to bloom into a magnificent being and show our true colours

We are done concealing our true identities
We fly high and free, and feel warm sun in our wings

But we butterflies are sensitive
An insult causes us to wilt and fall
So be kind to us, and cherish us
For we do not last forever

My Home

By Tor Broughton, age 12

In my recent TED Talk I mention JT. [1]
And how he passed Bill C-16.

I've been told he's the reason I'm now safe, but I'm quick to deny it.
Because matter of the fact is, the first pride march was a riot.

Led by black trans women throwing bricks at white cops.
Because the police tried to make their queer lives stop.

Marsha P. Johnson is the real reason we have parades.
And those riots are why we don't need ones for straights.

Because they aren't harassed for their gender or love.
Not somewhat or even kind of.

Canada is surely leading in the world's queer justice.
But that doesn't mean we've run out of room for more acceptance.

Other countries are succeeding at high rates.
India just legalized gay sex on September's first Thursday.

Obama gave same-sex marriage a try.
And now it's just called "marriage" by any good ally.

It was recently queer people were still hated. In fact, I remember.
Because the truth is, people still think there's only two genders.

You know in our world there's something wrong
Because if there wasn't, wouldn't we all just get along?

And yeah, Canada could be doing worse
I mean, on our team we have MPs, mayors, and we're pretty damn diverse

Down south they're doing bad
This Cheeto guy got the whole country in his hands.

And his ignorance is a kind of hate
That ignorance causes kids pain

Did you know that GSAs save lives
Kids without 'em kill themselves 33% of the time

But if they're accepted in the classroom
Only 17% fall victim to the suicide doom

Some people still don't know what LGBTQ stands for.
Let me explain so they understand more.

Lesbian and gay are the simple first two.
Then bisexual means you like girls and guys too.

Transgender, that's me!
Simply put, my mind doesn't match my body.

And the Q, that means queer.
Which back in the day was a word used to cause fear.

But now we've reclaimed it and it's an umbrella word.
It's simply a term for all us folks to be referred.

But there's many other identities than just those few.
Such as demi, poly, and asexual too.

For some, labels are a social construct, designed to tear you down.
For others, labels are the only thing keeping their frown upside down.

And, you need to respect that.
Because truthfully, it's a personally preference.

And the world is changing step by step.
Every single country becoming more progressive.

Accepting diversity is going to change our society.
Because people are like ice cream, we're better with more variety.

And with this
I wanna change the world.
To be more colourful and full of bliss.

You see, I'm white and privileged and most certainly lucky.
But it's surely not ideal to be born in the wrong body.

Now other folks might argue that my body is not wrong. And I strongly agree.
The thing is, this body just doesn't suit me.

Personally, I believe that everyone's body is a place to live.
While all the cishets were gifted a home or a temple.
I was merely given an apartment for rental.

While my home is under construction I've been given somewhere to stay.
And it's not quite time to move in yet, I'll have to wait a few more days.

So why not make this house as cozy as I can.
Because for now, this is the home of a handsome young man.

NOTE

1. JT refers to Canadian prime minister Justin Trudeau.

Life Itself: Trans Youth, Their Bodies, and the Freedom They Are Owed

By Dr. Jake Pyne

The body tends to feature prominently in discussions about trans lives. The covers of books about trans topics are populated by the blurry bodies of gender-ambiguous figures (see Namaste, 2000; Salamon, 2010; Stryker & Whittle, 2006) and often sport titles such as "A Stranger in My Own Body" (Di Ceglie & Freedman, 1998), "Assuming a Body" (Salamon, 2010), "No Body" (Rosello-Penaloza, 2018), or "Trans Bodies, Trans Selves" (Erickson-Schroth, 2014). Trans bodies are of increasing concern to right wing lawmakers in the US, with an onslaught of bills proposing to regulate what trans bodies can do in public space, in sports, schools, washrooms, and so on (Grinberg, 2019). The extent and the nature of violence against young trans women of colour has made it unmistakable that Black trans feminine bodies are, as Laverne Cox declared, "under attack" (Democracy Now!, 2014). Young trans bodies are a worry to Canadian conservative politicians as well, who recently succeeded in stripping Ontario's school sex education curriculum of references to "gender identity" (Canadian Press, 2019). Even twenty years after Dutch media first lost their wits over the phenomenon of trans youth taking puberty blockers (Schöttelndreier, 1999), recurring cycles of media alarm continue to erupt with each pundit seeming to believe in the originality of their own social panic—a panic suggesting trans youth are somehow departing from nature or from life itself (Wente, 2014). In short, what trans youth do or don't do with their bodies seems to inspire a great deal of societal hand-wringing.

In 1996, trans woman and sociologist Carol Riddell responded to the publication of a particularly transphobic text by writing: "My living space is threatened by this book" (Riddell, 1996, p. 189). In the present day, young trans people are also fighting back against threats to their living space. At the level of cultural production, trans youth produce art with statements like "trans bodies are beautiful" (Bothways, 2018) and "trans bodies deserve love" (Ashenden & Braidwood, 2018). Trans youth craft new language to tell a more complex story about the gendered body (NBD Campaign, 2018). With support from allies, they launch successful legal challenges (Vikander, 2019). Some make themselves visible, despite the endangering aspects of visibility, especially for racialized youth (Gossett, Stanley, & Burton, 2017). At times, trans youth refuse to answer to transphobia, and instead start new conversations on their own terms.

The nine pieces of trans youth writing and art in this collection talk back to public conversations about trans bodies in intriguing ways. In order to contextualize the important ideas that these young authors and artists are surfacing, I put their work into conversation with theory in trans studies, with current social science and trans health research, and with other forms of trans poetry and life writing. Specifically, this chapter considers the images and metaphors these young people draw on to describe the experience of their bodies—the body as a prison, the body as a home, and the multiple meanings of the mirror. With their poetic choices, I suggest these youth reveal glimpses of their bodily worlds to us—worlds in which their complex trajectories represent not a departure from life, but life itself. I distill three lessons that they share: trans youth need space, trans youth need a place, and trans youth "need your help to get free" (Vaid-Menon, as cited in Lerner, 2016).[1]

THE TRANS BODY IN TIME: THINKING ABOUT RACE AND SPACE

In 2019, we are roughly a century past the point when people we now call trans began to publish writing about their lives (see Body, [1907] 2006; Hoyer, [1933] 2004).[2] Curious similarities persist across descriptions of their bodies, yet even more curious differences are evident, indicating that lives can and will be storied in uncooperative ways across time and place. It is beginning to be more widely acknowledged that those most commonly named as important figures in trans history, those who are usually publicly credited with having made possible future trans generations, are almost always white. Within recent years, however, criticism has become louder with respect to this dangerously incomplete version of history. In the book *Black on Both Sides: A Racial History of Transgender Identity*, C. Riley Snorton (2017) reads the archives of the postwar Black press for stories of Black trans life that have otherwise been left out of trans histories. While it is also commonplace to refer to trans history as a history of adulthood and trans children and youth as "new," Jules Gill-Peterson (2018) writes about the forgotten history of young trans people of colour who not only *existed* in the past, but were active change-makers. For example, Latina trans woman Sylvia Rivera was living on the streets in New York City by age eleven and went on to establish the organization STAR: Street Transvestite Action Revolutionaries. Together with Black trans activist Marsha P. Johnson, Rivera also played a key role in the 1969 Stonewall Riots, generally understood as the birthplace of the North American gay liberation movement (Gill-Peterson, 2018).

In her text *Transgender History*, Susan Stryker notes that many who led both the 1969 Stonewall Riots and the 1966 Compton Cafeteria Riot in San Francisco would today be called trans youth of colour (Stryker, 2018). While trans history includes individuals who quietly and privately found ways to express themselves in a stifling time, Stryker (2018) writes that this history also includes young trans people, often racialized and often poor, who used their bodies to openly fight for space in the streets during some of our most formative historical moments. For this reason, when trans youth in this collection speak of feeling their body is a prison, or that their body often leaves them without a feeling of home, it is important to also reflect on those trans youth, often racialized and poor, who experience literal imprisonment and homelessness, and whose bodies our rights are often built upon (Stanley & Smith, 2015). In his poem "My Home," Tor recognizes these predecessors as the reason he has some semblance of safety now:

In my recent TED Talk I mention JT.[3]
And how he passed Bill C-16.
I've been told he's the reason I'm now safe, but I'm quick to deny it.
Because matter of the fact is, the first pride march was a riot.
Led by black trans women throwing bricks at white cops.
Because the police tried to make their queer lives stop.
Marsha P. Johnson is the real reason we have parades.
And those riots are why we don't need ones for straights.

I turn now to the poetic and artistic works in this collection and the embedded ideas of space, place, and freedom—a freedom that we must insist trans youth are owed.

THE BODY AS A PRISON: TRANS YOUTH NEED SPACE

In the poem "My Body," Jaxon writes "my body feels like a prison," gesturing to over a century of self-representations by trans and gender nonconforming writers who came before him. The particular type of "unfreedom"[4] conjured by the image of the prison shows up in multiple forms in this collection. In the poem "Strength," Lupus writes about being "trapped in a cage" and waiting "to be freed." Tor writes that he was "born in the wrong body" and that "this body doesn't suit me." Maisie speaks of hiding, and Jaxon remarks on the need to "escape" and leave behind the bleak space of a body that "feels suffocating." Trans youth, according to these young authors, need out of their confines—they need room to breathe and space to live—and while these narratives might be new for some, historically they are in good company.

In the 1860s, German attorney Karl Ulrichs published a series of pamphlets describing those who were "female souls in a male body" ([1864] 1994, p. 363). Though Ulrichs might be considered a gay man by today's standards, transsexuals[5] came to describe their predicament as a state of being "trapped in the wrong body" (Meyerowitz, 2002; Stryker, 2018). In the poem "My Home," youth writer Tor notes the potential and the limitations of framing his body as having something *wrong*: "Now other folks might argue that my body is not wrong. And I strongly agree. / The thing is, this body just doesn't suit me." While some trans scholars propose that "trapped" is simply what being trans feels like (Prosser, 1998), others suggest the statement has a purpose—to resist the problematization of trans minds, therefore resisting reparative or conversion therapies aiming to "fix" trans minds (Bettcher, 2014).[6]

In their writing, several of these youth authors use the term "dysphoria" to describe their relationship to their bodies. In the poem "Dysphoria," A.J. describes this as an "intense" and "weird feeling"—a feeling of "something not matching." Lupus speaks of a "blinding pain" and "hating" oneself because of feeling that they are "not in the right body." Maisie describes an "ugly" feeling. Sam writes that he feels "disproportionate." Jaxon simply expresses the problem with the word "too"—the sense that his body is too this, or too that, and in some way "never felt quite right." A.J. remarks that dysphoria is "kicking his ass" and ultimately offers: "Bodies suck sometimes."

As these young writers reach for metaphors to describe their sensations, their accounts of gender dysphoria are consistent with how the term is clinically used (American Psychiatric Association, 2013). According to the Canadian Psychological Association, gender dysphoria is an "unhappiness that some people feel with their physical sex and/or gender role" (2015). Though criteria shift over time, a diagnosis of gender dysphoria is generally part of assessing trans youth who seek gender confirming medical options such as puberty blockers, hormones, or surgery. The frequency with which the term gender dysphoria is used to describe trans people, however, might lead one to believe that *only* trans people experience this. A recent study found otherwise.

In 2013, a team of social scientists surveyed over 2000 people about their gender identity and their relationships with their bodies, 99 per cent of them cisgender (Joel et al., 2013). The survey questions were those typically asked only of trans people. Even though only 1 per cent of those surveyed were trans, 36.6 per cent felt sometimes as the other gender, 41.9 per cent were sometimes discontent with their sexed body (gender dysphoria), and 63.7 per cent sometimes wished to be of the other gender (Joel et al., 2013). In pointing to this, I do not mean to suggest that trans people and the space and supports they require are not significant. However, clearly these desires can be seen as part of a spectrum of human experience.

When Jaxon repeats three times that his body "feels like a prison," he communicates his need to put space between himself and a body that he finds "suffocating." Some trans youth might create that space by trying out a different name or pronoun, or changing their clothing, hair, etc. (often called social transition). Other trans youth might choose to create that space with medical transition steps. Listening to public debate, one could get the sense that such medical procedures are new or have yet to be thoroughly studied or tested. Yet this is not the case, because hormone therapies, puberty blockers, and similar surgical procedures have often been used uncontroversially with cisgender people. For example, in the 1950s, cis girls were given high doses of estrogen to prevent them from growing to a height that was deemed "too tall," and men have often taken testosterone to alter muscle growth or sex drive. Puberty blockers (GnRH analogues) are often described as new and even as a risky idea, yet they have been studied and prescribed for over three decades to pause puberty when physicians determine a young person has entered puberty too soon.[7] Even trans surgeries are not as unique as some might think. T. Garner (2014) writes about the overlap between male gynecomastia surgeries (the removal of unwanted male breast tissue) and the chest surgeries some trans men choose. Garner points out that the rationale for gynecomastia surgery is the same as that for trans chest surgery (not feeling comfortable in one's own skin) and is therefore the same technique done for the same reason. Garner (2014) concludes that desire for this surgery is treated as non-psychiatric for cis men because it takes their body toward, rather than away from, the norm.

In his poem "Dysphoria," A.J. writes about the feeling that one's body "doesn't belong to" them. A.J. asks: "Is that my voice? Is that *my* voice?", gesturing to the sense of dislocation some trans youth feel in their bodies, the sense that it is not their own. "It isn't me," Jaxon states bluntly in the poem "My Body." While this sensation is often pathologized in trans people, the idea that a feeling of estrangement from the body could be a part of human experience is not new within the history of philosophy. In the 1940s, French philosopher Jean-Paul Sartre considered that everyone's experience of their body is fragmented, and that profound alienation results if one's view of one's own body is replaced by another's view of it (Sartre, [1943] 1984). Again in the 1940s, French philosopher Maurice Merleau-Ponty wrote about those who perceive limbs they do not have (phantom limbs) or fail to perceive limbs they do have (anosognosia), noting that body image does not always reflect the physical body ([1945] 2012). Trans studies scholar Henry Rubin (1998) applied these concepts to trans bodies, proposing that trans people's body image is not an error but a type of "embodied knowledge" (p. 271). Feminist philosopher Gayle Salamon (2010) suggests that our understanding of all bodies will remain partial until we take trans bodies seriously. Nikki Sullivan (2006) maintains that not only is "being" important for humans, but also "becoming," and proposes trans lives as reflective of the human need for transformation. What critical body scholars suggest, then, is that the line separating "natural" bodies from trans bodies is the result of political maneuvers, and is itself not natural (Moore & Casper, 2015).

Lastly, in the framing of their bodily experience as one of imprisonment, as Jaxon does, the youth writers in this collection insist that their search for a better "living space" is reasonable (Riddell, 1996). Indeed, with the metaphors they draw on and the images they bring into view, they push back on the assumption that trans bodies are unnatural. In "Butterflies," Maisie imagines the process of coming out or transitioning as emerging from a chrysalis, blooming into a "magnificent being" and flying "high and free" with "the sun on our wings." In "My Home," Tor wishes for a world that might be "more colourful" because "we're better with more variety." In "Disproportionate," Sam likens their experience to "hibernation" and "suffocating under the cold," but with a chance to "blossom and bloom from the pressure" in "new colours." With imagery of birth, death, and rebirth, they reclaim the often-powerless position trans youth are left in when they seek recognition from the adults around them. Gesturing to a sense of freedom, they declare their independence as beings in their own right, rather than the property of adults. In Samuel's view, his need to "wait" in "dark space" before "spring is here," before he can finally "grow ... out of winter skins," is akin to nature's story of a seed waiting for life to shoot upwards; a reminder that "small things are still whole." In essence, with their metaphors of natural phenomena, these young writers locate themselves firmly in the natural world, with coming out or transition as part of a legitimate life course; not a departure from life, but life itself. As poet Mary Oliver (1986) wrote in "Wild Geese," these youth "[announce their]place in the family of things" (p. 14). The next section considers how these authors engage with the idea of place.

THE BODY AS HOME: TRANS YOUTH NEED A PLACE

A.J. writes that to have "gender dysphoria" is to feel your body "doesn't belong to you." Yet as the young writers in this collection show us, this feeling is not inevitable and there is much to learn from the steps trans youth take to make their bodies their own—steps that, in their own words, take them home.

In the aptly named piece "My Home," Tor proposes that "everyone's body is a place to live." Yet he distinguishes between his "place to live" and that of others. According to Tor, the "cishets," by which he means cisgender heterosexual people, "were gifted a home or a temple," yet he was "merely given an apartment for rental." Tor gestures to a feeling of impermanence, a lack of ownership or full authority with which to inhabit his body. Yet Tor also points to a hopeful possibility—his home is "under construction," and his current body has been given to him as "somewhere to stay" in the meantime. "It's not quite time to move in yet," Tor adds; "I'll have to wait a few more days."

In his book *Second Skins: The Body Narratives of Transsexuality*, trans theorist Jay Prosser (1998) asks if the willingness of (some) trans people to alter their bodies suggests, on the one hand, that the body is *unimportant* to trans people, or on the other hand, that the body is *highly important* to trans people. In "My Body," Jaxon speaks to this puzzle, noting on the one hand that his body is "just the vessel," and then clarifying that, despite this, it is a body that "must carry me through my life." Jaxon shows us that for some trans youth, it is crucial that they alter their homes so that they work for and not against them.

The concept of the body as home, or transition as a homecoming, is not new in trans studies or in the public narration of trans lives. Twentieth-century transsexual autobiographers would sometimes narrate their transitions as a type of emigration to a new place or a return to an old home. In the article "No Place Like Home," Prosser (1995) writes that the trans desire to change the body is an instance in which "the familiar is felt as most strange" (491). According to Prosser (1995), transition can be a way of coming home to the self, a sense of nostalgia for a body one has never had. Lucas Crawford (2010) notes that our terms for describing bodies are often architectural (a temple, a home, a frame) and suggests that, in one way or another, gender has always been wrapped up with structure. Writing about trans people of colour and migration, Nael Bhanji (2013) on the other hand suggests we should be mindful of which trans people can comfortably claim a home, on the basis of race and national belonging. Indeed, in "My Home," Tor uses the concept of home to mean both the body and the nation, though he refuses to credit the Trudeau government's human rights legislation (Bill C-16) for trans rights, reminding us that Stonewall, the birthplace of these rights, "was a riot." Additionally, Prosser (1998) insists on the importance of embodiment and specificity, since for trans people, not just any name or pronoun will do, and not just any body. In the essay "Hair Expression," Tor writes, "My hair is me, and that's who I am."

Elsewhere I have proposed that both space and place are important for trans individuals, though not necessarily for the same individuals, since *space* may be more important to non-binary folks and genderqueers and *place* may be more important to transsexuals

(Pyne, 2017). While some (non-binary, genderqueers) aim to dwell between or outside of gender, other trans individuals require a dwelling, a place to be, and not just any place, but a home. When Jaxon expresses his sense of ownership over his body in saying that he "can alter it any way" he pleases, he is in fact supported by a recent court decision of the British Columbia Supreme Court that found that a fourteen-year-old trans boy was legally entitled to access transition care despite the strong objections of one of his parents (Vikander, 2019). Indeed, the judge stated that refusal to grant access to his transition was a form of family violence. Additionally, such parental rejection can result in literal homelessness. In the Trans PULSE study, 100 per cent of trans youth who had strong parental support for their gender identity were adequately housed, compared to only 45 per cent of those without this support (Travers et al., 2012). For Indigenous trans and Two-Spirit youth, to be without a "home" can have an additional depth of meaning, including a lost relationship and legal title to land through the devastation of colonialism (see Thistle, 2017).

In the poem "Strength," Lupus notes the most frightening struggle in some trans lives: "You must fight the urge to end it all." Research confirms what Lupus is describing, that some trans youth are unable to easily inhabit their bodies and can struggle with self-harm. In a Canadian survey, Veale et al. (2015) found that nearly two-thirds of trans youth reported self-harm in the past year. The Ontario Trans PULSE study found higher levels of suicidality among trans youth than trans adults (Scanlon et al., 2010). Yet research also shows this is not inevitable and can be altered, and I elaborate on this in the following section. In recent years, there has been considerable concern and debate in the public realm regarding trans youth and whether they will "desist"—changing their minds and no longer identifying as trans. Statistics proposing high rates of "desistance" have been circulated in attempts to dissuade professionals and parents from supporting a young person's transition. Yet other clinicians, researchers, and advocates have rejected the research relied on to obtain those figures. Indeed, a special issue of the *International Journal of Transgenderism* recently hosted a debate on the topic (Temple Newhook et al., 2018). Instead of curtailing young people's futures, Temple Newhook et al. (2018) conclude that we must instead prioritize respect for trans youth autonomy in the present— prioritizing respect for their bodies as their own—because for all of the studies of gender nonconforming youth, we ultimately stand to learn more by simply listening to them.

To listen to the voices of trans youth in this collection is to understand the possibility that the body can mean different things than we might expect. Tor writes that while he waits for his body (his home) to better reflect his sense of self, he can "make this house as cozy" as possible in the meantime. Jaxon writes: "My body still doesn't feel quite like it was made for me, / But it feels just a little less alien." He goes on to say that his body is "starting to feel like less of a prison." Tor concludes his poem by stating: "Because for now, this is the home of a handsome young man." Writing in a different text about a feeling of disconnection/connection to the body, trans poet Ali Blythe (2019) writes: "I jump and the man's / skin comes with me" (p. 24).

In "My Body," Jaxon repeats three times that his body "feels like a prison." Yet as he moves toward transition this begins to shift:

I'm now three and a half months on T.
My voice has dropped,
My face has changed,
And I'm starting to feel stronger.

He writes: "Maybe, / Just maybe, / My body is finally starting to feel like home." The many references in this collection both to bodies as prisons and bodies as homes demand that we acknowledge there is a world of difference between a prison and a home, and that the difference is one of choice, will, and freedom. The next section explores how the young writers in this collection express their desire to be mirrored and their need to be free.

THE MEANING OF THE MIRROR: TRANS YOUTH "NEED YOUR HELP TO GET FREE"[8]

In the visual art contribution by Ajam entitled "Reflection," we see a mirror image that differs noticeably from the individual standing before it. Maisie's Life Journey pieces similarly show two different images of the same person. As a depiction of the "gender dysphoria" that other contributors have described, these images are simpatico with Jaxon's description of his body: "It does not show people who I am. / It isn't me." Similarly, in "Strength," Lupus writes: "You must live with what you have until you are freed."

In *Second Skins* (1998), Prosser devotes a chapter to "Mirror Images," in which he discusses the disorienting mirror scenes that appear consistently throughout twentieth-century transsexual autobiographies. "My life was a series of distorted mirrors," writes autobiographer Mario Martino, describing the pain and struggle that led him to transition in the 1960s (as cited in Prosser, 1998, p. 100). Reading the youth writings in this collection, we are witness also to their pain and struggle, yet there is more to such difficulties than just "gender dysphoria," and more than merely witnessing is required of us as an audience. As these young authors hold up a mirror to this society, that we might see it through their eyes, we are called upon to return their gaze and reflect back the leadership they show us. In short, we are called upon to be their mirrors.

The struggles of trans youth are more widely reported on than ever before, in particular, troubling levels of suicidality. In 2015, the Canadian Trans Youth Health Survey found that 65 per cent of trans youth (ages fourteen to eighteen years) had attempted suicide in the past year, and 37 per cent had seriously considered it (Veale et al., 2015). Yet crucially, research also shows that important aspects of trans suicidality are driven by factors within their social world, rather than solely internal to that individual. For instance, in a Trans PULSE (2013) survey of 433 trans people in Ontario age sixteen and older showed that, when trans youth had strong parental support for their gender identity, their risk of attempting suicide decreased by a staggering 93 per cent (Travers et al., 2012). An American study found that trans youth who are able to use their chosen name are at a reduced risk for suicide, with the risk decreasing for every context in which they are able to use their name (Russell et al., 2018). The Trans PULSE study also found that suicide risk is lowered when trans people have social support, identity documents that match their lived gender, and parental support for their gender through adulthood (Bauer et al., 2015). The same study found that experiencing transphobic violence is associated with a seven-fold increase in suicide risk. Furthermore, those who desired medical transition but had not yet begun were twenty-seven times more likely to have attempted suicide in the past year than those who had completed transition, by their own definition (Bauer et al., 2013). Thus, while some professionals extend the wait time for transition under the assumption that taking more time will increase youth safety, there is some evidence that the pre-transition time (for those who desire medical transition) can be a dangerous time that should be shortened. What remains hopeful about these otherwise troubling statistics is that societal attitudes are clearly alterable and within our power to change.

In "My Home," Tor remarks on the impact of transphobia on trans youth:

That ignorance causes kids pain
Did you know that GSAs save lives
Kids without 'em kill themselves 33% of the time
But if they're accepted in the classroom
Only 17% fall victim to the suicide doom.

As Tor points out, this raises the importance of looking beyond an individual definition of gender dysphoria and toward the aspects of "dysphoria" that belong to a human community that is failing trans youth. Trans poet Joy Ladin (n.d.) remarks: "A diagnosis of gender dysphoria, then, is a diagnosis not just of an individual, but of a culture: the client diagnosed with gender dysphoria is manifesting the culture's failure to support the articulation, understanding, expression, development, and integration of transgender selves" (p. 3). In short, Ladin points to a society that fails to mirror back trans people's personhood. In his article "Trans Bodies and the Failure of Mirrors," Langer (2016) writes that young trans people's psyches are damaged by "repeated failures in misattuned mirroring" by the adults around them (p. 308).

In recognition of the importance of mirroring for trans youth, the dominant model for responding to trans youth has shifted over time, from a reparative or corrective approach to an affirming approach. In the 1960s and 1970s, a subfield of sexology, psychology, and psychiatry began to systematically study and "treat" gender nonconforming children, most often those they termed "feminine boys," with the goal of preventing them from growing up to be gay men or trans women (Bryant, 2006). Influential psychiatrist Richard Green wrote: "My focus will be on what we might call the prevention of transsexualism" (1971, p. 167). Children who differed from expectations were classified as disordered. Elsewhere, I've written that supportive parents were also pathologized and trained to reject their child's identity (Pyne, 2014; 2016). Over time, the affirming model has challenged the truth claims of the reparative approach, and it now parts ways in philosophy and goal. Aiming to support young people's authentic gender health (Hidalgo et al., 2013), in the affirming model parents are encouraged to be "child-taught" and to celebrate the child no matter their current or future identity (Hill & Menvielle, 2009).

Many historical events played a role in the paradigm shift toward an affirming model, including but not limited to:

- Exposure by journalists (Burke, 1996);
- Critique by researchers (Hird, 2003; Grace, 2015; Langer & Martin, 2004; Pyne, 2014; Tosh, 2011);
- Advocacy by mental health clinicians (Ehrensaft, 2011; Hill & Menvielle, 2009; Pickstone-Taylor, 2003; Wallace & Russell, 2013; Wong, 2014);
- Local, online, and media activism challenging pathologizing treatment (Pyne, 2015a; 2015b; Tosh, 2011; Williams, 2017; Winters, 2006);
- Research showing negative results associated with rejecting a trans child's identity (Travers et al., 2012; Turban et al., 2018);
- Research showing positive results associated with affirmation (Hill et al., 2010; Olson et al., 2016);
- Supportive parent leadership (Manning et al., 2015);
- Legal change, including the banning of "conversion therapy" in some jurisdictions (Legislative Assembly of Ontario, 2015);
- A growing list of professional position statements supporting trans children and denouncing "conversion therapy" by the World Professional Association for Transgender Health (2011), the Canadian Professional Association for Transgender Health (2015), the Canadian Psychological Association (2015), the Canadian Association for Social Work Education (2015), the American Psychological Association (Drescher & Pula 2014), the American Academy of Pediatrics (Rafferty 2018), and the American Academy of Child and Adolescent Psychiatry (2018).

While there remain parents who refuse to affirm trans children, the North American clinical approach is now firmly rooted in affirmation. As mentioned, the British Columbia Supreme Court ruled that a parent misgendering a trans youth can constitute child abuse (Vikander, 2019).

In the poem "Strength," Lupus writes that "no one can help you find yourself." Here I might offer an alternative perspective, supported by philosophy, suggesting that perhaps other people can help us find ourselves, but only if they do not neglect their responsibilities. Within moral and political philosophy, there is a tradition of theorizing the concept of "recognition" in light of the intersubjective nature of the self (Hegel, [1807] 2009). We rely on others for our own "self-relation," Williams (2017) argues, and we develop our self-worth in relationship with others rather than in solitary self-reflection (151). Sartre ([1943] 1984) wrote: "The road of interiority passes through the Other" (p. 236). In this light, recognition is a basic human need, not a mere courtesy. Moreover, on the larger political stage, philosophers have argued that the withholding of legitimate recognition for devalued persons constitutes an act of injustice (Honneth, 1995; Taylor, 1994). In her poem "Butterflies," Maisie writes: "But we butterflies are sensitive / An insult causes us to wilt and fall." What I understand Maisie to be saying is that our self-concept is affected by others' concept of us, at times to a staggering degree. Trans poet Joy Ladin writes: "That's the scandal and glory of identity: our sense of self is not ours alone ..." (2014). It must be noted, however, that for Indigenous communities, these are not new ideas, but part of a rich tradition of viewing one's life as inseparable from "all our relations" (Talaga, 2018). We rely on one another to "get free" (Vaid-Menon, quoted in Chakraborty, 2016).

In Lupus's poem "Strength," he references the struggles some trans youth can have with suicidality: "You must fight the urge to end it all, because you know deep down inside that / your spark is very important and your life is your reward." In this collection, these authors teach us not only about these potential brushes with death, but also the profound steps taken to live and to face the world on their own terms. For some this involves taking important medical transition steps, and for others, being true to themselves consists of linguistic innovations—shifting to non-binary ways of speaking to make room for one another. In the social sciences, language is studied for what it does—not just as a way of describing reality, but a way of *doing* it (Gibbs, 2015). Therefore when A.J. writes "A boy with curves? You bet your bottom dollar that's what I am!," he expands the possibilities for *boy*. When he writes "I got myself a real thick, pudgy body, but that's just more of me to love!," he expands the possibilities for which bodies can be loved and loveable. Finally, A.J. offers a loving and humorous way to recognize and mirror back other trans youth and their bodily struggles:

> Are you missing parts or have ones you don't want? That's okay. Sometimes when you build furniture from a certain Nordic-themed store, they give you extra pieces that don't make sense, or they forget one or two. That's okay—it just is something that makes you, well, *you!*

CONCLUSION

In a social sphere in which there are few to no words with which to celebrate diverse genders, it should come as no surprise that a sense of silence and dislocation tends to follow gender nonconforming people. Yet here in this collection, these young authors are finding the words, and with them, they're also finding worlds. Through metaphors and poetic imagery, they tell us of experiencing the body as a prison, the body as a home, and the need to be mirrored as the people they know themselves to be. In their journeys to tell us who they are, these young authors come to *be* who they are—they write themselves into the story and build the very world they need. Despite their astonishing bravery and independence, I would add, however, that they still deserve our help "to get free" (Vaid-Menon, quoted in Chakraborty, 2016). As they hold a mirror up to our world, that we might see it through their eyes, their declarations of self demand that we mirror back to them our recognition, not only recognition of their struggles, but also of their imaginings of new ways to live. While critics of trans rights will sometimes claim that trans youth are departing from nature, the young artists and authors in this collection show us that the trajectory they take is not a departure from life, but is life itself. How fortunate we are to bear witness as they open and step through what trans poet Joy Ladin (2012) calls "the door of life."

TIPS FOR SUPPORTING THE BODILY AUTONOMY OF TRANS YOUTH:

✓ **Encourage body autonomy.** If you're a parent or caregiver, consider ways to increase the decisions that your child (trans or cis) makes about their body. How can you maximize their choices in how they dress, groom, and present themselves? Depending on the age of your child and whether they are seeking any medical transition steps, consider if there is emotional work you might need to do as a parent in order to let go of the choices your child might make about their body. Be mindful that having a complex relationship to one's body is not uncommon for many people, trans or cis, and needn't be pathologized. Remember that the steps that some trans people take in order to feel at home in their bodies might be different from what you imagined for your child. Trans or cis, we all need to feel that our bodies are our own.

✓ **Speak up.** Service providers in particular need to respond to all harmful statements made about trans people. For example, parents will sometimes make transphobic remarks as they struggle to learn how to accept and celebrate their child. As a service provider, people look to you for guidance on acceptable boundaries which means that your actions and inactions carry extra significance. Practise the strategies you will need for challenging transphobic statements with a friend or colleague before you need to use them. You can intervene in instances of transphobia, while still remaining supportive to the parents who need your care.

✓ **Centre the experiences of racialized and more marginalized trans youth.** If you are a service provider, be mindful of how trans youth on the margins—due to their status as Indigenous or racialized youth, or due to disability, poverty, and other factors—can face more exposure to brutal living conditions and require our ongoing commitment to address their needs. Anticipate a diverse range of trans and non-binary youth in your service setting, rather than waiting for racialized or disabled trans youth to tell you that your services are not accessible or relevant. Bringing in speakers or launching a targeted hiring is one way to welcome a wider range of perspectives into your agency. Lending your support for local social movements, such as supporting Indigenous land defence actions, will help to connect you and your agency to a wider range of communities.

✓ **Arm yourself with resources to advocate for trans and non-binary youth.** Especially as parents, caregivers, educators, or service providers, you need to be aware of the research supporting your affirmation of trans and non-binary youth. The research cited in this chapter and elsewhere in this book can help to demonstrate how impactful affirmation is for trans youth, including social support, their ability to use their chosen name, and their access to medical transition steps if desired. Try to collect the references and resources you need so they are available to you if your support for trans youth is called into question. While being able to explain your position is helpful, ultimately, we must demand that others justify their *lack* of support for trans youth.

✓ **Pay attention to language.** Notice how trans and non-binary youth describe their identities and bodies themselves. Mirror that language back when speaking to or about them. You might not get everyone's pronouns right all the time, and mistakes do happen, but you can apologize and then remember it for next time. It will mean a lot to trans and non-binary youth to know that someone cares and is trying.

NOTES

1. The phrase "I need your help to get free" comes from the recent public performance of non-binary artist Alok Vaid-Menon (see Lerner, 2016) and from historical writings in Black feminist thought (Taylor, 2017).
2. What one considers the first trans autobiography is debatable, first regarding who might be called trans, and second regarding whether individuals authored their own texts or were written about by others.
3. "JT" is a short form for Justin Trudeau, the prime minister of Canada at the time of writing.
4. The term "unfreedom" is used by Black scholars such as Okolo (1984) to describe the results of anti-Black racism.
5. The term *trans* or *transgender* is more commonly used today; however, some identify with the term *transsexual*. See *Trans / Transgender* in the glossary at the end of this volume.
6. Yet it is also becoming important to acknowledge that the need to have a so-called "right mind" in order to be eligible for transition can negatively affect disabled trans youth, those with mental health concerns, and autistic trans youth.
7. The first trans youth was given puberty blocking treatment in the Netherlands in the early 1990s, and Dutch studies have found no negative outcomes or serious side effects after a twenty-two-year follow-up study (Cohen-Kettenis et al., 2011). The Endocrine Society declared that the benefits of puberty blockers outweigh the risks (Hembree et al., 2009). In Canada, approximately twelve clinics provide this treatment to trans youth, and the research study TransYouthCAN aims to better understand these young people's health and well-being (TransYouthCAN Project, 2018).
8. Alok Vaid-Menon (see Lerner, 2016).

REFERENCES

American Academy of Child and Adolescent Psychiatry. (2018). *Conversion therapy*. Retrieved from https://www.aacap.org/AACAP/Policy_Statements/2018/Conversion_Therapy.aspx.

American Psychiatric Association. (2013). *Diagnostic and statistical manual of mental disorders* (5th ed.). Arlington, VA: American Psychiatric Press.

Ashenden, A., & Braidwood, E. (2018, October 4). *Trans bodies deserve love – this campaign celebrates their beauty.* Pink News. Retrieved from https://www.pinknews.co.uk/2018/10/04/trans-bodies-deserve-love-this-campaign-celebrates-their-beauty/.

Bauer, G., Pyne, J., Francino, M., & Hammond, R. (2013). Suicidality among trans people in Ontario: Implications for social work and social justice. *Service Social, 59*(1), 35–62.

Bauer, G., Scheim, A., Pyne, J., Travers, R., & Hammond, R. (2015). Intervenable factors associated with suicide risk in transgender persons: A respondent-driven sampling study in Ontario, Canada. *BMC Public Health, 15*(525), 1–15.

Bettcher, T. (2014). Trapped in the wrong theory. *Signs, 39*(2), 383–406.

Bhanji, N. (2013). TRANS/SCRIPTIONS: Homing desires, trans(sexual) citizenship and racialized bodies. In S. Stryker and A. Aizura (Eds.), *The transgender studies reader 2* (pp. 512–527). New York: Routledge.

Blythe, A. (2019). *Hymnswitch.* Fredericton, NB: Goose Lane Editions.

Body, N. O. ([1907] 2006). *Memoirs of a man's maiden years.* Philadelphia: University of Pennsylvania Press.

Bothways, E. (2018). *Trans Bodies Are Beautiful.* World Alternative Crown at World Burlesque Games 2018. Retrieved from https://vimeo.com/300097918.

Bryant, K. (2006). Making gender identity disorder of childhood: Historical lessons for contemporary debates. *Sexuality Research and Social Policy, 3*(3), 23–39.

Burke, P. (1996). *Gender shock: Exploding the myths of male and female.* New York: Anchor Books.

Canadian Association for Social Work Education. (2015). *Joint statement on the affirmation of gender diverse children and youth.* Canadian Association of Social Workers and Canadian Association for Social Work Education. Retrieved from http://caswe-acfts.ca/joint-statement-on-the-affirmation-of-gender-diverse-children-and-youth/.

Canadian Press. (2019, January 21). *Sex-ed curriculum rollback endangers transgender girl, human rights tribunal told.* CBC. Retrieved from https://www.cbc.ca/news/canada/toronto/human-rights-tribunal-hearing-challenge-rollback-sex-ed-curriculum-1.4987157.

Canadian Professional Association for Transgender Health. (2015). *Submission to the standing committee on justice policy re: Bill 77, Affirming Sexual Orientation and Gender Identity Act, 2015.* Retrieved from http://www.cpath.ca/wp-content/uploads/2016/02/2015-06-03-CPATH-Submission-Re-Bill-77-Affirming-Sexual-Orientation-and-Gender-Identity-Act-2015.pdf.

Canadian Psychological Association. (2015). *Psychology Works Factsheet: Gender Dysphoria in Children.* Retrieved from https://www.cpa.ca/docs/File/Publications/FactSheets/PsychologyWorksFactSheet_GenderDysphoriaInChildren.pdf.

Chakraborty, D. (2016, September 6). *Trans artist Alok Vaid-Menon explains why taking a selfie is an act of empowerment.* Vagabond. Retrieved from https://www.vagabomb.com/Trans-Artist-Alok-VaidMenon-Explains-Why-Taking-a-Selfie-Is-an-Act-of-Empowerment/?fbclid=IwAR1mWJYi1IoUJt0Zzs8dZE6DOTBoA6ICpW0We-3_Is95kWsWJ5Xb5gkNxtg.

Cohen-Kettenis, P. T., Schagen, S. E. E., Steensma, T. D., de Vries, A. L. C., & Delemarre-van de Waal, H. A. (2011). Puberty suppression in a gender-dysphoric adolescent: A 22-year follow-up. *Archives of Sexual Behavior, 40*(4), 843–847.

Crawford, L. (2010). Breaking ground on a theory of transgender architecture. *Seattle Journal for Social Justice, 8*(2), 515–539.

Democracy Now!. (2014, February 19). "Black trans bodies are under attack": Freed activist Cece McDonald, actress Laverne Cox speak out. Retrieved from https://www.democracynow. org/2014/2/19/black_trans_bodies_are_under_attack.

Di Ceglie, D., & Freedman, D. (1998). *A stranger in my own body: Atypical gender identity development and mental health.* London: Karnac Books.

Drescher, J., & Pula, J. (2014). *Ethical Issues raised by the treatment of gender-variant prepubescent children.* LGBT Bioethics: Visibility, Disparities, and Dialogue, *Hastings Center Report, 44*(5), 17–22.

Ehrensaft, D. (2011). *Gender born, gender made.* New York: The Experiment.

Erickson-Schroth, L. (2014). *Trans bodies, trans selves: A resource guide for the transgender community.* New York: Oxford University Press.

Garner, T. (2014). Chest surgeries of a different "nature." *Annual Review of Critical Psychology, 11,* 337–356.

Gibbs, G. (2015). *Discourse analysis part I: Discursive psychology* [video file]. University of Huddersfield. Retrieved from https://www.youtube.com/watch?v=F5rEy1lbvlw.

Gill-Peterson, J. (2018). *Histories of the transgender child.* Minneapolis: University of Minnesota Press.

Gossett, R., Stanley, E., & Burton, J. (2017). *Trapdoor: Trans cultural production and the politics of visibility.* Cambridge, MA: MIT Press.

Grace, A. (2015). *Growing into resilience: Sexual and gender minority youth in Canada.* Toronto: University of Toronto Press.

Green, R. (1971). Diagnosis and treatment of gender identity disorders during childhood. *Archives of Sexual Behavior, 1*(2), 167–173.

Grinberg, E. (2019, February 28). *These bills could make life harder for transgender people, civil rights goups say.* CNN. Retrieved from https://www.cnn.com/2019/02/27/us/transgender-bills-2019/index.html.

Hegel, G. F. ([1807] 2009). *Phenomenology of spirit.* Translated by J.B. Baillie. Available from digireads.com.

Hembree, W. C., Cohen-Kettenis, P., Delemarre-van de Waal, H. A., Gooren, L. J., Meyer, W. J. III, Spack, N. P., Tangpricha, V., & Montori, V. M. (2009). Endocrine treatment of transsexual persons: An endocrine society clinical practice guideline. *Journal of Clinical Endocrinology & Metabolism, 94*(9), 3132–3154.

Hidalgo, M., Ehrensaft, D., Tishelman, A., Clark, L., Garofalo, R., Rosenthal, S., & Olson, J. (2013). The gender affirmative model: What we know and what we aim to learn. *Human Development, 56,* 285–290.

Hill, D. B., & Menvielle, E. J. (2009). "You have to give them a place where they feel protected and safe and loved": The views of parents who have gender-variant children and adolescents. *Journal of LGBT Youth, 6*(2–3), 243–271.

Hill, D., Menvielle, E., Sica, K., & Johnson, A. (2010). An affirmative intervention for families with gender variant children: Parental ratings of child mental health and gender. *Journal of Sex & Marital Therapy, 36*, 6–23.

Hird, M. (2003). A typical gender identity conference? Some disturbing reports from the therapeutic front lines. *Feminism & Psychology, 13*(2), 181–199.

Honneth, A. (1995). *The struggle for recognition: A moral grammar of social conflicts*. Boston: Polity Press.

Hoyer, N. ([1933] 2004). *Man into woman: The first sex change*. Blue Boat Books.

Joel, D., Tarrasch, R., Berman, Z., Mukamel, M., & Ziv, E. (2013). Queering gender: Studying gender identity in "normative" individuals. *Psychology & Sexuality, 5*(4), 1–31.

Ladin, J. (2012). *Through the door of life: A Jewish journey between genders*. Madison, WI: University of Wisconsin Press.

Ladin, J. (2014). *I am not not me*. Presentation at Writing Trans Genres conference in Winnipeg, MB. Retrieved from http://www.writingtransgenres.com/.

Ladin, J. (n.d.). *What we talk about when we talk about "gender dysphoria": An address to psychotherapists*. Retrieved from https://www.academia.edu/23409519/ What_We_Talk_About_When_We_Talk_About_Gender_Dysphoria_.

Langer, S. J. (2016). Trans bodies and the failure of mirrors. *Studies in Gender and Sexuality, 17*(4), 306–319.

Langer, S. J., & Martin, J. I. (2004). How dresses can make you mentally ill: Examining gender identity disorder in children. *Child and Adolescent Social Work Journal, 21*(1), 5–23.

Legislative Assembly of Ontario. (2015). *Bill 77, Affirming Sexual Orientation and Gender Identity Act, 2015*. Retrieved from http://www.ontla.on.ca/web/bills/bills_detail. do?localeDen&BillIDD3197.

Lerner, S. (2016, September 8). *A total stranger stared at them and asked them what they were. This is their response*. Aplus. Retrieved from https://articles.aplus.com/a/alok-vaid-menon-selfie -facebook.

Manning, K., Holmes, C., Pullen-Sansfacon, A., Temple Newhook, J., & Travers, A. (2015). Fighting for trans* kids: Academic parent activism in the 21st century. *Studies in Social Justice, 9*(1), 118–135.

Merleau-Ponty, M. ([1945] 2012). *Phenomenology of Perception*. Translated by Donald Landes. New York: Routledge.

Meyerowitz, J. (2002). *How sex changed: A history of transsexuality in the United States*. Cambridge, MA: Harvard University Press.

Moore, L.J., & Casper, M. (2015). *The body: Social and cultural dissections*. New York: Routledge.

Namaste, V. (2000). *Invisible lives: The erasure of transsexual and transgendered people*. Chicago: University of Chicago Press.

NBD Campaign. (2018). *I'll use your pronoun*. No Big Deal Campaign. Retrieved from: https://www.nbdcampaign.ca/

Okolo, C.B. (1984). Apartheid as unfreedom. *Presence Africaine, 129*, 20–37.

Oliver, M. (1986). Wild geese. In M. Oliver (Ed.), *Dream Work* (p. 14). New York: Atlantic Monthly Press.

Olson, K., Durwood, L., DeMeules, M., & McLaughlin, K. (2016). Mental health of transgender children who are supported in their identities. *Pediatrics, 137*(3), 1–8.

Pickstone-Taylor, S. (2003). Children with gender nonconformity. *Journal of the American Academy of Child and Adolescent Psychiatry, 42*, 266.

Prosser, J. (1995). No place like home: The transgendered narrative of Leslie Feinberg's *Stone Butch Blues. Modern Fiction Studies, 41*(3-4), 483–514.

Prosser, J. (1998). *Second skins: The body narratives of transsexuality.* New York: Columbia University Press.

Pyne, J. (2014). The governance of gender non-conforming children: A dangerous enclosure. *Annual Review of Critical Psychology, 11*, 79–96.

Pyne, J. (2015a, January 14). *Fix society please: Final Words of transgender teen are a wake-up call to stop fixing trans kids and start repairing their broken worlds.* NOW Magazine.

Pyne, J. (2015b, December 17). *Discredited treatment of trans kids at CAMH shouldn't shock us.* Toronto Star.

Pyne, J. (2016). Parenting is not a job … it's a relationship: Recognition and relational knowledge among parents of gender non-conforming children. *Journal of Progressive Human Service, 27*(1), 21–48.

Pyne, J. (2017). Arresting Ashley X: Trans youth, puberty blockers, and the question of whether time is on your side. *Somatechnics, 7*(1), 95–123.

Rafferty, J. (2018). Ensuring comprehensive care and support for transgender and gender-diverse children and adolescents. *Pediatrics, 142*(4), 1–14.

Riddell, C. (1996). Divided sisterhood: A critical review of Janice Raymond's transsexual empire. In R. Ekins and D. King (Eds.), *Blending genders: Social aspects of cross-dressing and sex-changing* (pp. 171–189). London: Routledge.

Rosello-Penaloza, M. (2018). *No body: Clinical Constructions of gender and transsexuality – pathologization, violence and deconstruction.* New York: Routledge.

Rubin, H. (1998). Phenomenology as method in trans studies. *GLQ, 4*(2), 263–281.

Russell, S. T., Pollitt, A. M., Li, G., & Grossman, A. H. (2018). Chosen name use is linked to reduced depressive symptoms, suicidal ideation, and suicidal behaviour among transgender youth. *Journal of Adolescent Health, 63*(4), 503–505.

Salamon, G. (2010). *Assuming a body: Transgender and rhetorics of materiality.* New York: Columbia University Press.

Sartre, J. P. ([1943] 1984). *Being and nothingness: A phenomenological essay on ontology.* New York: Washington Square Press.

Scanlon, K., Travers, R., Coleman, T., Bauer, G., & Boyce, M. (2010). *Ontario's trans communities and suicide: Transphobia is bad for our health.* Trans PULSE. Retrieved from http://transpulseproject.ca/wp-content/uploads/2010/11/E2English.pdf.

Schöttelndreier, M. (1999, November 13). *Kinderen van het verkeerde geslacht.* Algemeen Dagblad. Retrieved from http://www.ad.nl/ad/nl/4560/Gezond /article/detail/ 514097/1999/11/13/ Kinderen-van-het-verkeerde-geslacht.dhtml.

Snorton, C. R. (2017). *Black on both sides: A racial history of trans identity.* Minneapolis: University of Minnesota Press.

Stanley, E., & Smith, N. (2015). *Captive genders: Trans embodiment and the prison industrial complex*. Oakland, CA: AK Press.

Stryker, S. (2018). *Transgender history, revised edition: The roots of today's revolution*. New York: Seal Press.

Stryker, S., & Whittle, S. (2006). *The transgender studies reader*. New York: Routledge.

Sullivan, N. (2006). Transmogrification: The (un)becoming other(s). In S. Stryker & S. Whittle (Eds.), *The transgender studies reader* (pp. 552–564). New York: Routledge.

Talaga, T. (2018). *All our relations: Finding the path forward*. CBC Massey Lectures. Toronto: House of Anansi Press.

Taylor, C. (1994). The politics of recognition. In A. Gutmann (Ed.), *Multiculturalism: Examining the politics of recognition* (pp. 25–73). Princeton, NJ: Princeton University Press.

Taylor, K.Y. (2017). *How we get free: Black feminism and the Combahee River Collective*. Chicago: Haymarket Books.

Temple Newhook, J., Pyne, J., Winters, K., Feder, S., Holmes, C., Tosh, J., Sinnott, M., Jamieson, A., & Pickett, S. (2018). A critical commentary on follow-up studies and "desistance" theories about transgender and gender non-conforming children. *International Journal of Transgenderism, 19*(2), 212–224.

Thistle, J. (2017). *Indigenous definition of homelessness in canada*. Toronto: Canadian Observatory on Homelessness Press.

Tosh, J. (2011). "Zuck off!" A commentary on the protest against Ken Zucker and his "treatment" of childhood gender identity disorder. *Psychology of Women Section Review, 13*(1), 10–16.

TransYouthCan Project. (2018). *About*. Retrieved from http://transyouthcan.ca/.

Travers, R., Bauer, G., Pyne, J., Bradley, K., Gale, L., & Papadimitriou, M. (2012). *Impacts of strong parental support fort trans youth: A report prepared for Children's Aid Society of Toronto and Delisle Youth Services*. Toronto: Trans PULSE.

Turban, J., Beckwith, N., Reisner, S., & Keuroghlian, A. (2018). Exposure to conversion therapy for gender identity is associated with poor adult mental health outcomes among transgender people in the US. *Journal of the American Academy of Child and Adolescent Psychiatry, 57*(10), S208.

Ulrichs, K. H. ([1864] 1994). *The riddle of "man-manly" love*, 2 volumes. Translated by Michael A. Lombardi-Nash. Buffalo: New York.

Veale, J., Saewyc, E., Frohard-Dourlent, H., Dobson, S., Clark, B., & the Canadian Trans Youth Health Survey Research Group. (2015). *Being safe, being me: Results of the Canadian trans youth health survey*. Vancouver: Stigma and Resilience Among Vulnerable Youth Centre, School of Nursing, University of British Columbia.

Vikander, T. (2019, March 12). Misgendering Kids and preventing transitioning can constitute child abuse, BC Supreme Court rules. *The Star Vancouver*. Retrieved from https://www.thestar.com/vancouver/2019/03/12/misgendering-kids-and-preventing-transitioning-can-constitute-child-abuse-following-bc-supreme-court-ruling.html.

Wallace, R., & Russell, H. (2013). Attachment and shame in gender-nonconforming children and their families: Toward a theoretical framework for evaluating clinical interventions. *International Journal of Transgenderism, 14*, 113–126.

Wente, M. (2014, February 15). Transgender kids: Have we gone too far?. *The Globe and Mail.* Retrieved from https://www.theglobeandmail.com/opinion/transgender-kids-have-we-gone-too-far/article16897043/.

Williams, C. (2017). Disco sexology. *Trans Advocate.* Retrieved from https://www.transadvocate.com/part-i-the-rise-and-fall-of-discosexology-dr-zucker-camh-conversion-therapy_n_19556.htm.

Winters, K. (2006). Gender dissonance: Diagnostic reform of gender identity disorder for adults. *Journal of Psychology & Human Sexuality, 17*(3–4), 71–89.

World Professional Association for Transgender Health (2011). *Standards of care: For the health of transsexual, transgender and gender non-conforming people* (7th ed.). World Professional Association for Transgender Health.

Wong, W. (2014). Using a family and multi-systems treatment approach: Working with gender variant children. In D. Irving and R. Raj (Eds.), *Trans activism in Canada: A reader* (pp. 235–246). Toronto: Canadian Scholars' Press.

CHAPTER FOUR

Everyday Life

KEY THEMES

- Pronouns, names, and gendered language
- Polarization of transgender lives and issues
- Navigating transphobia from microaggressions to violence

CRITICAL QUESTIONS

- What everyday activities, such as travelling, using social media, or practising your faith, are more difficult or complicated because of your social identities, or who you are?
- What everyday activities in your life might be different if your gender expression changed?
- How are everyday spaces and things, such as washrooms and ID cards, designed to reinforce the gender binary? How could you reimagine them as more inclusive?

BOOKS WE LOVE

Picture Books

Anderson, A. (2018). *Neither!*. New York: Little Brown Books
Gonzales, M. C., & Sg., M. (2017). *They, she, he, me: Free to be!*. San Francisco: Reflection Press.
Labelle, S. (2018). *Rachel's Christmas boat*. Toronto: Flamingo Rampant.
Roher, M. (2012). *Transgender children of God*. San Francisco: Wilgefortis Press.
Silverman, E., & Hatman, H. (2018). *Jack (not Jackie)*. New York: Little Bee Books.

YA and Graphic Novels

Bongiovanni, A., & Jimerson, T. (2018). *A quick & easy guide to they/them pronouns*. Portland: Limerence Press.
Fisher, F., & Fisher, O. (2018). *Trans teen survival guide*. London: Jessica Kingsley Publishers.
Gillman, M. (2017). *As the crow flies*. Chicago: Iron Circus Comics.
Jiménez, K. P. (2021). *The street belongs to US*. Vancouver: Arsenal Pulp Press.
O'Hara, J. (2013). *Two-Spirit acts*. Toronto: Playwrights Canada Press.

General Audience

Airton, L. (2018). *Gender: Your guide – a gender-friendly primer on what to know, what to say, and what to do in the new gender culture.* Avon, MA: Adams Media.

Halberstam, J. (2018). *Trans: A quick and quirky account of gender variability.* Jackson: University of California Press.

Hartke, A. (2018). *Transforming: The Bible and the lives of transgender Christians.* Louisville, KY: Westminster John Knox Press.

Plett, C., & Bolton, S. (2014). *A safe girl to love.* New York: Topside Press.

Snorton, C. R. (2018). *Black on both sides: A racial history of trans identity.* Minneapolis: University of Minnesota Press.

Memoirs/First Person Narratives

Belcourt, B. R. (2019). *This wound is a world.* Minneapolis: University of Minnesota Press. *Also available in French*

Jennings, J. (2017). *Being Jazz: My life as a (transgender) teen.* New York: Crown.

McBride, S. (2018). *Tomorrow will be different: Love, loss, and the fight for trans equality.* New York: Random House.

Shenher, L. (2019). *This one looks like a boy: My gender journey to life as a man.* Vancouver: Greystone Books.

Stein, A. (2019). *Becoming Eve: My journey from ultra-orthodox rabbi to transgender woman.* New York: Hachette Book Group.

Government Buildings

By Ajam, age 14

Airport

By Jasper Ledgerwood, age 14

I am in an airport, and I am afraid.

I'm fourteen years old.
It's only my third time traveling alone.
This should be what scares me,
But it's not.

46% of people hate me for who I am.
20% hate me for who I love.

Is it the middle-aged man
Reading the newspaper in the seat next to me?

Is it the exhausted mother,
Two kids in tow?

I am in an airport, and I am afraid.
Someone like me is murdered every 31 hours.
I have to be on my guard,
Carefully calculate everything I do.
I already have a target on my back.
Don't want to make it worse.

My life is like a game of roulette.
Am I next?
Am I doing enough to ensure my parents won't get a call
Telling them their kid won't be coming home?
Which bathroom can I use without drawing attention to myself?
Will I even reach adulthood?

I am in an airport, and I am afraid.

The Plan

By Christopher, age 17

I'm not religious, but you could call me a romantic in that I like to think this world has a plan. Out there somewhere, I trust in a blueprint, and from primordial ooze to the inevitable, sun-scorched grave, every base on this planet seems to be covered. Except one.

As it turns out, the plan has no place for me. That's what they've hammered into me since the day I learned my own name: I am the mutation, the broken puzzle piece, the fatal detour off the straight and narrow. When they tell me I shouldn't exist, I sputter, as anyone would—but then I begin to panic. My alarm bells ring, not because they say it, but because for a moment I believe them.

And so the search begins. Before their accusations can settle, I'm scouring, frantic, for my rebuttal—some kind of secret code, written into the earth itself, that will wave a steady hand and tell them, "Don't worry. He is as natural as you are." I trust only experts, so I turn to those wardens of the world who predate our petty arguments, and hope they'll point me toward an age-old precedent for lives like mine. They should know, after all. They are the animals, they are the plants, and they are the stars.

Unfortunately, they're also cryptic bastards, and I find no easy answer. Penguins fall in love, the earth reshapes itself, and stars explode, but girls do not turn into boys. If I squint hard enough, I might see traces of myself in mysterious fish and poisonous frogs that transform from one thing to another. I might pretend that I, too, am a courageous pioneer of evolution, elaborately constructed to push the species forth. But no ancient animal has ever been so contentious, and unlike the rest of them, I did not strategize this. I am a fluke, a dent in nature's rules. Maybe I'm all the things people say about me. Impractical. Haphazard. Absurd.

Either way, they're right about one thing: I am not simple. At best, I am a question that begs asking; at worst, I am the brick that toppled their masterpiece. When I see it through their eyes, I realize they're mourning not just a convention of biology, but [also] something sacred, something they could understand without effort and trust without risk. They found comfort in simplicity—simple men, simple women—and I cut it to swathes.

So I forgive them for calling me broken, and stupid, and unnatural. It was only their attempt to make sense of things. In time, I forgive myself, too, for breaking the heirloom the universe gave them. I learn to accept my title as the one who made things complicated, who strayed from the earth's tradition and stumbled into territory that is uniquely human.

And I wonder if I'm going crazy or if the world just delivered my answer.

Because the truth is, we are not the animals, and we are not the plants, and we are not the stars. We are human beings, and maybe the simplest thing about us is that we defy every rule we write. We are so desperate for a cure to our own natural chaos that we look for it in all the wrong places, and try to force answers where questions should be. It's a strange kind of masochism, our attempts to explain ourselves. No one knows it better than I do.

But in the absence of answers, I have found the only thing that makes sense. I do not follow the rules of the rest of the world, but I follow the rules of being human. Hidden between the lines of code in this universe is the verdict, plain and simple, that not all things are meant to be so easily understood.

Something tells me that was part of the plan all along.

Untitled-2

By Riley, age 17

We nest in the tall grass, metal mouths full of acid and wrapped about 40s
I touch knees with her, bear hug and angel kiss
Have you ever seen a place so closely resemble neverland?
Lost boys hell bent on never coming home
Your love is yellow, shining through my sunglasses, sticking to my shiny skin
Your laughter whistles through the air, sonic waves of hysteria
I smile cat-like, your sober observer
She tells me I ground you all, like a river stone, like an A minor chord

We roll and leap and separate, tender hearts full of folk punk, wrapped around each other
Tonight it's simple, who needs triangles when you have shrooms?
Have you ever seen a family so closely resemble inmates
Sewing each other together back to front, never leave me, never leave
Our songs filter through my shadow almost coming from a half mile down the pat bay
I feel far but way too close, hand over ears yet your hand sticking in my heart
Pushing through my ribcage like it's nothing
You tell me I ground you, even with piss and blood and shitty poetry leaking from my gash

We come and go in the atrium of open meadow, voices raw and keening
Songs melt together, smoke-filled and honest
I've never been fit so closely by friendship and terror
The night grows long and swollen with confessions and laughter
Joy climbs trees, kisses goodbye, goes home for the night as reckless abandon takes over
I watch through a crack in the door, a stone in my throat
I know death and she comes quick and blind
You tell me I ground you and I smile till my gums bleed. Don't die.

Dysphoria

By Isaiah Hagerman, age 19

Dysphoria and I whispered at your door. Not wanting to be heard. We waited for five minutes, then you answered. My eyes upon you and yours upon me. You smiled—oh, that smile—I blushed—damn this anxiety—Dysphoria screamed at me—I deepened my voice. We sat on the couch. You unknowingly went face to face with an extra guest. You asked me to tell you about myself. Dysphoria laughed and grew. My hands that I wouldn't allow you to hold dripped with sweat.

Then you called me handsome. Dysphoria shrieked in pain, starting to sizzle away.
You leaned in to kiss me, and with one final cry,
Dysphoria vanished into thin air.
You touched me, and love appeared in the vacant seat.

The Dream

By Maisie Bodrug, age 13

Hidden Transphobia

By Tor Broughton, age 12

"They/them is plural though," he says.

"No it's not! You're being transphobic!" I viciously reply.

"That's not transphobic!" I hear that lie echo in my ears all too often. Whether it's people who truly believe they aren't doing anything wrong or people who are just flat-out bad, we need to pay more attention to these things.

People tend to subconsciously be racist, sexist, transphobic, homophobic, or discriminatory without even noticing. It's human nature to try and judge people based on looks when we first see them; it's a survival skill. We look and judge to see if someone's a threat. It's not in human nature to discriminate against someone. People are oblivious to their bad actions. We are taught to hate. We are taught to discriminate. It's not natural to verbally or physically hate on someone due to gender, race, sexuality, social class, or any other difference.

You can be posting all the posts you want about "I love trans people," but if your love doesn't include people of colour, obese people, tall, short, weak, strong, autistic, broke, depressed, non-Christian, disabled, non-binary, questioning people, and women, it's not real love. If your feminism is based off of the uterus and not off women, it's not real feminism. Include trans people!

I understand if it's against your religious morals or beliefs to be LGBTQ+. But that doesn't mean you suddenly have the power to discriminate. You might think that what you're saying isn't hurtful or transphobic/trans ignorant. But if a trans person tells you that it is, it is. You do not have the power to decide if you're being transphobic. Also, just because you are LGB or BIPOC or a woman or any other minority, that doesn't make you immune to being transphobic. If someone transgender or a non-binary person tells you that you're being transphobic, you are, end of story.

Simply put, watch what you're saying and look out for others. Respect people's differences and be kind. Listen to them when they tell you that you're being discriminatory and then change! When life is unfair, you don't have to be.

Raise Your Voice

By Jasper Ledgerwood, age 14

You tell me to stop.
To quiet down.
"You don't need to tell everybody"
But … I do.

You're the one who made it the sole part of my identity.
When my siblings were dying off.
An invisible assassin among us,
You made it clear.

We weren't to be touched.
We were a disgrace.
We were diseased.
That was all we would ever be.

When we were disgraced in almost every community.
"You're just dressing up as something you're not."
When we were and still are murdered for being ourselves.
You made it clear.

You didn't want us.
We disgusted you.
We were not welcome with you.
That was all we would ever be.

We told you we were more.
Told you we were your children, neighbours, friends.
You didn't care.
You told us this small bit of us was all we would ever be.

You did this to us.
You were the ones who told us we were limited
To this one thing,
This one miniscule thing that shouldn't even matter.

Being trans is not a pride parade every day.
It is not something I glorify.
It is not something I ever would have wished for,
I don't think.

But when you tell me
I'm worthless because of this small part of who I am
It makes me angry.
No. It makes me fucking furious.

It makes me want to shout from the rooftops,
"YES, I'M TRANS. WHAT THE HELL ARE YOU GOING TO DO
ABOUT IT?"
Because you have no right.
No right at all.

To tell me I'm not good enough,
To tell me to keep it bottled in,
Because secrets will be tolerated, but being myself will not.
Because you are so goddamn afraid of me.

I'm sorry.
Sorry for having the audacity to be comfortable with who I am.
Sorry you think you have the right
To tell me what to do with my life.

No, I'm not sorry.
The only people I need to apologize to
Are the people who feel this pain every day.
The people like me.

You don't deserve to be treated badly.
You deserve love, kindness, compassion.
You deserve much more than you're given,
But I believe in you.

You are strong, and you can make it through.
I believe in the resilience our community has shown.
I believe in you having the best life you possibly can.
I believe in love.

Maybe that makes me sappy or cliché.
I don't really care.
All I want is acceptance.
I have hope.

We can all raise our voices
And hope they'll be heard.
In the end, that's what matters.

Queer, But Still a Christian

By Alexander M-G, age 13

Why is it us
the bullied ones who rise to new heights when all is lost
Why is it us the abused ones who stand up for the survivors
Why is it us
the misunderstood ones who listen to crazy ideas when others can not
Why is it us the hated ones that will love when strong ones won't
Why is it us
the feared ones that will show others not t fear when others refuse

Alexander

Being queer but also a Christian is hard but also rewarding because in the queer community, most people talk about how Christians don't accept queer people, while most Christians talk about how queer people are bad. So I'm caught between two worlds, and I wanted to show that in my work.

Tools of the Transgender Teen

By Tor Broughton, age 12

Being trans is neat
Except when people are mean
Why can't we be kind
Binders, lupron, T
Tools of the transgender teen
Keeping us alive
That is why we need to be kind

Everyone Has an Everyday Life

By Dr. Lee Airton

> *"I am in an airport, and I am afraid."*
> —Jasper Ledgerwood, "Airport"

When I was heading home after the Trans Tipping Point (now called Gender Generations Project, or GGP) retreat in February 2018, where I had given a workshop on self-advocacy, I found myself waiting to board the same plane as one of the youth participants. Tired after a very full two days, we chatted for a while and then each got down to passing the time in our own way. My friend took out his phone. I did too, but only to look busy. While "just on my phone," I was actually doing some research and a risk assessment, or preparing to step up for my friend in case things got heavy when we presented our IDs to board the plane. Given my friend's age, I guessed that he wouldn't yet have changed the sex marker on his passport. Would he be denied boarding due to the "mismatch" between his masculine gender expression and the (incorrect) information on his passport?

As we lined up, I stood behind him and steeled myself as he handed his documents to the friendly gate agent. She looked over his passport and boarding pass, and then loudly wished some girl a good flight, effusively booming that girl name to reassure an unaccompanied minor. My friend took back his documents without a word and proceeded down the jet bridge, while the gate agent extended her hand to receive my own. I felt a bit silly. There was no fire here: just casual everyday misgendering. It may seem like "nothing happened," but actually something did: the extra energy expenditure required of transgender people of all ages in order to move through these ordinary moments in time (see Pullen Sansfaçon et al., 2018).

The epigraph is from Jasper Ledgerwood's first poem in the Everyday Life section, which features writings and art that convey some of what it is like to be a trans youth just going about your business, whether this means falling in love, having conversations, staying out all night, or playing music. In "Airport," Jasper speaks about what it is like for him to pass time in a site moved through by millions of people on a yearly basis. As a transgender adult, airports are also not my favourite places, because people in airports are bored. They cast about in search of some kind of stimulation to make the time pass more quickly, and someone who stands out is an easy target for one's restless attention. And in airports, we have to produce proof that we are who we say we are. For many transgender people, our identification documents do not say anything true about us. We are not just getting a thing out of our wallet, but getting ourselves ready for yet another moment of gender scrutiny and casual misrecognition, or worse.

Everyday life for transgender people can be remarkably exhausting, even when it looks uneventful or even boring on the surface, and even when it is devoid of explicit anti-trans harassment and violence. Trans youth face documented barriers to accessing the kinds of things that look like "normal life" for a young person. Three-quarters of the older youth who responded to the Canadian Trans Youth Health Survey (Veale et al., 2015) reported that most of their days at school or work were "a bit" or "quite a bit" stressful, with "almost half of younger youth feeling stressed to the point that they could not do their work or deal with things during the last 30 days" (p. 40). The vast majority of youth respondents reported that they never participate in physical activities that include a coach, which begs the question of whether transgender youth are able to access recreational activities that help reduce stress and anxiety (see also GLSEN, 2013). Other research has shown that public bathroom access—which means finding a safe bathroom in a shopping mall or community centre—is a powerful barrier to many transgender people's participation in public life. Anticipating conflict deters many transgender people from drinking and eating before they leave home for an extended period (James et al., 2016). Some trans people also report developing kidney or urinary tract infections from "holding it" for too long (ibid.). The idea of "everyday life" as being in any way ordinary can go out the window when we consider the everyday lives of many transgender youth.

On the flip side, however, the pleasures that everyday life brings can be a source of tremendous joy and invigoration for transgender youth and people of all ages. In this section, Ajam, Jasper, Christopher, Riley, Isaiah, Alexander, and Tor throw these joys and some challenges of everyday trans life into relief via acrylic, prose, and poetry. My task in responding to these pieces is to connect their themes to relevant scholarly literature, and then offer some suggestions for what you can do to pitch in.

I will begin by linking Jasper's two poems "Airport" and "Raise Your Voice" to an ongoing conversation among researchers about how gender and sexual minority youth are represented in research (see Airton, 2013; Bryan & Maycock, 2012; Sinclair-Palm & Gilbert, 2018; Talburt & Rasmussen, 2010): more specifically, about the unintended consequences of generating and publicizing reams of data on transgender youth suffering, risk factors, and resilience (where the latter is often held to put more of a positive spin on this representation). Ask any transgender kid with Internet access about research on people like them, and they will bring up rates of things like violence, suicide, and self-harm. Findings like the following from the Canadian Trans Youth Health Survey (Veale et al., 2015) are less commonly circulated and, I would argue, far less likely to penetrate public conversations in which transgender youth continually encounter themselves through the lens of risk alone: "It is important to note that not every transgender youth is similarly distressed. Around a quarter of the transgender youth in our study reported that their overall mental health was good or excellent" (p. 47). In "Raise Your Voice," Jasper expresses what it is like to bear the weight of the knowledge that, per these statistics, his siblings are "dying off, / An invisible assassin among us." In "Airport," he writes from this knowledge with cutting, numerical precision:

Someone like me is murdered every 31 hours.
I have to be on my guard,
Carefully calculate everything I do.
I already have a target on my back.
Don't want to make it worse.

Notably, in these poems Jasper does not describe things that have actually happened to him personally, but zeroes in on the difficult experience of moving about in everyday life knowing that—statistically-speaking—he is "at-risk." All this is to say that, while considerable attention paid to risk data has led to the creation of supportive policies and programs, this may have come at the expense of propagating more varied research stories about being a transgender youth. Missing stories might centre trans youths' experiences of joy and affirmation, but not only. The best corrective will not be going to the opposite end of the spectrum and only telling research stories about ideal trans youth lives free of strife. Rather, as Julia Sinclair-Palm and Jen Gilbert (2018) remind us, "our narratives of trans youth must stay open to young people's exploration of gender and desire ... and the ordinary challenges and pleasures that trans youth experience as part of growing up through adolescence" (p. 323). Like other youth, transgender youth are entitled to complex and ambivalent experiences *and* representations, not only those centred either on risk or its overcoming.

Several pieces in this section stage this complexity and ambivalence, re-casting typical teenage experiences such as being kissed by your crush or getting high and singing with your friends in a field. In reading these pieces, however, we lean in to the extra headiness and euphoria of such typical teenage things because the youth experiencing them are trans. In "Dysphoria," Isaiah knocks on his crush's door and interminably waits for them to open it. But he has not come alone. Rather, Isaiah has brought dysphoria with him: a pervasive feeling of discomfort with one's body and its relationship with one's gender identity. Affirmation from his crush vanquishes Isaiah's dysphoria when his crush pronounces him handsome and leans in for a kiss. In "Untitled 2," Riley writes evocatively of a night spent in a field with friends who offer far more than friendship. Riley shares all the ways their friends show them they are the centre and the glue that binds this family together, even while stating that they have "never been fit so closely by friendship and terror." Riley's terror comes at the spectre of death taking away these friends and this life-giving scene. Friendship is more than friendship for Riley, just as crushing is more than crushing for Isaiah. These pieces add a more visceral knowledge base alongside research findings that substantiate what ought to be common sense: that relationships of recognition are key to the "thrival" (Greteman, 2017) and not just bare survival of gender and sexual minority youth, regardless of how transness may intersect with one's other identities and social positions (see Arnold & Bailey, 2009; Singh, 2013). We know that transgender people who report strong self-esteem, social support, and healthy relationships with peers whether online or offline have better health and mental health outcomes, and that the opposite also holds true (Bauer et al., 2015; Johns et al., 2018; McConnell, Birkett, & Mustanski 2016; Pullen Sansfaçon et al., 2018; Veale et al., 2015).

What are these findings other than a testament to the significance of everyday life for transgender youth, whose well-being is so often conceptualized in policy as hinging on exceptional situations of crisis and transition? In fact, this section finds the authors expressing outrage at being made into an exception against their will, whether as an exception to biology, to normalcy, or the range of basic human needs. In "Raise Your

Voice," Jasper expresses anger at how his transness is blown out of proportion when it is, in fact, "this small part of who I am." "Being trans is not a pride parade every day," Jasper writes, insisting on his right to be more and other than his gender pathway, or to just be. In Tor's poem "Tools of the Transgender Teen," he describes the things that many trans youth need that set them apart from other youth, while also juxtaposing these needs with something everyone needs: kindness. Many things trans youth need are not, in fact, exceptional. In "Queer, But Still a Christian," Alexander M-G meditates on some contradictions of their Christian and trans identities, which are just different parts of their whole self. The illustrated figure is protective, watching over the bullied, abused, misunderstood, hated, and feared ones who do the radical yet ordinary work of accepting others using the strength conferred by our own experiences of otherness. Dressed for a summer's day picnic with the sun reflecting in their lustrous hair, the figure reminds us that this work takes place everywhere trans people live our lives.

That said, it can be challenging or even downright impossible to have one's ordinary needs met if you are constantly called on to prove that you are who you say you are. Everyday life for trans youth entails extra labour to advocate not only for their needs but for their very identities. What does "everyday life" mean when, in the course of everyday life, you must regularly engage in conversations with (even well-meaning) people who want to take on your existence like a high school debating society? In his essay "The Plan," Christopher articulates a desire to speak back to people who tell him that being transgender is "unnatural." He turns to those he identifies as experts "who predate our petty arguments"—"they are the animals, they are the plants, and they are the stars"—but only finds there a path back to a too-simple model of static binary sex differentiation that again suggests his transness to be unnatural. Frustrated, Christopher settles on naming transness as an extra-human quality because, in his rendering, complexity is a characteristic of humans alone. The people who call him unnatural have "found comfort in simplicity—simple men, simple women," and he says, " I cut it to swathes." Tor's essay "Hidden Transphobia" questions whose knowledge counts when it comes to knowing whether trans people are "real" or whether something counts as harm against trans people. Having to justify your own realness and assert authority over your own self-knowledge is a burden born by many trans people, including these youth, and sometimes before breakfast. To make matters more complicated, the transness that the cisnormative world respects and understands the most is one that is consistent, persistent (see Temple Newhook et al., 2018), and binary, whereas transness looks different for different trans people. Youth who are gender-fluid or non-binary are likely subjected to more frequent and ardent demands to prove the realness of their genders, including by some parents and family members (Aramburu Alegría, 2018). It is unsurprising that non-binary participants reported worse health and mental health on the Canadian Trans Youth Health Survey (Veale et al., 2015), which

> could be due to added stigma experienced by this group for not conforming to Canadian society's (or Western society's) binary gender expectations. ... This

group is likely to be less understood and acknowledged than transgender youth whose gender identity fits into the man/woman binary, and this may mean non-binary youth are less likely to have social support. (p. 48)

It is by now indisputable that "being able to live in one's felt gender—in the gender that feels the most right—is positively linked with trans youth's health" (p. 68). And yet we currently live in the "free speech" era, which means that trans youth see the legitimacy of their existence and their everyday needs (e.g., being referred to with the correct name and gender pronoun—see Russell et al., 2018) regularly debated by pundits and columnists with nationwide exposure and thousands of online followers. Having to prove you are real and valid may be a unique, corrosive feature of everyday trans youth life for a while to come.

Before I move into practical suggestions, I will share an interpretation of Ajam's acrylic painting titled "Government Buildings," which I think offers a caution. In the painting, Ajam has rendered a building that looks like the stereotypical image of a parliament building or legislature, complete with domes and turrets. Ajam's government building is conflicted, however. It is at once draped in the colours of the trans pride flag—seemingly offering a welcome—*and* peppered with ominous doors and windows that reveal nothing of the interior and from which no light shines. While there has been a recent abundance of transgender-supportive policies and laws—things created in government buildings—the painting reminds us that these macro approaches only touch everyday life with great difficulty. These larger structures might wear our flag these days—which I think is a positive development—but that does not mean that everyday life for trans people is made better by them without work. And it remains an open question whether the increased visibility of transness in public life and governance is exclusively beneficial (Pullen Sansfaçon et al., 2018; see also Gossett, Stanley, & Burton 2017).

My response to the pieces in the Everyday Life section has focused on a few themes that I saw as emerging across this body of work: how an ordinary day for trans youth is ordinarily exhausting; that there are unintended consequences of propagating data on trans youth suffering, including how this can be burdensome on the very youth that this propagation aims to protect; that "typical teenage" things can take on a different and possibly more heady significance for teenagers who are transgender; that trans youth have ordinary needs just like other people; and that an ordinary part of being a trans youth is battling against arguments that you and your gender are not real or are otherwise invalid. With all of these in mind, here are some suggestions for taking action in relation to these themes, wherever you are:

✓ **(Diverse) representation matters.** Be mindful of when and where you present, reiterate, retweet, or re-post damage-centred (Tuck, 2009) research findings about trans youth or trans people more broadly. This can be a good plan for swaying people in power, but likely is not necessary (and can be very grating) when your audience, classroom, or social media feed includes trans people. If you are a teacher or if you work with youth (trans or no) in a similar capacity, ensure that resources or books about transgender youth do not only share stories of crisis and transition, as this is not the whole story. Try to give all students access to representations of transgender-spectrum people doing very ordinary things.

✓ **Trans youth are more than just "the trans kid."** When you infer or find out that a kid is transgender and/or non-binary, do your best not to convey the assumption that a thing they go through is necessarily related to gender. It can be very tiresome to be seen only through that lens.

✓ **Being trans can sometimes make "normal" experiences harder.** Conversely, the loss of a friend or date, or moving to new place, or even being separated from their devices for prolonged periods of time can be particularly painful for transgender youth if this also means straining relationships in which they were/are particularly seen or supported. Reducing their feelings to "teenage troubles" or moods might not do them justice. Bear this in mind, and keep lines of communication open.

✓ **Affirm that there are *lots* of ways to be trans.** There are many different ways in which trans youth articulate their transness, and you might feel like you have more of an understanding of some of these than of others. That is not a problem, provided that you try your best not to call youth's identities into question when they let you know who they are. There are so many occasions upon which trans youth are required to advocate for their very realness and validity, and a great gift you can give is believing them and, moreover, making this belief obvious, palpable, and dependable.

✓ **Speak up.** Intervene in "devil's advocate" or "free speech" conversations that involve a trans youth. This is not something that trans people in general need, and trans youth may find themselves in a power imbalance with someone wanting to go down this road. There are many other, more valuable ways for trans youth to expend their energy.

REFERENCES

Airton, L. (2013). Leave "those kids" alone: On the conflation of school homophobia and suffering queers. *Curriculum Inquiry, 43*(5), 532–562.

Aramburu Alegría, C. (2018). Supporting families of transgender children/youth: Parents speak on their experiences, identity, and views. *International Journal of Transgenderism, 19*(2), 132–143.

Arnold, E. A., & Bailey, M. M. (2009). Constructing home and family: How the ballroom community supports African American GLBTQ youth in the face of HIV/AIDS. *Journal of Gay & Lesbian Social Services: Issues in Practice, Policy & Research, 21*, 171–188.

Bauer, G. R., Scheim, A. I., Pyne, J., Travers, R., & Hammond, R. (2015). Intervenable factors associated with suicide risk in transgender persons: A respondent driven sampling study in Ontario, Canada. *BMC Public Health, 15*(1), 525.

Bryan, A., & Mayock, P. (2012). Speaking back to dominant constructions of LGBT lives: Complexifying "at riskness" for self-harm and suicidality among lesbian, gay, bisexual and transgender youth. *Irish Journal of Anthropology, 15*(2), 8–15.

GLSEN. (2013). *The experiences of LGBT students in school athletics* [Research Brief]. New York: GLSEN. Retrieved from https://www.glsen.org/learn/research/athletics-brief.

Gossett, R., Stanley, E. A., & Burton, J. (2017). *Trap door: Trans cultural production and the politics of visibility.* Cambridge, MA: MIT Press.

Greteman, A. J. (2016). Queer thrival. In N. M. Rodriguez, W. J. Martino, J. C. Ingrey, & E. Brockenbrough (Eds.), *Critical Concepts in Queer Studies and Education* (pp. 309–317). New York: Palgrave Macmillan.

James, S. E., Herman, J. L., Rankin, S., Keisling, M., Mottet, L., & Anafi, M. (2016). *The report of the 2015 U.S. transgender survey.* Washington: National Center for Transgender Equality.

Johns, M. M., Beltran, O., Armstrong, H. L., Jayne, P. E., & Barrios, L. C. (2018). Protective factors among transgender and gender variant youth: A systematic review by socioecological level. *The Journal of Primary Prevention, 39*(3), 263–301.

McConnell, E. A., Birkett, M., & Mustanski, B. (2016). Families matter: Social support and mental health trajectories among lesbian, gay, bisexual, and transgender youth. *Journal of Adolescent Health, 59*(6), 674–680.

Pullen Sansfaçon, A., Hébert, W., Lee, E. O. J., Faddoul, M., Tourki, D., & Bellot, C. (2018). Digging beneath the surface: Results from stage one of a qualitative analysis of factors influencing the well-being of trans youth in Quebec. *International Journal of Transgenderism, 19*(2), 184–202.

Russell, S. T., Pollitt, A. M., Li, G., & Grossman, A. H. (2018). Chosen name use is linked to reduced depressive symptoms, suicidal ideation, and suicidal behavior among transgender youth. *Journal of Adolescent Health,* Advanced online publication.

Sinclair-Palm, J., & Gilbert, J. (2018). Naming new realities: Supporting trans youth in education. *Sex Education, 18*(4), 321–327.

Singh, A. A. (2013). Transgender youth of color and resilience: Negotiating oppression and finding support. *Sex Roles, 68*(11–12), 690–702.

Talburt, S., & Rasmussen, M. L. (2010). "After-queer" tendencies in queer research. *International Journal of Qualitative Studies in Education, 23*(1), 1–14.

Temple Newhook, J., Pyne, J., Winters, K., Feder, S., Holmes, C., Tosh, J., Sinnot, M-L., Jamieson, A., & Pickett, S. (2018). A critical commentary on follow-up studies and "desistance" theories about transgender and gender-nonconforming children. *International Journal of Transgenderism, 19*(2), 212–224.

Tuck, E. (2009). Suspending damage: A letter to communities. *Harvard Educational Review, 79*(3), 409–428.

Veale, J., Saewyc, E., Frohard-Dourlent, H., Dobson, S., Clark, B., & the Canadian Trans Youth Health Survey Research Group. (2015). *Being safe, being me: Results of the Canadian trans youth health survey.* Vancouver, BC: Stigma and Resilience Among Vulnerable Youth Centre, School of Nursing, University of British Columbia.

CHAPTER FIVE

Schools

KEY THEMES

- Educational policy and trans rights
- Bullying and transphobia
- Gender-segregated sports and washrooms

CRITICAL QUESTIONS

- Think about the bullying you witnessed or experienced in your childhood. In what ways was that bullying gendered?
- How does the gender segregation of certain school activities pose barriers for trans youth? For all youth?
- How does educational policy either encourage or prevent transphobia in schools?

BOOKS WE LOVE

Picture Books

Baldacchino, C., & Malenfant, I. (2014). *Morris Micklewhite and the tangerine dress.* Toronto: Groundwood Books. *Also available in French*

Gonzalez, M. G., & Sg, M. (2019). *They, she, he, easy as ABC.* San Francisco: Reflection Press.

Moradian, A., & Bogade, M. (2018). *Jamie is Jamie: A book about being yourself and playing your way.* Minneapolis: Free Spirit Publishing.

Thom, K. C., Ching, K. Y., & Li, W-Y. (2017). *From the stars in the sky to the fish in the sea.* Vancouver: Arsenal Pulp Press. *Also available in French*

Smith, H., & Carter, A. (2018). *Angus all aglow.* Victoria: Orca Books.

YA and Graphic Novels

Gregorio, I. W. (2015). *None of the above.* New York: Balzer and Bray.

Labelle, S. (2020). *Ciel.* Toronto: Second Story Press. *Also available in French*

Mardell, A. (2016). *The ABCs of LGBT (gender identity book for teens).* Coral Gables, FL: Mango Media.

Polonsky, A. (2016). *Gracefully Grayson.* New York: Scholastic Inc. *Also available in French*

Williamson, L. (2016). *The art of being normal*. Oxford, UK: David Fickling Books. *Also available in French*

General Audience

Butler-Wall, A., Cosier, K., & Harper, R. L. S. (2016). *Rethinking sexism, gender, and sexuality*. Milwalkee, WI: Rethinking Schools.

Jiménez, K. P. (2016). *Tomboys and other gender heroes: Confessions from the classroom*. New York: Peter Lang.

Jones, A. (2017). *Warrior anthology: LGBTQIA short stories*. UK: Ink and Locket Press.

Killerman, S. (2017). *A guide to gender: The social justice advocate's handbook* (2nd ed.). Austin, TX: Impetus Books.

Woolley, S. W., & Airton, L. (2020). *Teaching about gender diversity: Teacher-Tested lesson plans for K–12 classrooms*. Toronto: Canadian Scholars' Press.

Memoirs/First-Person Narratives

Andrews, A., & Hill, K. R. (2014). *Some assembly required*. New York: Simon & Schuster.

Coyote, I. E. (2018). *Tomboy survival guide*. Vancouver: Arsenal Pulp Press.

Dugan, J. T. (2015). *Every breath we drew*. Hillsborough, NC: Daylight Books.

Ramirez, M. G., & Partnoy, A. (2019). *Happier as a woman: Transforming friendships, transforming lives*. Jersey City, NJ: Cleis Press.

Rajunov., M., & Duane, A. S. (2019). *Nonbinary: Memoirs of gender and identity*. New York: University of Columbia Press.

Where Do We Draw the Dividing Line?

By Ajam, age 14

A Day in the Life of One Trans Person

By Maisie Bodrug, age 13

My boobs are made of silicone (I sometimes forget to put them on).
Forget them one day and poof! They're gone.

When I'm at school, I'm kinda stealth (and take vitamin D for my health).
You call me a freak, I'll call you a fool.
Just 'cause I'm unique doesn't mean I'm not cool.

When it's time for bed, I remove my boobs and shout,
"I am awesome!"
Then I hit the lights out.

I wake up in the morning, I rub my eyes and yawn,
Walk up to the bedside table, turn the lamp on.
My mom calls up, "It's breakfast!" and I say "Just a minute!"
She made me an omelet; I wonder what's in it.

I finish up my breakfast, and I go and pack my bag,
Then run into a bigot. He starts calling me a fag.
I go and confront him—I say, "Leave me alone."
He tells me that I'm garbage and that he sits on the throne!
I tell him, "That does it." I'm boiling with rage.
I tell him he's a douchebag and that he should act his age.

I get to class and take my seat; we're doing science! It's gonna be sweet!
We're studying hormones! What a surprise!
Estrogen! Testosterone! I can't believe my eyes!
I go to lunch—it's a burger and fries!
Then someone calls me a tranny and part of me dies.

Student Letter Responding to the Backlash on the Sexual Orientation and Gender Identity (SOGI) Curriculum

By Anonymous, a transgender student, between ages 14 and 17

I don't want to be afraid to go to school. I don't want to have to tear down signs and notes stuck on my locker, I don't want to have to wear my headphones while I walk in the halls so I don't have to hear the things these kids say about me ...

You say that you don't want the school experience to be ruined for your kids with teaching of SOGI, but my school experience has been forever tainted by the unkind things said and done by *those* kids. They tell me that a man I don't even know hates me, and that I'm going to Hell for being who I am; they tell me that I am disgusting and a disgrace. There are so many other words that they've said to me that have become ingrained in my mind so deeply that I was convinced I didn't even deserve to be alive. The number of days I lie in bed terrified to go to school far outweigh the number of days that I'm not.

Do you know how it feels to be afraid to walk down the hallways, terrified that everyone around you is talking about you behind your back? To be terrified that someone might hurt you or shout at you? Do you know how it feels to walk up to your locker and see words scrawled across it, and papers pasted to it with words that hurt more than any punch ever could? Every single day, I am terrified to go to school, to go to a place built on learning and love, but that's filled with hatred. I'm terrified to check my social media ever since someone posted a picture of me with a noose drawn around my neck. I'm terrified to live.

If students knew that I am no different than they are, maybe I wouldn't have to be so terrified. Maybe I would be able to live my life carefree, like I did when I was a young child. If we could teach at a young age that being transgender, or being queer in general, is okay, maybe I wouldn't have lost as many friends as I have. If we could teach children that it is okay to be themselves, think of how much happier they could be. When I was 10 years old and said that I liked people of the same gender, I had two different responses from the people around me: they were either indifferent, or they were violently grossed out and were quick to judge. I wish they didn't care. I wish I never had to hear people telling me that "that's not what God intended," or "that's a sin," or "that's gross."

I was a young kid—no, I was a *child*.

People say that we are pushing our "agenda" onto kids, yet we see babies and toddlers wearing clothing with slogans like "ladies' man" and "chick magnet" amongst many others, so it begs the question: Whose alleged "agenda" is being forced on whom? We don't have an *agenda*. We just want to educate kids and teens to make them understand that it's okay to be "different." I wish that this was part of the curriculum when I was younger. I wish that I could have said "yes, I am transgender" without people asking me what "turned me" this way, or what "made me feel like" I had to be. Nothing made me *want* to be trans, nothing *made me* want to be "different," I just wanted to be **me**, and wanted to be accepted.

I'm lucky because I have family who support me; I'm lucky because I at least still have some friends who weren't appalled by my existence. Some kids aren't. I've lost friends who weren't accepted by their families, and peers to suicide. These deaths weren't because they weren't brave enough or strong enough like some may say. It was because they had to fight every day and they were in a place that they could not win. They were beaten and bruised with words and fists and notes. They were disrespected and harassed by people around them, and this group has the audacity to say that they don't tolerate hate? How dare you. How dare you let these kids suffer and lead themselves to destruction because you don't want your children to know that they exist. How dare you say that you won't tolerate hate, when it is the same people who attack me and my friends. How dare you say that you want what is best for the kids when the only kids you care about are the "normal" ones.

My teachers, counsellors, and the other staff at my school ... they have done so much to support me, they have done so much to be inclusive and to be respectful to *all* students. We aren't asking for "special rights." We are just asking to be acknowledged and respected. We aren't asking for "more." We are asking for the same respect that all students deserve. We're asking to be treated like *people*. That's all I want. I just want to be treated like a *person*.

Discovery

By Max, age 13

"Alice, snap out of it, we're almost there." I slowly drop the elbow I had propped up on the window of my mom's silver Toyota and roll my eyes and slowly grab my figure skating bag from beside me. The car rolls to a stop when I get out, wishing I didn't have to be here.

I look at my feet as I walk to the ice rink, the doors opening automatically for me as I enter. I see the familiar faces of the hockey team, leaving because their practices start right before figure skating.

Since I was little, I always begged my mom to let me join hockey instead of figure skating: my earliest memory of it is being dragged into the change room by my arm, when I was only five. It was my first day ever figure skating. I pleaded and cried for my mom to let me join hockey, saying it will help with teamwork, and that I will get stronger, but she insisted that it was a "boys' sport." I tried to tell her that I didn't care, and I wanted short hair, but she just rolled her eyes at me, telling me that I am a girl and I am just being silly. After weeks of begging, I just gave up. I decided I'd just stay in figure skating and stop arguing because she wasn't going to change her mind.

I snap out of my daydreaming and look up to see all the hockey players gone, and all the people on my figure skating team in their place. (It doesn't help that I have nothing in common with any of the girls on the team.)

I run into the change room, then into a bathroom stall. I change out of my black skinny jeans, blue sweater, and AC/DC shirt and quickly into the tights and zip-up sweater required for skating. I throw on my white figure skates and rush out of the change room, seeing the glances of girls staring at me for changing in the stall. I'm used to it.

I walk through the large doors that exit out onto the ice rink and start skating around. Even though I hate skating, I'm still one of the best skaters on the team and am always picked to go to events and competitions. I do a quick warm up and start practising my new routine for my competition. Not long after, my coach calls everyone in and everyone gracefully skates over with smiles on their faces. I roll my eyes at them and skate over. He talks to us about the competition coming up, and wants to show us a new move, a triple axel, something that I had learned a couple years ago. He pulls me up and asks me to demonstrate, which I sigh and then do. Everyone watches with envy. They know that I hate doing this, but I'm still one of the best skaters on the team. For the rest of practice everyone tries to do a triple axel but avoids asking me how to since none of them like me.

Practice is soon over, and I rush to the stall in the change room to change back into my AC/DC shirt, sweater, and black skinny jeans, and pull my hood over my head to hide my hair. As I change, I can hear the girls talking: "Omigosh why does Alice have to be such a show off, she doesn't even want to be here."

"She? More like 'it.' Alice doesn't even act like a girl. 'It' shouldn't be allowed on the team." They start giggling and I finish packing everything up and storm out of the change room and run out to my mom's car, which is waiting there for me. I put my earbuds in my super old iPod shuffle and listen to Panic! at the Disco on repeat the whole way home, avoiding talking to my mom.

I step into my house, a decent sized building, with a top floor, where the living room, kitchen, dining room, my sister's room, and my parents' room is, and a basement, where my room is. As I enter, I try to avoid my dad and start to make my way down to my room, but he catches me first. "How was practice?" he says cheerfully.

"It was fine," I respond blankly, trying to get this conversation over with.

"I'm glad it went well! So, your mom and I have a surprise for you. Since you just turned 14, we decided that it was time we got you an actual phone!" My eyes light up as he says this. I was never allowed electronics except for school work on the family computer and now I'm getting my own phone!

"Thanks, Dad!" I say excitedly as he hands it to me.

"Now use it wisely; don't talk to strangers online," he warns.

"Yeah, yeah, I know, whatever, but thank you!" I say then give him a hug and run downstairs to my room—a room with cream coloured walls, a bookshelf covered in different books, sketchbooks, notebooks, some comics and pop vinyls, and an electronic piano.

I flop down onto my bed and take out my phone, immediately downloading a bunch of songs onto it, all punk, classic rock, and alternative songs. I put on "Run Boy Run" by Woodkid and start to look at apps. I see a social media app called Blogr in the top and decide to download it. It turns out to be an app for, well … blogs … and you can post whatever you want. I try to think up a name. I see the cactus on my window sill and decide to call my blog "Lonely-Cactus." I smile a bit and search around for different things. I decide to look up to see if there are any other people like me, girls who don't feel like girls, who feel like they are trapped and just want to jump out and escape themselves and be a boy. I start to write something out: "I feel like I'm trapped. A boy stuck in the prison of a girl's body and I don't know what to do. I don't know what I am." I take a deep breath and post it onto the website with the tags "boy," "girl," "gender," "confused."

I decide to close the app and go onto YouTube to distract myself. I watch videos on TV shows and movie theories for a few hours, when I get a notification from Blogr. I decide to open it and see someone has messaged me: "Hey there! I'm Adam, and I think I might know what you're going through. You might be what is called 'transgender,' that's what I am, you were born assigned as a girl but you feel mentally like a boy, or the other way around for some people, if you have any questions feel free to ask me about it!" I read this a few times. This is exactly how I feel …

"Could I be transgender?" I think to myself then decide to respond. "Thank you for your help, Adam. I'm going to research into what transgender is, because that is exactly how I feel." I send the message, then search in tags for "transgender." I knew what LGBT was, well at least what gay, lesbian, and bisexual meant, but I never really thought about the "T" or really knew what it meant. When I search it, lots of posts come up, people talking about experiences in being transgender, or trans for short. I find that I relate to a lot of these people, feeling like I'm trapped in the body of someone I am not, feeling like I was assigned the wrong gender. It's like everything clicked.

I find out that what I think I'm experiencing is called "gender dysphoria," negative feelings toward being referred to, seen as, looking like, and having the body of your assigned gender. I spend all night researching about it and keep messaging Adam about what to do. I soon look at the time on my phone to see it is already 3 am, and I have to go to school tomorrow. I message Adam a quick "goodnight, thank you so much for helping me through tonight, talk later?" He responds with, "No problem, and sure, goodnight!"

I set an alarm to wake up and put the phone down, lie on my side, and slowly drift into sleep. That night I dreamt about being a boy, a not-uncommon dream for me, but this time it was different. I was slowly transforming, from the body I had that I hated, to a more masculine body and face, with a strong jawline, and short hair, and less prominent hip bones.

At 6 am my alarm went off, giving me a total of three hours of sleep that night. I throw on a black and red plaid button up and a pair of black jeans again, with a toque to cover my hair, then run upstairs and eat breakfast. When I get to school I go to my English/Social studies class, with my favourite teacher, Ms. Holmes (yes, like Sherlock Holmes). In class we are learning about the Renaissance, and we have to do a creative project on it. Even though it's my favourite class, the whole time I was distracted, anxious for lunch to come so that I could talk to Adam again.

I raise my hand and ask to go to the washroom. As I stand up I pull my shirt forward a bit, so it looks baggier and covers my chest. I go into the bathroom then into a stall and grab my phone out and check my Blogr. A couple people reblogged my post, so I decided to make another one: "I have now found out what Transgender means, and think it is possible that I am but I don't know, and have become more informed about the LGBT+ community, although I still do not know much since this is new to me, so any information on what to do next or explaining things would be appreciated!" I add the tags "transgender," "trans," "lgbt," "lgbt+," "girl," "boy," and "gender." I post it then run back upstairs to my class to work on my project, which is a Renaissance-style painting with a modern outlook and theme to it. The two blocks of class seem to take forever to finish, but as I am finishing sketching out the idea for the painting the bell rings. I shove it into my notebook and shove that into my backpack then walk down to the library and sit down on a beanbag chair and take out my phone. I see three new messages for me on Blogr. The first one I open is from "trans-advice-blog":

"Hey! It's okay to be confused on what your gender is, there are lots of people who don't identify with any gender, or feeling like both genders! Dysphoria can really suck, but there are always ways to help cope, but never ever ever try to bind your chest with ace bandages, they will just hurt you." I search up what ace bandages are and find out they are the tight bandages you put around yourself when you get hurt, and I vow to never use them on myself no matter what. The other two messages are from a trans guy named Alex, and a trans girl named Cleo, who explained to me what it's like being a trans girl in comparison to what her friends who are trans guys have told her. I start to learn a lot more, in the struggles that people face every day, and continue to message back and forth with trans-advice-blog, just asking little things like how to bind safely (a binder is your best option, but layering two sports bras or wearing one a size too small won't hurt you, but never wear any sort of binder for more than eight hours a day).

The time quickly flies by and soon lunch is over. My last two blocks fly by quickly, as I feel a small bit of happiness on knowing that I'm not the only one who feels like this and that there are ways to help.

As soon as I get off the school bus, I run home and go downstairs to look for an extra sports bra to layer over the one I'm already wearing. I throw on my shirt and sweater over it and look at myself in the mirror and see myself flat chested. A smile forms on my face as I imagine that being how I always look.

That night I talked to Adam, who is fifteen and lives in Wellington, New Zealand, so it is hard to find times when we can both talk. We spent the whole night talking and he finally asked, "Hey, what name do you want me to call you? If you want me to call you anything." My heart started to beat when he asked that question; what do I want him to call me? I don't want him to call me Alice, because that's a "girl name" but I don't have any other name to say. I just respond with "I'm not sure … I'm still trying to figure out all this gender stuff and I don't know what I want to be called (other than I sure as heck don't want to be called by the name my parents gave me)." He was cool with it and we continued our conversation as normal, learning new things about each other, like how he's been out for one year, and has two brothers, a sister, and a dog. At around midnight I say goodnight to Adam and put my phone away, a smile on my face for the first time in a while.

In the morning I throw on the double layer of sports bras, a black t-shirt, my blue hoodie, and dark blue jeans. I go through my normal morning routine, then go to school. My first block is Math, so I go upstairs to the math room and sit down in my seat. I am the first one there but soon one of the "popular" kids comes in after me. "So, are you a boy or a girl?" I ignore him and continue to write in my notebook so he pushes me: "You going to answer me?" I roll my eyes at him.

"None of your business." I'm not normally rude to people but this guy is getting on my nerves. He eventually just laughs at me and walks away to where his friends are. For the rest of class I keep my head down, and can't finish my work. All that is bouncing through my head is his voice, "So, are you a boy or a girl?" I couldn't answer it. I didn't know.

My head is down on my desk when the bell rings, which startles me up and I grab my bag and walk to the library for break. The rest of the day is kind of a haze. I go through all my classes but can't really focus on anything at all.

As soon as I get home I started texting Adam about what happened. I don't know why it affected me so much, I can normally handle that sort of thing, but this time it wouldn't go away. After texting Adam, my mom calls me upstairs for dinner before going to figure skating. We have spaghetti, and figure skating just goes by in a blur like school had.

While my mom and I are in the car on the way back from skating she tells me, "Since you are going to a National competition for the first time I think I need to get you something."

I look at her quizzically: "What?"

"Anything you want, it's a present for you doing so well." She's never done anything like this before and I think for a second then my face lights up.

"I can see you've decided on something," she laughs.

"I want to get my hair cut!" I say excitedly.

"You get your hair cut all the time, what's so special about this?"

"No, like, cut short."

She looks at me with a shocked expression."No, you can't do that, you need long hair for figure skating."

"Please, please, please! You said anything!" I beg.

"Fine, but not too short, only to your ears," she says, defeated.

"Thank you so much, Mom!" I know it isn't much, and I still won't have the "boy" short haircut I want, but it's something.

That night I can barely sleep. We made an appointment for after school the next day, so I stay up texting Adam, and he can tell how excited I am to get my hair cut. For the first time in a while, school goes by happily. Nobody makes fun of me, I don't feel bad, I'm just excited to get my hair cut off. I hang out with my friend, Jax, at lunch time and tell him I am going to cut my hair. He is super supportive and says it's going to look awesome.

When I get home, I call my mom to the door. We go to the car, and start to drive to the hair salon. "Are you sure you want to do this, Alice?" she says, slightly sadly.

"Yes, I am one hundred percent sure I want to do this."

"Okay …" she responds. It takes about five minutes to drive to the salon, and once we get there I jump out of the car and speed walk to the salon.

I enter and say, "I have an appointment to get my hair cut. It should be under the name Alice." The receptionist is nice and she shows me to the salon chair and sits me down, then the hairdresser comes. Her name is Jade, and she has awesome, short hair dyed a silvery-blue colour with an un-dyed undercut. She asks me what I want and I say, "well, I want it all off, but the most my mom will let me is up to my ears." She gives a little laugh and starts to cut my hair. It takes about an hour but once it's done it is *amazing*. My blonde hair looks layered, and Jade had cut it to look more masculine for me as I had asked. It looks so much better, and even though it isn't as short as I want it, it still feels like a massive weight is lifted off my chest, or at least my head. My mom seems to actually like how it looks, although she comments on how masculine it is. I fall asleep texting Adam again. I send him a picture of my hair (with my face scribbled out) and he says it looks awesome.

The next morning I wake up at 5 am to leave for my competition, which is happening tonight. We have to take a ferry to the island for it. On the ferry ride I start to look at names, specifically masculine/boys names. I have made many posts since my first two and want to change my name, so I can tell my fifty followers, as well as Adam, to address me by name. I want a name that means something, not just a random name that sounds nice, so I search names on Blogr, and some baby name website. I don't find anything that is similar to Alice, or that means something to me, and then I think about my grandfather, who died the previous year. I'll name myself after him and keep a family name since I was very close to him. His name was Magnus, meaning "great." I love how the name sounds and think it matches me, while also carrying on my grandfather's legacy. I message Adam on the ferry and tell him.

"Hey, I've picked a name for myself. I'm going to use Magnus. It was my grandfather's name and I feel like it represents me."

Adam agrees and says that it is great! "Magnus is a really cool name, and it's awesome that you're naming yourself after your grandpa."

"Thanks! Okay, I gotta go, text ya later Adam."

"Bye, Magnus."

Seeing that name typed out, directed to me feels so good, at least someone understands. I post to my Blogr, telling everyone what my name is and why I chose it. I'm elated, everything seems to be going up, but that fantasy comes crashing down pretty soon when the ferry slows.

My mom grabs my arm and says, "C'mon, Alice, we have to get down to the car and get to your competition." The drive to the hotel is about fifteen minutes, and I drop my bags off there, then get all my figure skating stuff ready. My mom does my hair to make it more feminine, and I can't wear two sports bras to cover my chest. It feels like I am back at square one, a super feminine-looking figure skater, which is the opposite of what I want but I'm not going to let it affect my performance. I have to do this for my mom. Everything feels wrong, like it always did, but being on the ice helps, even though I don't like figure skating. I have always loved skating and being on the ice, which is why I want to do hockey. I take a deep breath and step onto the ice, channeling all my frustrations into it.

After it's over, my coach comes up to me. "That was the best performance you have ever done, Alice! You could see the passion, the anger, the loneliness, the sadness, it was amazing." I feel myself blush a bit at the praise and just say a quiet thank you in response.

***

I have to skate in a competition three times the following week, so I'm off school for half the week. I got 2nd place overall, and won a $100,000 scholarship to whatever university I want! I'm super excited for the scholarship, and everyone seems to be really happy for me, but I should be happier. I can't be, with my brain nagging at me, telling me, "They just see you as a girl," "You'll never be a real boy," "You'll be stuck like this forever." I've always had that voice in my head, but it seems to be a lot worse right now. I struggle to keep smiling.

When we finally get home I'm exhausted from an entire week of skating and super feminine sparkly costumes. My parents let me take Thursday off to relax, but I have a math test on Friday they aren't going to let me miss. Adam is being super encouraging about how well I've done, and keeps reassuring me that I do look masculine.

On Thursday, I text Adam all day. We talk about everything, and I start to open up about my dysphoria and he comforts me, telling me he feels the same way. On Friday, I'm the first into math class and, again, the "popular" kid—I can't even remember his name—comes up to me and starts making fun of me, especially since now I have short hair. He seems to have thought of the same thing as the people on my figure skating team since he starts calling me "it," which is so much worse than someone just saying "she." I try to ignore him but, when I get home, I immediately go downstairs and cry into my pillow, even though I'm not typically an emotional person.

I can't take it anymore.

I imagine telling my parents that I'm trans, but my mom is fairly strict and religious. I don't think my dad would overreact too much, but I'm still scared. I don't do anything that weekend, my parents let me stay home from Saturday's practice and on Sunday I go to church then stay home talking to Adam all day. We are getting closer and closer every day.

I decide that before telling my parents I'm going to try to tell someone I think will be more accepting. On Monday, at the beginning of class, I ask Jax if I can talk to him about something at lunch. I'm so nervous but I feel like I'm ready to tell him. All through English and Social Studies I freak out about telling him, but I promise myself that I won't chicken out.

At lunchtime, Jax and I meet in the library where we normally hang out, and I pull him off to the side. "Um … Jax… there's something I need to tell you," I say nervously, a feeling in my stomach like I'm about to puke.

"Yeah, what is it?" he says, looking very confused.

"So … I'm transgender," I say then turn away, knowing he is going to hate me, but he just smiles.

"Okay."

I stare at him for a bit. "Wait, actually?"

"Yeah, I'm cool with it, my cousin is actually trans." He laughs quietly. "What name do you want me to use for you?"

"Um … Magnus, it was my grandfather's name." I take a huge sigh of relief. For the rest of lunch we just talk like normal, we laugh and hang out. I feel amazing for the rest of the day, every class seems to be a thousand times better, it feels like a cinder block has been taken off of my chest. Over the next few days, Jax slowly gets the hang of calling me Magnus and it feels amazing.

That weekend I decide it's time. I'm going to tell my dad first because I think he's going to be more accepting of it, then my mom depending on how it goes with him. I message Adam and he's super supportive, just making sure that it would be safe to tell, but I know no matter what happens, I won't be kicked out of my house. The next day at school I tell Jax that I'm going to tell my parents. I can't go by "Alice" any longer. I need to be myself. I psych myself up on Saturday, since my mom is going to be away for the day, and then I go to my dad and take a deep breath …

When You Call Me "She"

By Owen Miller, age 16

When you speak with someone who thinks you're someone you're not,
You begin to feel every word is a lie.

Every sound over my lips feels lipstick-stained.
It feels like dead girl's blood is smeared across my mouth.
It drips over the apple at my throat and dries like wax.
It stings when I try to scrape it off: it yanks the hair from my skin.

When someone calls me "she,"
It's grade four again, and my world is upside down.
I'm peeling duct tape off my calf with one hand,
The other sticking to the cold pole by the sweat on my palm.
I'm struggling to keep the blood from rushing to my head,
Struggling to keep the name that isn't mine out of my mind,
But they force it through my ears like claps of thunder.
Stones hail my body and their echoes crack the asphalt.
My bare, innocent skin swirls into a storm of red, orange, blue, and purple.
Raindrops glide off my jaw and paint the daisies red.
When someone calls me "she,"
I hear it again:
"Freak." "Tranny." "Dyke."

When you call me "she,"
I'm in grade eight again.
I'm sitting in an empty bathtub, the hairs on my neck raised.
The humid air around me seems to vibrate,
Settling on the curve of my shoulders and hips, hair sticking to my clammy skin.
Rich red streams gush down my forearm and scarlet tendrils dribble into my trembling palm,
Their deathly fingertips struggling to intertwine with mine.
I live in a hazy world that barely feels real, even under the light of dusk.
I try to dig past this foreign skin
And find relief in the realization that I am nothing but blood, skin, bones:
I'm bound to no expectations: none of your creations.
Sunlight makes my head spin and my stomach churn.
My teacher asks me why I'm not handing in my schoolwork
And why when I could be skipping grades, I'm skipping classes.
I felt insane,
So I assumed I was.

When you call me "she,"
You're talking past me.
Though I know you have no malicious intent,
I see sun-kissed skin setting to ash,
Droplets on my water bottle slipping into bloody rivulets down the drain,
Musty mildew asphyxiating brisk dawn airways.
You're making a game out of fight or flight:
My heartbeat slams adrenaline through my veins at the thought of going back to that place.

It's grade ten.
I'm learning to speak
As none other than myself
Through chest-hollowing gasps,
White fire locked under my tongue,
Frustration bubbling like bile in my throat.
I accept that I'm no she,
Struggle against their animosity,
And choke back the shame.

Four years reborn and I've never wanted to kill myself.
The most anxiety I get is worrying about exam marks
Until you call me "she."
So yes, my pronoun is a big deal to me,
And it's not okay when you don't use it.

Being transgender isn't a mental illness;
The denial of someone's right to identity is.

Boy or Girl?

By Luna Orion, age 14

I shuffle toward my closet and sigh. "Here we go again," I mumble. One by one, I push every shirt I have to the side until I find my favorite flannel. Grey, just like my mood. I plop a black beanie on my head and I'm ready to go. I try to wear dark clothing to hide what my mom always calls "the beautiful curves that God gave me." She thinks that I need to start to embrace the body that I was given, but really, what good is that going to do if it's the wrong one? I don't tell her this, of course, because I would just get the same response I always do.

"You are perfect just the way you are. You were given the body you have for a reason."

Now, my mom is a wonderful woman, don't get me wrong, but (a) I am not about to start "embracing myself" for her and (b) I'm not out to her yet. She just doesn't understand. Which is why I haven't come out in the first place. Trying to help her understand would be insurmountable. I found the label "non-binary" sometime last year when I was scouting online for internet friends. There were a bunch of accounts that I found where people would put their sexual orientations and gender identities in their bios. At that time, I had no idea that gender identities other than the binary existed.

When I came across "non-binary," it felt like something clicked inside me and I finally understood why I had felt so out of place for so long. All of a sudden, I was a part of something so unique and wonderful while also finding a piece of my identity jigsaw.

A vibration in my back pocket interrupts my thoughts. It's a text from my best friend Isabella.

"Morning Georgia:)"

My heart sinks. I'm not out to anyone except for my online friends. I want to come out to Isabella, but I just don't think she'll understand. We've been best friends since we were really little, and even though I am very "tomboyish," as she would say, she knows me as a girl and wouldn't be able to see otherwise. I'm going to have to say something soon, though. I can't stand not being able to tell her the truth.

"morning bella"

"did you hear that charlie is actually a boy now?" I ask, testing the water.

"Yea! It's so awesome and brave of him! I'm happy that he can finally express himself like he wants to."

Whew! That went way better than I thought it would. Maybe coming out won't be as hard as I thought.

"I know right?! anyway I'll see you at school"

Hope lights up inside me. "I can do this," I whisper to myself. "One person at a time." I sling my backpack over my shoulder and grab a waffle off the kitchen counter. "Bye, Mom!" I yell from the front door.

"Goodbye! Have a nice day, sweetheart!"

The walk to my school isn't that far, so I'm always early. The chilly November wind on top of the overcast sky makes the schoolyard look especially deserted today. When I'm out to everyone I want to start going by the name Grey because it reminds me of these kinds of days. Overcast skies may seem kind of yucky to most, but I love them. They mean that rain is on its way, and rain is spectacular. As I am unlocking my locker, I hear a snicker from behind me. I turn around to find three girls that I used to be friends with chuckling and pointing at me. Ashley, Mackenzie, and Justice are always harassing someone. I take things really personally so I'm the most fun to pick on.

"What are you even wearing?" says Ashley, wearing a cruel grin.

"Flannels are for dykes," adds Justice, venomously.

I feel my face go bright red. I grab my books and slam my locker door, turn quickly in the opposite direction and speed walk down the hallway, straight into the bathroom. Luckily, it's empty.

Looking at myself in the mirror, I immediately regret picking out this shirt, even though it's my favourite. In a stall I take it off and throw on a baggy hoodie that hides the things I don't like. No matter how hard I try, the stupid things those girls say to me still bother me. They pick on everything that I hate, as if my self esteem isn't low enough already.

Back in the hallway Bella comes up behind me and jumps on my back. "Hey G!"

"Hello, Bella," I say back, with a smile. She always brightens my day.

"Look, there's Charlie!" Isabella nods in his direction.

"Yeah. He's pretty great. I'm kinda envious of his bravery."

Isabella gets off my back and starts walking beside me. "Me too! He's just so proud to be himself and nothing anyone says brings him down. He's kind of my school idol." This is a very good thing.

"What do you think about transgender people?" I ask, timid.

She smiles widely at me. "I think that they are very bold and should be able to be whoever they want to be without any repercussions. Anyway, I have English—maybe we can talk more at lunch?"

I nod eagerly and feel butterflies spring to life in my belly. "See you then!"

10:42. The clock could not possibly go any slower. 10:56. My humanities teacher is droning on and on about Galileo and I cannot stop thinking about what to say to Bella. Finally, at 11:05 the bell rings and I hop up from my seat and bound out the door, into the crowded artery of a hallway.

"Meet me in the caf?" I text Bella. She quickly responds with a thumbs up.

On my way to the cafeteria I decide to take a pit stop in the bathroom. Bad idea. Two girls jump as I enter and giggle.

"You're in the wrong bathroom! The boys' washroom is around the corner."

I laugh along with them and dart back into the hallway. I'll just hold it until I get home.

Isabella is waiting in line to buy a wrap for lunch. "Hey," I whisper in her ear, sneaking up on her.

"Jeez, you scared me half to death!" she says holding a hand overtop her heart. "How was class?"

"Boring as usual." I roll my eyes. "How was your class?"

She shrugs. "You know I love English, but we are doing some dull novel study and I just want to do poetry."

I laugh. "You are such a nerd."

She grins widely at me. "I take pride in it. Now, what were we talking about before school?"

Yes! This is what I've been waiting for. "Charlie. And then we were talking about transgender people," I say.

"Oh yes. I think that they are awesome!" She pays for her wrap and we head to our small little corner of the cafeteria that we've unofficially claimed.

"Me too. Have you heard of other gender identities, like non-binary, for example?"

She tilts her head ever so slightly, thinking, and then says, "I've heard of it, but I'm not quite sure what it means." Well, at least she's heard of it.

"It's pretty much an umbrella term for people who identify with genders that are not exclusively masculine or feminine or genders outside of the binary." Isabella's eyes widen and she puts her hand up.

"Wait, hold on. There are more genders?" She says, already confused. This might take a while.

By the end of lunch, I think she has somewhat of an idea of what I'm talking about when I use the term non-binary. Personally, I believe we've made great progress.

"So, why are you telling me all this stuff, G?" Isabella asks me as we walk to Biology. I feel my whole body start to shake. I take a tentative glance toward Bella, who is smiling at me patiently.

"I, uh, well. I kind of think I am non-binary, I guess." I mumble as I become very fascinated with a scuff on the white tip of my Converse.

"Are you kidding?" She says, looking at me with wide eyes.

"No?" I say, getting progressively more anxious.

"No, I mean, that's super awesome!!!" Bella smiles excitedly and hops around a little. "See? You are already cool and now you are even cooler! Why do you look so nervous?"

"I just had no idea that you would take this so well! I'll see you after school, okay?" She nods and skips down the hallway to her last class. I can't help but smile like an idiot the rest of the day.

"So, can you explain more about this stuff to me? Like how it relates to you, I mean?" Bella asks as we walk to my house. She comes over almost every day.

"Of course. I guess I can start off by saying that I personally identify as neither man nor woman but somewhere in between whereas some others who identify with the term non-binary may identify as more masculine, more feminine, or maybe something completely separate."

She nods slowly. "So, it doesn't matter what sex you were assigned at birth?"

"No. It's more about how you feel about your gender inside."

"That makes sense." I smile softly and walk very lightly the rest of the way home. Just when we are about to reach the front door she breaks the peaceful silence. "Well, what do I call you?"

I quickly open the door and rush Isabella upstairs to my bedroom, closing the door quietly.

"Well, you are the first person I've told all this, so you can't call me anything aloud yet, but I've always wanted my name to be Grey." I look at my feet, embarrassed.

"That's a great name for you, G," She says with a loving smile. "You know that I will always love you, no matter your gender or who you fall in love with or whatever. I'll always be here for you, okay?"

I look up at Bella, who is smiling softly as she pulls me into a hug. "Okay, Bella. I love you. Thank you so much for being my best friend."

"I love you too, G. Always." We hug for a while and then do our homework together.

After she's left, my mom comes up to my bedroom door and knocks three times. "Hey, can I come in?" She says softly.

"Yeah sure." The door creaks as she pushes it open slowly. I swivel around in my desk chair to face her. She sits on the end of my bed and looks around my room for a few seconds before looking at me.

"I, uh, heard what you and Isabella were talking about, and I just want you to know that you can be whoever you want to be and I will still love you. I will never stop loving you or hold who you are or who you love against you." She smiles lovingly.

"Thanks, Mum. I'm sorry that you found all this stuff out this way instead of me telling you directly, but if you ever have questions I'm here. I really appreciate you telling me this."

"Of course. I'm your mom!" She rises from my bed and flattens the sheets where she was sitting. Standing in the doorway she says, "We're having spaghetti for dinner. It should be done in about ten minutes. Come down when you are ready." She strides out of the room and closes the door behind her.

So, I think to myself, even though there are some horrible people that do horrible things and some people who will never accept people like me, if I focus on all of the wonderful and accepting people in my life, maybe all this won't be as hard.

Strength

By Finn Lewis, age 13

"This art piece is meant to express the feelings of being transgender in some rough school surroundings. The rainbow-coloured head in the air is my character and expresses my feelings of creativity. Also, the clouds are the city I've created."

Are We There Yet? Making a Roadmap Toward Thriving for Trans, Gender-Creative, Two-Spirit, Intersex, and Queer Youth in Schools

By Lindsay Cavanaugh

While considering what I could say in this chapter as a cisgender queer educator, I had a conversation with a dear friend. It was fall. We were sitting in our respective living rooms, and they had recently moved to another city. This meant that our usual catch-ups, sipping tea at a local café, became bi-weekly Skype dates. As fellow queer educators, we were discussing what we often did, the joys and frustrations of teaching, especially as they relate to gender and sexual diversity in schools. A few weeks prior, my teacher friend had told me gleefully that their school's Gender and Sexuality Alliance (GSA) was creating posters. My friend had spent months establishing this club and was excited to see the youth plan an initiative. The students decided they wanted to build awareness about gender and sexual diversity through adorable meme posters. But that day, my friend's excitement for poster making had faded. That day, while we sipped tea from our living rooms, they recounted how students had ripped down the posters the GSA had made. Their voice was slow and cracking. They said: I mean, how is it still like this, Lindsay? How has it not changed more?

They described seeing students vandalize the posters and pull them violently off the wall. We've come so far. Stuff like this shouldn't still be happening! When my teacher friend told their GSA about the incident, the students nodded solemnly: We're not that surprised. We kind of expected that. They then exchanged stories of indignities. Of being pushed. Of being harassed. Of not feeling safe.

I wish that my friend's story surprised me. I wish that the youth stories in this collection surprised me. But sadly, I am not shocked that Maisie's speaker is called bigoted names, that Max's character Magnus is called "It," that Luna's character G is told that "flannel is for dykes," and that Finn's drawn figure is crying blue, pink, and white tears. I witnessed many instances of bullying and gender-policing both from my time attending school and working as a teacher in multiple provinces. Research reflects a similar story. In one national Canadian study, researchers found that, on average, less than half of trans teens reported feeling connected to their schools (Veale et. al, 2015). Around 90 per cent of trans teens reported hearing transphobic comments daily (Taylor & Peter, 2011), 78 per cent reported feeling unsafe (Taylor & Peter, 2011), and 55 per cent reported being bullied at least once while at school (Veale et. al, 2015). It is not a rude awakening therefore that the anonymous writer felt "terrified that someone might hurt" them. The sad reality is that bullying, harassment, and discrimination are frequent events for trans, gender-creative, two-spirit/Two-Spirit, intersex, and queer people in schools. Moreover, Indigenous, Black, and brown gender variant youth are especially vulnerable to instances of violence and harassment (Brockenbrough, 2015).

Even cisgender and heterosexual youth are experiencing gender-based harassment when they are perceived as gender nonconforming or non-heterosexual (Taylor & Peter, 2011). While not news to me, these youth pieces remind me that even though we have come a long way in some respects for LGBTQIA2S+ rights in general, we still have a long, long way to go—particularly when it comes to policies, protections, and rights for gender diverse folks. We have not arrived at a place of thriving for LGBTQIA2S+ people in schools and society yet. So, where do we go from here?

We need to start by acknowledging that there is a problem with school cultures and take responsibility for shifting our schooling system. The final line from Luna's story reminds me of this when they write: "I think to myself, even though there are some horrible people that do horrible things … if I focus on all the wonderful and accepting people in my life, maybe all this won't be so hard." Their words reminded me of how trans youth and people are cultivating communities and experiences of joy in spite of and in resistance to violence, discrimination, and exclusion. Finn's drawing also showcases this duality of love and pain. Their illustration depicts a person crying tears, coloured pink, blue, and white, a nod to the trans pride flag. The person in the drawing has two outstretched hands: one clenched and empty and one open holding two hearts (one with the colours of the LGBTQ+ pride flag and one with the colours of the trans pride flag). Like Luna's story, Finn's painting seems to be gesturing toward the ways that trans people have to hold two things: the "horrible people that do horrible things" and also the "wonderful and accepting people." While I agree that it is powerful to focus on the good people in one's life, I struggle to accept Luna's sentiment that there are "horrible things" that trans people must still experience in the first place. This is because trans, gender-creative, two-spirit/Two-Spirit, intersex, and queer folks deserve so much more than survival in schools and society at large—they deserve to thrive. So how do we shift toward thriving?

As educators, community members, and administrators—regardless of our gender or sexual identities—we need to take responsibility for fostering environments where trans, gender nonconforming, and queer people can thrive. As Meyer, Tilland-Stafford, and Airton (2016) argue, it should not be on the shoulders of trans and gender-creative youth to educate cisgender people about their identities or how to create affirming spaces for them. Even if someone is "the first apparent trans or gender-creative student in a school," they should not have to "sacrifice their right to privacy, among other things, in order to bring attention to the lack of gender inclusion in a school community" (Meyer, Tilland-Stafford, & Airton, 2016, p. 57). In other words, schools should not be waiting for the presence of trans and gender-creative people to act or depend on trans and gender-creative youth or adults to start efforts to support themselves. Instead, schools should take responsibility for educating staff and students about gender and sexual diversity in sensitive, compassionate, and affirming ways all the time.

In this response, I propose that schools take two approaches toward gender and sexual diversity. I suggest schools start with an approach that focuses on safety, protection, and inclusion. Then, once protective policies, gender-neutral washrooms, and student support groups have been established, I advocate that schools take a more radical stance: one that disrupts normative notions of gender and sexuality. To illustrate this two-pronged approach, I use the metaphor that we are a family about to embark on a road trip. Our destination is thriving for LGBTQIA2S+ people and everyone in schools. We are a large family: trans, gender-creative, and queer kids; youth, parents, teachers, and allies of various ages, ethnicities, racialized identities, class backgrounds, and abilities. We are crammed in an RV, driving along the freeway, looking for signs: rainbow flags, policies, protections, curriculum resources, anything resembling progress. This family, our family, is a bit lost because we do not have a map. We have not vacationed this way before. Like families often do, we begin to bicker. We do not know what direction to take. Some of us think it is better to turn onto Highway Inclusion, while others would prefer to turn down Disruption Lane. We also notice that there is construction. Some people are putting up roadblocks. They are shouting, wearing neon vests, holding warning signs, and telling us to turn back. But we do not turn back because there are others, waving us forward, paving new roads. Still, in the confusion, we do not know where to go. This chapter proposes that we turn down Highway Inclusion and then exit onto Disruption Lane once we have passed some basic landmarks.

HIGHWAY INCLUSION

We should start by turning down Highway Inclusion, which focuses on ensuring protections for LGBTQIA2S+ youth in schools because, without meeting safety concerns, other more lofty diversity goals are unlikely to happen. As the writers in this collection have indicated, trans and gender-creative people do not feel safe in schools. Too many students are "beaten, and bruised with words and fists and notes" (Student Letter, by Anonymous). Think of the verbal harassment that Maisie, Max, and Luna describe in their pieces. Think of the targeted harassment that the anonymous letter writer describes. Think of my teacher colleague describing a school culture where posters that affirm LGBTQIA2S+ people are being vandalized by students. I think of my friend's words: If this is upsetting for me—if this makes me feel unsafe as an adult queer person—I can only imagine what it feels like for my students. Safety is a basic need, and one that psychologist Maslow (1970) argues is necessary for personal growth. Maslow (1970) claims that for a person to be motivated, their physiological and safety needs must be met, then their belonging, love, and esteem needs, and then, only at that time, is a person able to self-actualize: realize their personal potential, and seek personal growth and self-fulfillment. I see Maslow's definition of self-actualization as synonymous with the sort of thriving I hope to see for children and youth in schools. But following Maslow's hierarchy of needs, gender variant folks are far away from self-actualization and thriving if their physiological and safety needs are not being met. Turning down Highway Inclusion is therefore about meeting those first basic needs.

So what does driving down Highway Inclusion look like in terms of action? This approach can look like:

- schools having anti-homophobia/transphobia initiatives and protection policies for trans and gender-creative people;

- some teachers or learners starting student support groups; and
- schools adopting gender-neutral washrooms.

The anonymous letter in this section describes how the "teachers, counsellors, and other staff at [their] school ... have done so much to support [them] ... to be inclusive and to be respectful for all students." This is a great start—having supportive staff that act as advocates in schools will help more students cultivate the sort of self-love that we see in Maisie's poem and the supportive friendships we see in Luna's and Max's stories. It is important to note, however, that driving down Highway Inclusion alone will not bring us to our final destination of thriving. It is unlikely that safety measures on their own will lead to thriving for gender variant and queer people in schools for two reasons. Firstly, such efforts do not address the belonging, love, and esteem needs of students. Secondly, focusing on LGBTQIA2S+ people as "at risk" and in need of interventions ignores the ways that cisgender and heterosexual people also need interventions: they need to learn more about non-dominant cultures and identities, and reflect on the ways the status quo limits possibilities for everyone (Airton, 2013; MacIntosh, 2007). In sum, policies, support groups, and gender-neutral washrooms are landmarks we need to pass, but to reach our destination we need more radical approaches. To reach our destination, I recommend we exit onto Disruption Lane.

DISRUPTION LANE

So what does driving down Disruption Lane offer us that Highway Inclusion does not? There are two big pieces of work that are missing in gender and sexual diversity efforts in schools.

Challenging Hetero/Cisnormativity

The first missing piece is ongoing actions that challenge normative understandings of gender and sexuality (hetero/cisnormativity). So what is hetero/cisnormativity exactly? Heteronormativity is the belief that heterosexuality is the only normative and desirable sexual orientation and often results in queer people needing to justify and negotiate their existence as they navigate hostile or unwelcoming environments (Toomey, McGuire, & Russell, 2012). Cisnormativity is the notion that gender is a fixed binary and that being cisgender, identifying with the biological sex one is assigned at birth, is the only normative and desirable gender identity. It often manifests in people assuming that everyone is cisgender, and leaves trans people having to announce their presence and fight to be recognized as valid. As García and Slesaransky-Poe (2010) explain, "[s]ociety, and consequently schools, feel most comfortable with what is considered 'normal' or 'normative' such as boys and girls following the script of what has been decided by the majority to be appropriate for boys and girls to do, act, like, and desire" (p. 248). One result of this discomfort toward anti-normativity or nonconformity is how children and adults often regulate gender and sexual expectations through language and behaviours (García & Slesaransky-Poe, 2010). We see this regulation in seemingly benign phrases like "boys and girls" and "ladies and gentlemen." We see it in the anonymous letter writer's observation that "we see babies and toddlers wearing clothing with slogans like 'ladies' man' and 'chick magnet.'" We see it in how teachers are addressed as Mr., Mrs., or Ms. (i.e., there is often no gender-neutral option such as Mx. in schools). We likewise see hetero/cisnormativity in the ways people try to shame certain gender and sexual identities. The anonymous writer provides an example of this when they describe some people's responses to them coming out as trans: "That's not what God intended," "that's a sin," or "that's gross." In schools, hetero/cisnormativity often lurks in the curriculum—what educators teach and do not teach (e.g., Connell & Elliott 2009)—and how students and teachers act and relate to one another (e.g., Simonsson & Angervall, 2016).

So why should we disrupt hetero/cisnormativity? We should challenge hetero/cisnormativity in schools because it incites and naturalizes homophobia, transphobia, and gender policing. It is a barrier to meeting the belonging, love, and esteem needs of trans and gender-creative students, educators, and community members in school spaces. As the anonymous student writes: "We aren't asking for 'special rights,' we're just asking to be acknowledged and respected.… We're asking to be treated like people." Without being "acknowledged and respected," which is incompatible with hetero/cisnormative beliefs, gender variant folks are unlikely to thrive in schools. But hetero/cisnormativity is not just harmful for LGBTQIA2S+ folks; it is also a barrier for thriving for cisgender and heterosexual people because, as educational theorist Freire (1970) argues, any form of oppression is dehumanizing for both the oppressed/oppressor. "Dehumanization, which marks not only those whose humanity has been stolen, but also (though in a different way) those who have stolen it, is a distortion of the vocation of becoming more fully human" (1). In other words, while it is an entirely different experience of dehumanization than that of those who are being harassed, bullied, and shamed, those who subtly or overtly police people's gender and sexualities are also disconnected from their humanity. Up to 58 per cent of straight cisgender students reported that they found it upsetting to hear homophobic comments—some because they felt empathy for the victims of the comments and others because they felt ashamed for participating or being bystanders (Taylor & Peter, 2011). As the youth in the collection remind us, everyone deserves to be treated like a person. We should therefore find ways to shift school cultures and our schooling system in general.

INTRODUCING MORE AFFIRMING NARRATIVES

The second missing piece is providing students with positive and affirming narratives about trans, gender-creative, and queer people in schools. Safety measures, while important, can "lead (albeit inadvertently) to an assumption that to be young and LGBT means facing adversity, thus minimising the potential for shared (public) stories of love, friendship, and happiness among LGBT young people" (Formby, 2015, p. 636). As Brockenbrough (2015) adds: noting only how LGBTQIA2S+ people suffer "downplays, or even misses, the transformative possibilities of queer youth agency" (p. 29). Instead of exclusively emphasizing how bad of a time LGBTQIA2S+ youth are having in schools, how trans and queer people are "at risk" or vulnerable, we should balance those stories with narratives of self-love, acceptance, resilience, love, and community. We should focus on the charming self-affirmation in Maisie's poem, which the speaker expresses in her nightly proclamation ("I'm awesome") and her awareness that "[j]ust 'cause I'm unique, doesn't mean I'm not cool." Or the hearts in Finn's illustration that float and sparkle in the air. Or the loving acceptance seen in Luna's story, when Bella replies to G's coming out with beaming excitement: "You are already cool and now you're even cooler!" Or Ajam's nuanced representation of gender fluidity in his watercolour painting, "Where Do We Draw the Dividing Line?" In his piece, he destabilizes the gender binary—the notion that there is just male or female—by positioning a person in the middle of a trans flag and illustrating clothing and mannerisms that have been socially coded as "masculine" on a pink backdrop and socially coded "feminine" clothing and mannerisms on a blue backdrop.

A part of telling these more positive LGBTQIA2S+ stories means teaching and learning about the unique insights and perspectives that may arise from living outside the boundaries of some social norms. Barnett, Choong, and Hudspith (2002)'s term "outsider status" fits well with the playful and confrontational mood of Ajam's painting and offers a more liberating perspective on marginalization. According to those scholars, "outsider status" is the quality of existing outside societal norms and is common in leaders who are marginalized. Barnett, Choong, and Hudspith (2002) note that this quality has "a powerful bearing on [a person's] innovative abilities" (p. 10) because through virtue of not fitting within certain norms, these people have the unique opportunity to see the world from a different lens. They are not tethered to certain societal norms and so, they argue, there is a potential for innovative, divergent thinking and action. This idea of "outsider status" connects to bell hooks's (1990) idea that living on the margins "offers radical perspectives from which to see and create, to imagine ... new worlds" (p. 6). In sum, we should not forget that trans, gender-creative, and queer people enrich the spaces they occupy; they do not just need protections—just like all people, they deserve opportunities to shine and share their insights.

So what does driving down Disruption Lane look like in terms of action? These are actions I witnessed as a volunteer with the Gender Generations Project. I saw the youth and mentors challenge norms in their compassionate and playful facilitation and bonding. These actions can be taken up by teachers and administrators. Driving down Disruption Lane for educators looks like them being able to:

- critically reflect on their own positionality;
- tell positive and nuanced stories about LGBTQIA2S+ people and all marginalized groups;
- acknowledge individuals who are gender variant and queer through their language, their behaviours, and what they teach;

- interrupt moments of gender-policing and facilitate learning for their students and colleagues about its harms;
- model acceptance, celebration, and love of nonconformity in its many iterations.

Driving down this lane also means critically reflecting on the ways we organize schools in general. It means taking a more expansive approach toward diversity in schools and shifting it from trying to make marginalized people fit into a pre-existing structure to changing the structure of schools itself. Unfortunately, we are still far away from this more expansive approach. We are moving forward, and it is powerful, as Luna wrote in their final sentence, "to focus on all the wonderful and accepting" things and people around us. I will end this response with a summary of each approach and practical suggestions for educators and administrators that combine the strengths of Highway Inclusion with the strengths of Disruption Lane. We have a long distance to go before we will arrive at an environment where all trans, gender-creative, Two-Spirit, intersex, and queer people are thriving in schools, but with each landmark we pass, we get a little bit closer to our destination.

Landmarks on Highway Inclusion

- Ensure your school has school and district policies that protect and support trans, gender-creative, and queer people
- Ensure your school has a support group for LGBTQIA2S+ youth (this could be a rainbow club, a gender and sexuality club, an inclusion club, etc.)
- Ensure your school has gender-neutral washrooms that are easily accessible

Landmarks on Disruption Lane

- Ensure that all educators, administrators, and staff in your school have an understanding of hetero/cisnormativity and are reflecting on how they can challenge dominant understandings of gender in their language, behaviours, and teaching
- Help educators, administrators, and staff learn about oppression, anti-oppressive education, and the ways that different forms of oppression are connected
- Come up with school-based strategies for disrupting hetero/cisnormativity and create plans of how to bring content about LGBTQIA2S+ people into various subjects (bring in community educators when stumped)
- Have educators talk about trans, gender-creative, two-spirit/Two-Spirit, intersex, and queer people in their teaching
- Ensure that students are hearing about positive LGBTQIA2S+ stories, and are learning about historical and current figures
- Create a culture of advocacy where students and educators are encouraged to support and fight for the rights and opportunities of others
- Teach students about difference, ambiguity, uncertainty, and nonconformity

WHAT NOW?

Wondering what you can do now? If you are an educator or administrator, here are some places to start:

✓ **Have conversations with your colleagues about how to support trans and gender-creative youth and make proactive strategies for supporting gender variant people.** Don't wait for visible trans people in your schools to develop supports—think about how you can change the culture and language you are currently using to support gender variant people. Do it now!

✓ **Learn about privilege and oppression on your own and in community.** Be kind to yourself as you learn while still holding yourself accountable to unlearning. Recognize we have all been socialized with white colonial hetero-cispatriarchal logics. If you are a cisgender (queer or heterosexual) educator, do not depend on trans, non-binary, two-spirit/Two-Spirit, and intersex educators or students to educate you about gender. Take responsibility for your own learning and compassionately work through the emotions that come up for you in ways that do not centre your privilege.

✓ **Understand that sexual orientation is different from gender identity** and that trans and gender-creative people often have different needs and experiences than people who identify as bisexual, queer, gay, lesbian, asexual, questioning, pansexual, etc. Remember to always keep learning. If you think you have arrived at a place of knowing, question yourself.

✓ **Educate yourself and others on the differences between biological sex, gender identity, gender expression, and sexual orientation** (bring community educators into your school if you need help learning/teaching). Recognize that different cultures have different understandings of gender and sexuality. There is not one singular understanding. It is okay to hold multiple truths.

✓ **Create a culture where people are sharing pronouns and challenging cis/heteronormative assumptions.** For example, have staff share their pronouns as a way to model support for trans and gender-creative folks (this can be in their email signature, when they write their names up on the board, etc.)

REFERENCES

Airton, L. (2013). Leave "those kids" alone: On the conflation of school homophobia and suffering queers. *Curriculum Inquiry, 43*(5), 532–562.

Barnett, R., Choong, D., & Hudspith, M. (2002). The lesbian innovation project: Identity politics and a new discourse on leadership. In A. MacNevin, E. O'Reilly, E. Leslau Silverman, & A. Tayler (Eds.), *Women and Leadership* (pp. 5–23). Ottawa: Canadian Research Institute for the Advancement of Women.

Brockenbrough, E. (2015). Queer of color agency in educational contexts: Analytic frameworks from a queer of color critique. *Educational Studies, 51*, 28–44.

Connell, C., & Elliott, S. (2009). Beyond the birds and the bees: Learning inequality through sexuality education. *American Journal of Sexuality Education, 4*(2), 83–102.

Formby, E. (2015). Limitations of focussing on homophobic, biphobic and transphobic "bullying" to understand and address LGBT Young people's experiences within and beyond school. *Sex Education, 15*(6), 626–640.

Freire, P. (1970). *Pedagogy of the oppressed.* New York: Continuum.

García, A.M., & Slesaransky-Poe, G. (2010). The heteronormative classroom: Questioning and liberating practices. *Teacher Educator, 45*(4), 244–256.

hooks, b. (1990). *Yearning: Race, gender, and cultural politics.* Boston: South End Press.

MacIntosh, L. (2007). Does anyone have a Band-Aid? Anti-homophobia discourses and pedagogical impossibilities. *Educational Studies, 41*(1), 33–44.

Maslow, A. H. (1970). *Motivation and personality.* New York: Harper & Row.

Meyer, E., Tilland-Stafford, A., & Airton, L. (2016). Transgender and gender creative students in PK-12 schools: What we can learn from their teachers. *Teacher College Record: The Voice of Scholarship in Education, 118*(8), 50.

Simonsson, A., & Angervall, P. (2016). Gay as classroom practice: A study on sexuality in a secondary classroom. *Confero, 4*(1), 37–70.

Taylor, C., & Peter, T. (Eds.). (2011). *Every class in every school: Final report on the first national climate survey on homophobia, biphobia, and transphobia in Canadian schools.* Toronto: Egale Canada Human Rights Trust.

Toomey, R. B., McGuire, J. K., & Russell, S. T. (2012). Heteronormativity, school climates, and perceived safety for gender nonconforming peers. *Journal of Adolescence, 35*(1), 187–196.

Veale, J., Saewyc, E., Frohard-Dourlent, H., Dobson, S., Clark, B., & the Canadian Trans Youth Health Survey Research Group. (2015). *Being safe, being me: Results of the Canadian trans youth health survey.* Vancouver: Stigma and Resilience Among Vulnerable Youth Centre, School of Nursing, University of British Columbia. Retrieved from http://www.saravyc.ubc.ca/2015/05/05/being-safe-being-me-results-of-thecanadian-trans-youth-health-survey/.

CHAPTER SIX

Mental Health

KEY THEMES

- Effects of transphobia and gender dysphoria on mental health
- Surviving depression, anxiety, and suicidal ideation
- Self and community care, and other forms of healing

CRITICAL QUESTIONS

- Have you or a loved one experienced mental illness? Did gender or gender expectations play into that unwellness?
- How do these pieces show the relationship between transphobia, gender dysphoria, and mental health?
- What patterns of coping, resilience, and thriving emerge from this chapter?

BOOKS WE LOVE

Picture Books

Boulay, S., & Bray-Bourret, A. (2020). *Riley can't stop crying*. Victoria: Orca Books. *Also available in French*

Doerrfeld, C. (2018). *The rabbit listened*. London: Scallywag Press. *Also available in French*

Howley, J. (2019). *Big boys cry*. New York: Random House.

Neal, D., Neal, T., & Twink, A. (2020). *My rainbow*. New York: Kokila.

Thorn, T., & Grigni, N. (2019). *It feels good to be yourself: A book about gender identity*. New York: Henry Holt & Co.

YA and Graphic Novels

Bornstein, K. (2006). *Hello, cruel world: 101 alternatives to suicide for teens, freaks, and other outlaws*. New York: Seven Stories Press.

Callender, K. (2020). *Felix ever after*. New York: Balzer & Bray/Harperteen.

Emezi, A. (2019). *Pet*. London: Faber & Faber.

Madrone, K. H. (2018). *LGBTQ: The Survival guide for lesbian, gay, bisexual, transgender, and questioning teens*. Minneapolis: Free Spirit Publishing.

Siebert, M., & Wuthrich, B. (2020). *Heads up: Changing minds on mental health*. Victoria: Orca Books.

General Audience

Fitzpatrick, C., & Plett, C. (2017). *Meanwhile, elsewhere: Science fiction and fantasy from transgender writers*. New York: Topside Press.

Singh, A. (2018). *The queer and transgender resilience workbook: Skills for navigating sexual orientation and gender expression*. Oakland, CA: New Harbinger Publishers.

Whitehead, J. (2018) *Jonny Appleseed: A novel*. Vancouver: Arsenal Pulp Press. *Also available in French*

Wilson-Yang, J. Q. (2018). *Small beauty*. Montréal: Metonymy Press.

Winter, K. (2013). *Annabel*. Toronto: House of Anansi Press.

Memoirs/First Person Narratives

Bennett, A. (2020). *Like a boy but not a boy: Navigating life, mental health, and parenthood outside the gender binary*. Vancouver: Arsenal Pulp Press.

Ferguson, L. M. (2019). *Me, myself, and them: Life beyond the binary*. Toronto: House of Anansi Press.

McBee, T. P. (2019). *Amateur: A reckoning with gender, identity, and masculinity*. Edinburgh: Canongate Books.

Shraya, V. (2018). *I'm afraid of men*. Toronto: Penguin Canada. *Also available in French*

Violet, M. (2018). *Yes, you are trans enough: My transition from self-loathing to self-love*. London: Jessica Kingsley Publishers.

Transcend

By Ajam, age 14

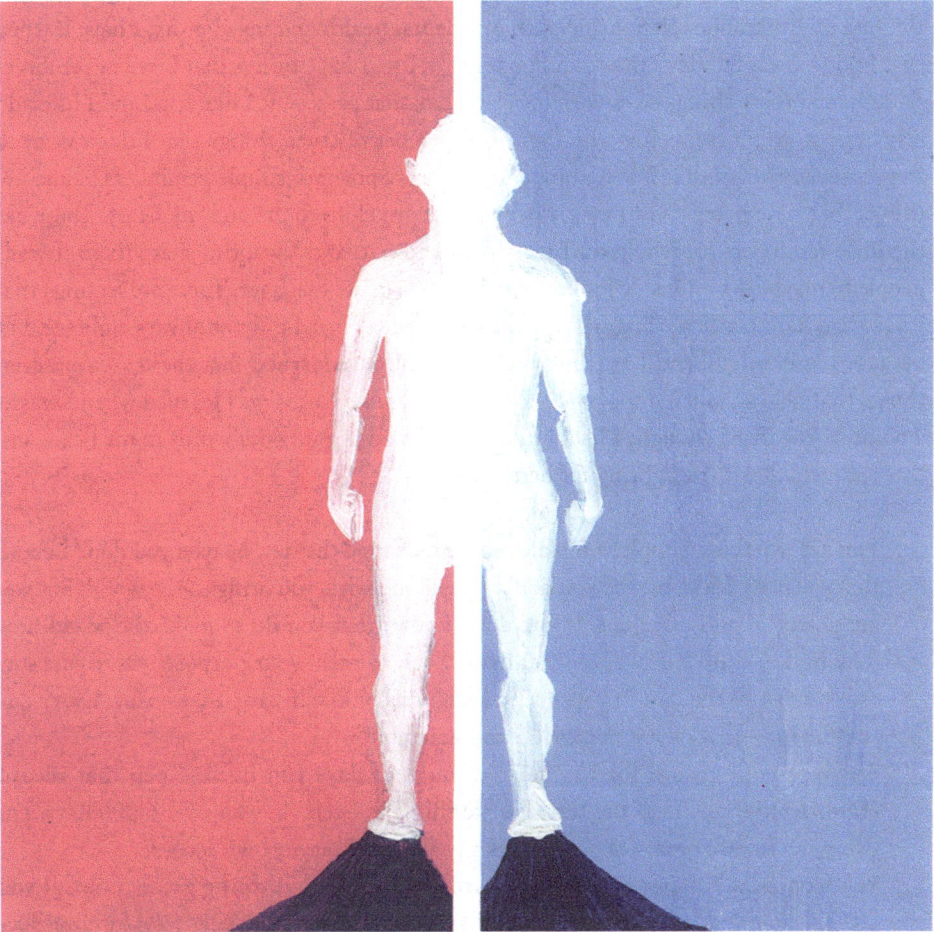

Self-Care

By A.J. Gabriel, age 17

Because of my strange relationship with my mental health and my identity, I have learned that I don't always understand what I'm doing in life. I have things that I will never forget though, and these things stick with me every day that passes by. I like lists, and I like odd numbers, so of course, being who I am, I have a list of seven things that I don't want to forget; seven things that I will always remember. Some are simple reminders, some are things that have been told to me by people that are close to me and my heart. These are the little reminders for whenever I feel down and out, and I want to share them. I want people to maybe get an inside look at the mind of a queer teenager. These are feelings that I have had hard times dealing with, and they are ideas that I did not always embrace, but because I am human, and I am always changing, I have learned that these are the seven things that hold so much importance to me. They are seven things I learned when I was at a point so low that I thought I had nothing left. I had nothing but words in my head, and these are what kept me fighting for better days.

1. **You are worth it.** Simple, simple words can change the day. Maybe you don't believe that you're worth it, maybe you don't understand what you bring to the world, but you are powerful and excellent. If you don't know what you do to make the world how it is, find it. Find the purpose you have. Even if today your purpose was to just stay asleep most of the day, or just wake up and do some self-care, that's okay. Every day is different—that's what makes life unpredictable.

2. **Today is your record for the most amount of days you lived. Keep that record climbing higher.** As of the time I write this, I've been alive for over 6,000 days. I'm going for 10,000 next. I'm gonna kick my ass and beat my own record!

3. **You have beat 100 per cent of your hardest days—you're doing great.** Look at you go, just winning, and living it up. All those shitty and relatively *yikes* kind of days you've had: you've come out alive! Sometimes that's all you can do; survive. But hey, that means you get more days to make things different! More days to find new hobbies, meet new people, get a new pet ... whatever it is that makes you feel a good feeling. You're doing amazing. I'm proud of you.

4. **There's something that's been keeping you here all this time. What is it?** Sometimes there's this feeling that nothing is worth it anymore. But you and your life are worth fighting for. You've stayed all this time when at any point you could have theoretically given up. Do you know why you're here? Do any of us know why we are where we are, or *who* we are? Find out, find yourself, find something new about yourself that you never knew.

5. **Sometimes you're lost, but you will always be found.** Maybe it won't be today, or tomorrow, or next week even. Life has a funny way of getting in the way when we

don't want it to. But something huge that I've learned is that you have to find yourself where you lost yourself, and from there, rebuild yourself even stronger than before.

6. **Just because today sucked doesn't mean tomorrow is gonna be just as awful.** Life's too short to be upset about everything all the time, yet here I am, the constant wet blanket of every event I go to. But hey, guess what? That's okay! It's okay to have feelings. It is also fine to have bad days. There are going to be days when all you want to do is give up. This is 100 per cent true and extremely understandable. On the flipside, there are going to be days when all you want is to keep going and keep fighting. Who knows what kind of day tomorrow will be? What will it bring? I guess the only way to find out is to stay and see.

7. **The past is the past, and the future will forever remain something to be desired.** This goes to say, things that happened in the past are just that—old news. But that doesn't mean that they weren't important or impactful. They always say in sci-fi-type movies that when you go back to the past not to change a thing because it will forever drastically alter the present. But why don't we think of our lives right *now* in the same light? If every little action can have a drastic effect on our future, why stay silent? If one small thing can change the present, what can we do with our future?

There are trillions of planets that exist in the galaxies here and further on. We were put on this planet for some reason, and we continue to change it every second of each day. I'm a strong believer in the butterfly effect, and I feel that everything that we do comes from something else that has affected us, and further goes to affect things around us. We are here for some weird, inexplicable reason, and sometimes it feels like we don't deserve to be here, don't deserve to take up the precious oxygen that we consume, or don't deserve to take up a place in society—especially if society has tried to outcast us for years. The world doesn't stop for anyone, and maybe the thought of disappearing is so strong that you feel that nothing will change without you; but that's just simply not true. Just because the world doesn't stop for anyone, doesn't mean that, to someone, you weren't their world. When there are really bad days when it seems impossible to do anything, just know that there is someone who exists that has been changed, in even the tiniest way, by knowing you. You, just as you are, are so important.

WORDS AND LISTS

Some words have a tendency to make you feel utterly horrible; so incredibly so that you wish you could be a turtle who could retract their neck and head inside of their body any time someone says *moist*; this is just a fact. I, for one, happen to have a journal that I keep and write down words and sentences that make me happy. I love little things and putting them together can make me feel less like a dumpster fire. I love lists, words, odd numbers, dogs, my hair, the concept of a clown-cowboy hybrid … but I don't always have all of those things on me when I'm upset. The things that I do have are words, and I have ones that I like to say just because they sound real nifty. Sometimes I'll just say them to myself when I'm upset or when I'm having a lot of anxiety or when don't know how to react to a situation.

The weird thing is that these words don't really mean much to me or hold any significant value. I just like the way they sound when I say them. It's strange how a series of syllables put together can make me convince myself that I'm doing well. I'm going to leave my list of words that I like to say, and I'm gonna encourage everyone who stumbles upon this piece to do the same.

- Castle
- Glass
- Pariah
- Duodenum
- Corrode
- Rhododendron
- Anecdotal
- Correlate
- Saoirse
- Juxtaposition
- Decrepit
- Chelicerates
- Thorn
- Lackadaisical
- Conundrum

When I'm having a big ol' bout of *STRESS*, I will just say these words either aloud or at least in my head. They make me feel calm, even though I only ever really say them when I am in fact *not* calm.

I Am Strong

By Tor Broughton, age 12

I am strong
As I look in the mirror trying to see myself
Releasing that he's not there
That's her
Victoria
That terrible word runs through my head
But I stand there telling myself who I am
I am strong
As I go to the gym and lift
I feel weak
When I see cis guys all muscular and lucky
As the pain of not being on T hits me
I keep lifting
I am strong
I get my blocker shot
The tears stream down into a waterfall of hopelessness
As I tell myself the shots aren't worth it
The pain I push through
I am strong
As I'm misgendered and told I'm not a real boy
While my grandparents tell me where I'm headed in the afterlife
Hell
The word I see written across the letter they wrote me
Hell
I put it away
I am strong
The cameras, lights and mics pushed into my face
Because I thanked the PM
Tears run again as he speaks to me
The tears I've been told were too feminine for me
I let them fall
I am strong

Why?

By Danny Charles, age 17

Why I didn't choose to feel this I didn't choose to have anxiety.

I can't talk, speak, make a sound, everyone told me my voice is heard, until I'm behind closed doors.

My voice is lost like my mind is crossed,
I can't run or hide my voice is implied,
When the door is finally open I push to speak about my incredible life, but really it's not.
I used to be my dad's little sparkle in his eye until he left without saying goodbye and my mom used to tell me these lies about how being alive is like trying to be a butterfly but really being alive means I'm trying to stay high on life and not live a lie.

My anxiety is like a storm, at first my eyes start to rain really hard, then my mind turns into a tornado of thoughts that drives me into an ocean of depression built up of pills and potions, where overdosing seems like my only way out.

When someone kills themself their suicide note was/is a story that needs to be heard, you know if they get stuck in their mind to the point that makes them feel so implied to sound so alive but their voice would still hide because they are afraid of lies.

Lying is like fake smiling no one knows.

Whose Whore?

By Ask Spirest (Spirit of the Forest), age 18

i was 16 when i exhaled,
lungs full of tar and despair,
rolling from a hit of molly that i couldn't
blame for wanting to die.

"you don't have to worry about hell ... you're living it."

i care about my parents ... i'd rather die than cause them such anguish,
yet my death would be more anguish ...
and guilt.

"Do you want to go to hell? Stop this! This is sinning! Sinners go to hell!"

4am he creaks up the stairs, cleaned restaurant.
i glide down the stairs in tune to the click of the bathroom door.

neither listen, nor hear enough to want to save me,
so i   s l i p   a w   a   y
and f
        l
            y.
down the hills,
levitating wand in hand,
fairy dust settling into my nervous system for a high to
last
another night.

i
crash.

still 16, the day after,

she drops me off on the side of the road to school
she speeds off,
i run off,
to.away from school to.running to.a bus to.find

16, hospital.

16, fuCK!

16, sex.

sex.

the first time.

Tuesday, November 22nd, 2016
"For fuck's sake
The first time I have penetrative sex, I get an STI.
Two rounds of antibiotics
and I didn't even get paid."

One stroke, one stroke, two strokes.
I complete the illusion of female form on the edges of my two eyes
for a man who's old enough
to have lived through
a few strokes himself.

I didn't want to have sex.
I wanted to have sex.
I reclaimed power over the flesh that houses and defines me.

I enter.

Why?
Freedom.
Free.
To be free.

Free sex to have freedom.

Freedom to pay for sex.

I move into my first home.

I haven't been able to call my parents' house my home for years.
Their demon child lurks in the shadows of their hellfire-lit Bibles.

I light my home with fairy lights and fairy dust.
Escapism rules my dreams and awakenings.
Clenched jaw,
throat raw,
molly, nightmare, night wear?

My first meal is ramen.
bought
with a pan I find in the mall,
paid for
with a $20 blowjob.
I knew him, but I never charge that
Little again.

20 dollars, to 40, to 60 ... year-old man.

I charge him $260,
his nails scrape my skin as I trace his skin with mine,
A silent plea for mimicked gentleness.

Tapestries fill my room now.
They travel with me, and are becoming of my space,
I sleep in corners on my floor, wrapped in tie-dyed fabrics.

~~~

I'm 18

I have found a safer haven

In the pink and Red Rooms of a massage parlour where I lay
Cold hands on warm skin.
Absorbing.

I charge triumphant.
Less than independence,
Worth the distance from my bedroom.

After,
the drive-through,
I smile at my lover,

"What do you want?"

"Don't spend it. That's your whoring money."

I turn away, and project my voice out to the speaker.
"I'm sorry. I just didn't want sugar at 12am."
He says,
Realizes.

I don't add.

We both know our youth.
Fast and easy money,
dangerous impulsive purchases.

My money is no different.

~~~

I shower the next morning, hot water burning life back into my muscles,

Fears of exposure following of excess.

Trans! Kinky! Whore! Queer!

I grasp the weapons and feel their weight and power,

An extension of my arm that I don't release.

Growing into the tendons of my arm, seeping into my heart,

I fight for freedom, fully armed.

~~~

My activism has empowered me to embrace all aspects of my identity and identifiers. I know better now how to stand up for myself, as I learn how to stand up for others with me. I still worry about being outed. There are things that I still wouldn't want my parents to hear about from someone else, like the way that being outed as trans eventually led to having to leave my parents' house earlier than I would have liked to.

Still, I am grateful for the growth and support of my chosen family and friends, and I can now see that the gains of being authentic can be worth the risk of pain and loss. I worry about not getting hired or accepted to schools if people know I'm trans and a sex worker, or freaky otherwise. Still, I know that the world I want to live in, the world I fight for, is one that is inclusive and celebrates all people for the good that we do and are.

Love,

Ask Spirest (Spirit of the Forest)

Life Letter

By Jaxon Steele, age 16

Inspired by Tanner Z

If you're reading this,
I am still alive.
Still breathing through constricted lungs,
Even though sometimes I think I would rather be still.

I'm still hurting and suffering and fighting the encroaching darkness.
I'm still having panic attacks and depressive episodes and nightmares that wake me up
in a cold sweat.
I'm still sparring with my inner demons and I'm still dysphoric as all hell.
I'm still struggling to get out of bed in the morning.

I'm still afraid.

I'm still battling against my own mind.
The only difference is,
Now I'm finally gaining some ground.

I am still alive.

I'm still learning and exploring and laughing.
I'm still creating and caring and loving with all my heart.
I'm still doing what I can to help others.

I'm still healing.

I am still writing my story.

I am still alive.

I'm now on my seventeenth orbit around the sun and I'm still here.
I never thought I would make it through my fourteenth.

I'm still here and I'm telling you my story.
Because maybe I'm still alive for a reason.
Maybe my purpose is to help others realize that suicide is not an option.
Maybe I'm here to tell them to write a life letter instead.

I'm now reading this,

Which means I'm still alive.

My heart is still beating even though my mind has been telling it to stop for the past eight years.

My lungs are still breathing even though I've imprisoned them within a tight binder.

My eyes are still opening and closing and taking in new sights even though I have prayed countless times to see only darkness.

Whether because of a miracle,

Or sheer stubbornness,

I am still alive.

A Perspective on Growth

By Alexander McIntyre, age 16

I still remember the smell of chemicals and blinding white walls of the hospital at 3 am.

It was six months after coming out to my family, six months of asking for help and getting emotional abuse instead of support. Six months after all this started was when I told my mother I was going to kill myself. I wasn't doing it for attention, or as a way to get what I wanted. It was a plea for help. It was the final card in my back pocket. It was the last resort. It was what I had to fall onto after putting up with my parents telling me that I was just going through another phase. After months of hiding out in my room as long as I could every day, because having any sort of conversation with them led to me feeling worse than being ignored. They were invalidating me. I kept asking for some sort of support to help me feel okay, but nothing seemed to make my parents understand the severity of the situation. The result of this led to where I was in December of 2016.

Sitting in a room with a doctor who knew literally nothing about the transgender community, and my mother who refused to admit that she was doing anything wrong. I remember looking out the window to the parking lot as the two adults talked, and planning out every route I could think of in order to get out of the hospital and where I could go from there. By the time I was allowed to leave, I was fifteen minutes away from jumping out of the window. I was desperate, and anywhere was better than there.

At this point in my transition, nothing had happened except getting a binder and my mother occasionally calling me by the right pronouns. I had gone to several school counsellors that had heavily suggested some sort of antidepressant medication, just until I could get further medical help. Both of my parents had refused to let me even try it out. I had asked numerous times if I could get in touch with a doctor to see what kind of hormone therapy was available to me. Neither of my parents thought that it was necessary. Despite my efforts to educate them on all the ways hormone therapy, or even hormone blockers could help me, they insisted that I was too young to make the decision for myself and I had to wait until I was 18. The irony in that promise was that by the time I was 18, I wouldn't need their consent any longer. It was their way of ignoring the problem and therefore not having to deal with backlash from the rest of my family. That was something that I had to cope with on my own. There were several times after coming out that one or both of my grandmothers would harass and disrespect my gender. The worst part was how neither of my parents stood up for me, and rather let their parents blatantly say things that disregarded my very real feelings.

The add-up of all this emotional abuse was what resulted in that midnight trip to the hospital. Strangely enough, I remember the sanitary smell of that place being almost more comforting than the smell of my own house. Looking back at it now, I understand why my mother did what she did. I understand that she was scared and confused and genuinely believed what she was doing was right. But after that night, it took almost a year before our relationship got any better. I ended up having to permanently move out of her house because the ignorance was too hard to handle. My father provided a safe place for me to live, and has learned over the years how to accept me for who I am, regardless of his personal opinion about it. The move wasn't emotionally easy in any way, but it was necessary. It provided my mother with time to come to terms with having a transgender son, and it showed her how serious the situation actually was.

I remember learning that sometimes you can give people all the information you have, provide them with a way of understanding you, but in the end it is their choice whether they want to accept you or not. They have to consciously make the choice to learn, and if they can't, then prying at them can often do more damage than good. I eventually had to accept that my mother wasn't ready to understand me. It hurt a lot, knowing that she couldn't accept me, but after living in a different house for almost a year our relationship had time to slowly start getting better. After leaving her, I got support from an amazing doctor, was put on a waiting list for top surgery, and started hormone therapy. Those things wouldn't have happened if I hadn't made the decisions I did. Although no one in my family agreed with these choices, my father came to terms with the fact that it wasn't his decision, and being away from my mother let her have time to accept her position as a parent of a transgender child.

I wish I had had someone to tell me that it isn't your fault if your parents or family members aren't accepting. Often, it is because they are going through something of their own. I had to learn to put myself in their shoes and try to understand the situation from their perspective. This is not to say that one must forgive toxic behaviour, but it's something I had to remember. It was easy to blame myself for my parents' unaccepting behaviours, but remembering the causes of it helped me cope.

Through my experiences, I remember being so alone in my thoughts. It's only now, several years later, that I can look back and see the whole picture. But I still wish I had had someone to make me feel less alone. Someone to tell me that things were going to be okay, and that I truly just needed to push through because things would get better. I'm no longer the broken boy sitting in a hospital waiting room at 3 am. This isn't to say that my life is perfect; I still have struggles and difficulties that I face every day. But even in my short years of life, I have seen things get better. I'm here to tell you that you can get through anything. The people who have the bravery to come out to the world, even just to accept themselves, can honestly do anything. You will find happiness. You will get through the times of hurt. You will un-familiarize yourself with the toxicity that comes along with an unaccepting family. I've done it, and I've seen many others do the same. No matter how much it feels like it, you are not alone.

Untitled-1

By Riley, age 17

We could all be swallowed by despair and no one would blame us

Murky tides could lull us to sleep, opiate daydreams and fearful keening
I could live in her wide, mascara-rimmed eyes, she looks at the sand, so much like all the other lost girls

I could live in the dark spots on his MRI or the empty 40s my brother drains

No one would blame me

But I need to choose their skin on mine, the feeling of driving fast through the night
The flutter in my stomach when I think about asking her on a date
Credence curling up on my lap as I read and sip coffee
There are too many beautiful things to choose instead of grief, though she will always live in my bones

How could she not?

Strength is not ignoring the hurt, it's softening into it and living through it
It's watering your roses with tears,
Holding your friends as they die over and over
Look her in her tear-soaked face and say "yeah, I know"

Dive into the ocean and lose yourself

We could be swallowed by grief
Lost in waiting rooms, rusty and jealous, minds in psychotic disrepair
No one would blame us
I could just never refill my prescriptions and spin spin spin spun into a manic haze

But instead I choose the boring work of recovery
Lay me down to sleep every night, eat everyday

Starry Stabby + Live + Love

By Ask Spirest, age 18

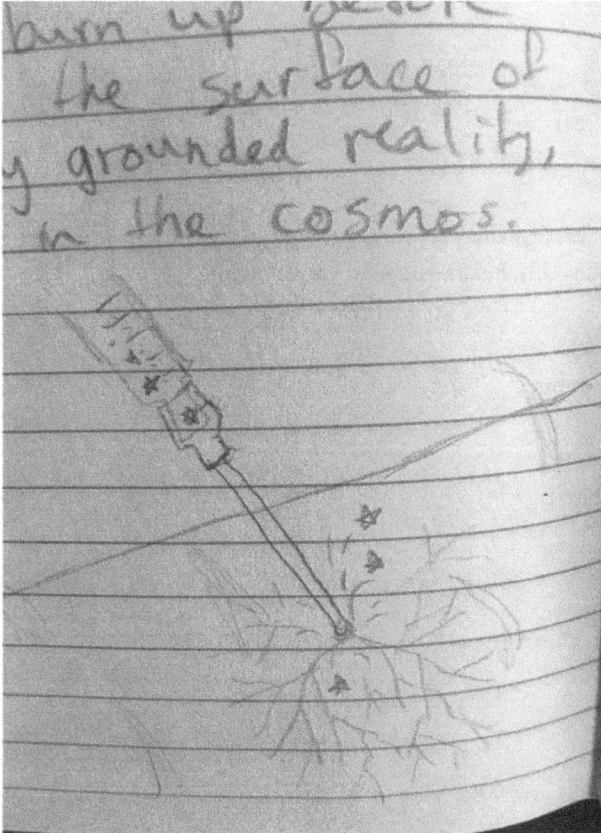

The constellations pricked into the surface of my upper thigh

Shoot stars deep inside my muscles
deliver crashing waves of hormones.
Hormones the societal atmosphere tries to burn up before reaching
the surface of my rocky ground,
floating in the cosmos

~~~

I'm going to live.

That feels selfish to think,
But people said it was selfish to leave them, too.

"Moderation in moderation."

I left, but I didn't leave.

I'm living.
~~

Be brave, you're real, and
Deserving of love, and celebration.

Be brave, you're worthy, and
Deserving of education, healthcare, and employment.

Be brave, still hurts, and
Support may seem far,

But really and truly,
We're here, my heart.

Poem for Your Troubles

By Maisie Bodrug, age 13

To all trans people, cold and alone,
I'm sorry your life has taken this tone.

But remember to love yourself, everyone else is taken.
Just remember these words, and your heart will awaken.

When you're feeling dark, just look for the sun,
And your happiness and joy will have begun.

Never turn to tobacco and drugs,
Turn to people who give you support and hugs.

The point of this poem is don't forget love,
Lest you forget, it will be gone like a dove.

Isolation

By Asa O'Connor-Jaeckel, age 13

Isolation is meant to represent shifting dynamics in social relationships during and after transition.

Resistance, Community Care, and Speaking Up: Thinking Through Trans and Non-Binary Youth Writings on Mental Health

By Astri Jack and J. Matsui De Roo

The collection of youth works in this chapter has offered us a glimpse into the tremendous acts of self-care and resistance of trans youth in the face of incredibly challenging circumstances. In this response, we will be engaging with the youths' works by discussing the history of trans healthcare, offering clinical reflections from practice experience, and exploring how trans youth doing whatever it takes to survive and reaching out to fellow youth is a form of radical resistance to transphobia.

A BRIEF HISTORY OF TRANS HEALTHCARE

The current standards of trans care are developed from the work of Harry Benjamin, a sexologist and endocrinologist who worked with hundreds of trans clients, helping them access hormones and surgery. He was renowned as a deeply compassionate man, beloved by many of his patients and keeping up correspondence with some of them his entire life. Benjamin's work helped established protocols of treatment, and in 1979 the Harry Benjamin Standards of Care were created. These standards are now on version 7 and are known as the World Professional Association of Transgender Health (WPATH) standards of care.

These standards of care were built on the best practices of a caring doctor living in an overtly transphobic and homophobic time. Benjamin was undoubtedly dedicated to ethical and accessible care, but the standards themselves were based on a paternalistic and gatekeeping medical model. Some of the restrictions of earlier standards of care included multiple assessments by psychiatrists or psychologists, and a real-life experience where the client was expected to live in their felt gender before they could access hormones or surgery—regardless of the fact that living this way before hormones and/or surgery may be actively dangerous. The earlier standards also reflected an understanding of gender that was entirely binary, assuming either male to female or female to male.

Standards were interpreted by clinicians who did not question the norms of their time. Matsui De Roo has heard stories from multiple clients and community members about how those restrictions affected the lives of trans people. Heterosexuality was assumed, so clients who were married were sometimes told they must dissolve their marriages to be allowed access to gender affirming care. Others were told that they must leave the place they lived and start anew to have any hope of succeeding, as a fresh start was seen as the only way of existing in a transphobic society. Frequently people were told they were not "true transsexuals" and assumed to be poor candidates for hormone therapy or surgery.

In the name of compassion, best practice, and "good outcomes," trans people were cut off, isolated, and denied care. People were harmed and even died due to this, and this harm continues to this day.

The current WPATH standards of care recognize more diverse expressions of gender, including non-binary identities, and no longer require a real-life experience to access hormones (WPATH, 2011). However, the quality of trans affirming care is still variable in Canada today. Many areas of the country lack trans-knowledgeable service providers, especially smaller or rural regions, and trans affirming mental health care may be limited or unavailable. As care providers, our job includes educating ourselves to develop trans affirming practices, unlearning harmful biases and outdated assumptions, and advocating for change.

THE DSM-5

A conversation about trans youth mental health cannot be had without discussing the Diagnostics and Statistical Manual of Mental Disorders (DSM), which is currently in its fifth edition (DSM-5). When Danny identifies himself as having anxiety and being driven into depression in his poem "Why?," and when Jaxon describes himself as "dysphoric as hell" in "Life Letter," they are both drawing on language that appears in the DSM-5. The DSM-5 has a litany of anxiety disorders and categories for depression (American Psychiatric Association, 2013), though we caution against diagnosing what may be a justified emotional response to challenging circumstances as a disorder. When Jaxon describes himself as dysphoric, he is gesturing toward the diagnosis of *gender dysphoria* in the DSM-5. Gender dysphoria is described as "a marked incongruence between one's experienced/expressed gender and assigned gender" (Gender Dysphoria section, p. 320) that causes "clinically significant distress" and must be accompanied by a minimum of six additional symptoms.

Because the DSM-5 holds tremendous clout in the medical community, we feel it is important to highlight the subjective and political nature of what appears in the DSM. As Stephen Madigan (2011) points out in his writing on the subjective nature of the DSM, the inclusion and exclusion of disorders in each edition does not bear the onus of scientific proof. Instead, what is included is decided by a majority vote. Consider this example that Madigan offers: when homosexuality as a mental illness was stricken from the DSM-III back in the 1970s, millions of people with same-sex attraction were transformed overnight from sick to healthy. This change did not happen because of the unearthing of new scientific data, but because of a cultural shift that led to the swaying of a vote on its inclusion.

It should be noted that there has been a meaningful shift in the wording of trans diagnoses. While the DSM-IV's diagnosis of *gender identity disorder* fully pathologized trans identities, its replacement with gender dysphoria in the DSM-5 has made a shift toward diagnosing the *distress* many trans people experience rather than diagnosing being trans as inherently disordered. The inclusion of gender dysphoria in the DSM-5 is in some ways useful to the trans community: it may help create medical legitimacy when seeking hormones and surgery and, as Nichols (2008) points out, "[p]sychiatric classification can initially increase public empathy for people who are seen as suffering from a 'disease' and can even enable oppressed groups to be treated more humanely" (p. 476). But, while these benefits may result in more humane treatment, they also risk positioning trans people as actually being less human, "reinforcing the belief that certain behaviors are deviant, sub-normal, or pathological, and therefore less deserving of genuinely equal rights" (Nichols, 2008, p. 476).

While the mental health struggles that trans youth are facing are real and urgent (the fact that Danny, Ask, Jaxon, and Riley all speak directly or allude to suicide makes this fact stingingly clear), we are critical of the inclusion of gender dysphoria in the DSM-5. One of the problems with having gender dysphoria listed as a diagnosable condition is that it positions trans people as sick, rather than viewing them as individuals on normal and legitimate gender journeys who often suffer because of the transphobic world we live in. What we are suggesting is that gender dysphoria is a symptom of oppression rather than a necessary part of being trans. Another way of articulating the relation-ship is the *minority stress model*. The minority stress model frames the health disparities (poorer health outcomes) faced by oppressed populations as the result of having to survive routine experiences of discrimination (Frost & Meyer, 2017). Experiences of oppression that contribute to minority stress for trans and gender nonconforming young people are well documented and are highlighted in the results of the Canadian Trans Youth Health Survey (Veale et al., 2015). The survey reveals that trans and gender nonconforming youth experience heightened levels of bullying, sexual harassment and assault, physical injury and threats of physical injury, homelessness, discrimination in healthcare settings, and violence in school and at home. As a result, it is unsurprising that many trans and gender nonconforming young people are at greater risk of substance use, suicidal ideation and attempts, feelings of hopelessness, and self-harm (Reisner et al., 2015; Veale et al., 2015).

Rather than positioning the experiences described by many of the youth in this chap-ter (such as depression, anxiety, suicidal ideation, substance use, sex work, or in some cases even gender dysphoria) as symptoms of being trans, or pathologizing the feelings of dis-tress regarding their gender expression through inclusion in the DSM, we encourage you to think of these experiences as being related to discrimination. What this tells us is that it is important not to think of trans and gender nonconforming youth as sick, but as a group of people who are doing their best to survive unfair and frequently cruel circumstances. In this way, we can also begin to think of some of the "symptoms" of minority stress as forms of self-care and resistance. These forms of resistance, such as the substance use that Riley speaks to, or the sex work Ask undertook to care for himself when he could no longer live at home, may not represent the type of youthhood many would describe as ideal, but they are ways of responding to and surviving tremendous challenges.

THE "WRONG BODY" NARRATIVE

As this book has shown us, not all young trans people have the same experience of their body. Tor and Ask, for example, provide strikingly different representations of their experiences relating to their bodies: while Tor describes the pain and jealousy that accompany being at the gym and seeing "cis guys all muscular and lucky" in his poem "I am Strong," Ask's poem "Starry Stabby + Live + Love" describes the marks left by hormone injections on his upper thigh as constellations, and the experience of taking hormones as a cosmic affront to societal norms. Despite the considerable diversity in how trans youth experience their bodies, there remains a heavy reliance on using the "wrong body" narrative (Long Chu, 2017) as the universal description of what it means to be trans.

Given the frequent assumption that gender is a biological fact, it is understandable that the "wrong body" narrative (Long Chu, 2017) as a way of understanding the trans experience has emerged. The wrong body narrative, which is the feeling that some trans people experience of being trapped in a body of the wrong sex, having their biological anatomy feel alien, or the gendered expectations of them not aligning with their felt self can often be incorrectly applied to all trans people (Long Chu, 2017). This understanding of transness also ties in neatly with the diagnostic criteria for gender dysphoria seen in the DSM-5, which could contribute to the prevalence of the wrong body narrative. To be clear, there is nothing inherently wrong with this narrative, and it describes a legitimate experience that many trans people have. It can also be one component of a complex and rich understanding of self and body that many trans people have, rather than a singular, defining feature of their transness. The danger comes in the way this narrative can get taken up by the medical community as a monolithic description of what it means to be trans or gender nonconforming. Furthermore, the idea that there is a wrong body experience can be wielded by healthcare providers to describe young trans people's bodies as sick by "efficiently construct[ing] a model of 'right body' experience" (Halberstam, 1998, p. 162).

Relying on the wrong body narrative as the only description of trans people's experiences allows healthcare professionals to incorrectly imagine they understand how trans people relate to their bodies without having to actually talk to individual patients. What Ask and Tor demonstrate in this chapter is that relying on the wrong body narrative to the exclusion of other stories is inadequate and that each trans youth's relationship with their body is unique and deserving of attention. Even more importantly, Ask and Tor show us that to be trans is not simply to hate one's body but something entirely more nuanced, complex, challenging, and beautiful.

CARING FOR YOUTH OR CARING FOR HEALTHCARE PROVIDERS?

Astri Jack has consistently seen trans and non-binary youth express fear of working with healthcare providers. One of the primary fears that she has heard from trans youth, and even more so from youth who identify as non-binary and Two-Spirit, is that they will not be considered "trans enough" to be provided with medical care. This is deeply troubling, especially given the close and complex relationships many young trans people have with the healthcare system both for reasons directly related to being trans for many youth (e.g., hormone blockers and hormone therapy), and for medical concerns that disproportionately impact trans youth (e.g., depression, anxiety, substance use, and suicidal ideation). In this section, Tor, Ask, Alexander, and Riley speak to their relationships with medications, healthcare providers, and medical institutions. This points to just how important it is for us to examine the ways the medical community both harms and supports trans youth.

In "A Perspective on Growth," Alexander documents multiple encounters with medical providers, including "sitting in a room with a doctor who knew nothing about the transgender community." Despite this experience, Alexander tells us that he still presented at the hospital when his mental health deteriorated and had the unsettling discovery that, even though the last medical provider had failed to provide him with adequate care, the hospital still smelled "almost more comforting than the smell of [his] own house." Further demonstrating the ambivalent relationship many trans youth have with the medical system, Tor reveals that when he was getting the hormone blocker injection that he and his family had tirelessly fought for, he had to muster strength to push through "the tears [that] stream[ed] down into a waterfall of hopelessness" as he worried that "the shots [weren't] worth it." While we are not explicitly told what all the factors were that made Tor wonder if the shots were "worth it," we suggest that the obstacles faced by trans youth, and especially younger trans youth, are such that what should have been an affirming and happy moment was tainted by hopelessness. Both Alexander and Tor demonstrate the complex relationship trans youth have with the medical system, and they highlight the ways young people are often both helped and harmed within it. With this in mind, it is important to provocatively consider who is really being offered care in this system: trans youth or healthcare providers?

In the face of a rapidly changing landscape of healthcare for young trans people, care providers are being asked to provide care in new ways. As we have made clear, there is a long history of medical providers telling trans youth they are sick. Even affirming providers may conceptualize working with trans youth as *treating* gender dysphoria rather than *supporting* trans youth along their journeys. We suggest that there is an important difference between treating a trans youth and supporting a trans youth to achieve a future that feels affirming for them and that practising the latter would be a meaningful shift in the way medical care is offered. However, there is good reason for why this shift is a challenging one to make for the medical community as a whole. Castañeda (2015) argues that one of the reasons medical providers position trans youth to be sick is because the medical model requires a patient that is sick in order for a healthcare provider to offer them treatment. Because of this, many trans youth are forced to be "diagnosed" as trans (specifically receiving a gender dysphoria diagnosis) in order to prevent the greater evil of going without medical care. This often unspoken requirement is made manifest in the WPATH (2011) Standards of Care, volume 7, which requires that trans and non-binary people exhibit "persistent, well-documented gender dysphoria" (p. 34) in order to access hormone therapy. As we have established, WPATH's work has been instrumental in the establishment of trans affirming healthcare in Canada and throughout the world. However, the Standards of Care are not without fault, and the recommendation that gender dysphoria be a prerequisite for the provision of medical care comes at the cost of relinquishing a young trans person's right to see their experience of gender as healthy and normal.

If we are to move away from the existing model wherein providing hormone therapy to trans youth is deemed a risk management strategy to treat (potentially lethal) psychiatric distress, and toward a demedicalized model, we may be faced with the task of combatting anxieties about liability and medical ethics among healthcare providers. If the healthcare provider can imagine that the trans child's mind or body is a risk to itself, the healthcare provider can legitimize their medical interventions as lifesaving care. If we argue that trans youth are not sick *and that they are still deserving of desired medical care* within our current model, which requires sickness before it offers care, the risk then shifts from the trans youths' bodies onto the healthcare provider. As White (2015) notes, we are "living in a time when the identification and management of risk has become a central preoccupation" (p. 504), and goes on to quote Mary Douglas's (1992) observation that "we are ready to treat every death as chargeable to someone's account, every accident as caused by someone's criminal negligence, [and] every sickness as a threatened prosecution" (p. 16). What are we telling trans youth when we uphold a system that is more interested in avoiding perceived risk for medical care providers than in affirming trans youths' selves and bodies as good and worthy of care?

CLINICAL REFLECTIONS

Whatever model of care we use, a holistic and contextual understanding of trans mental health is necessary. Gender affirming mental health care is so much more than access to hormones and surgery—although these are important! It includes having any aspect of lived experience and mental health addressed with respect by care providers. Many trans and non-binary youth find themselves silenced in health services, in family, in community, and in society. Whether we are mental health practitioners or lay people, we need to step away from diagnostic conceptualizations and move into the realm of lived experience. This is where truth lives, and from truth comes our healing. The stories in this book invite us to do that.

WITNESSING TRUTH

Telling our own stories is a fundamental human need. Sometimes, there may be no one there to listen. Other times, the uncomfortable truth in stories means they get denied, refuted, even overwritten with someone else's version of events. In Canada, we have seen the harm caused when settlers denied Indigenous knowledge, history, and experience, leaving the painful truths of cultural genocide and colonization out of the dominant narrative. The Truth and Reconciliation Commission of Canada created more space for Indigenous voices to be heard, but we need to commit to ongoing work for deeper healing to continue.

Speaking one's truth, and having it witnessed, is necessary for healing and health. Danny shares an uncomfortable truth but a powerful one: "When someone kills themselves their suicide note was/is a story that needs to be heard." Can we make space to hear the stories of the living as well as the dead? Danny writes eloquently about being alive but silent: "I can't talk, speak, make a sound." Paradoxically, he uses his writing to voice his own silencing, and in doing so, is heard. He allows us to witness his pain and his healing. Simply witnessing is one of the most powerful therapeutic tools we have. There is a reason that one of the core skills that therapists are taught is simply active listening.

As therapists, families, friends, allies, and peers of trans people, we can listen. You don't need to be a therapist to hold space for someone else's story. Being present, making space, and witnessing the stories that are entrusted to you can make a difference for trans youth.

SUPPORTING SELF-CARE

The next theme that emerges from these stories is self-care. Self-care is anything we do to keep ourselves alive and that helps us feel good in a world where oppression and harm are real. Ideally, self-care looks nurturing and affirming, but sometimes it involves behaviours or actions that are less ideal, but more accessible. Drugs, self-hurting, or other potentially harmful behaviours may seem maladaptive but may sometimes be necessary to tolerate the intolerable when no other resources are available.

A.J. shows us how self-care can involve changing thoughts, beliefs, and internalized stories from despair to hope and positivity, without denying the reality of systemic transphobia: "We are here for some weird, inexplicable reason, and sometimes it feels like we don't deserve to be here, don't deserve to take up the precious oxygen that we consume, or don't deserve to take up a place in society—especially if society has tried to outcast us for years." Self-worth comes out of self-care: "You, just as you are, are so important." Maisie echoes this belief, encouraging fellow trans people, even if they may be "cold and alone," to practise self-care through self-love. "Remember to love yourself, everyone else is taken."

Riley shows us another side to self-care: "Strength is not ignoring the hurt, it's softening into it and living through it." Riley witnesses and describes their brother's drinking as one option to survive in the world; when life is overwhelming, Riley feels that "we could be swallowed by grief." Despite this, they instead "choose the boring work of recovery."

Sometimes self-care also includes what looks like harmful behaviour. When we equate substance use with harm, we risk erasing someone else's narrative. Ask describes how substance use can lead to survival: "Fairy dust settling into my nervous system for a high to last another night." This is not necessarily self-harm; sometimes drugs are the only accessible form of self-care. This lack of access is a product of systemic inequalities that economically and socially disadvantage trans people (e.g., higher rates of unemployment and discrimination by healthcare and social service providers). These inequalities can prevent them from affording or accessing counselling, medications, and health and social supports that could support them in finding alternatives to substance use. Trans people are more likely to use drugs that cis people, and higher rates of drug use in trans people are associated with other risk factors for trauma, including history of transphobic assault, homelessness or underhousing, and sex work (Scheim, Bauer, & Shokooki, 2017). In clinical practice, it is important not to take away less helpful behaviours such as substance use without first introducing more helpful self-care measures to counter the effects of trauma.

RESILIENCE AND THE IMPORTANCE OF FAMILY SUPPORT

Youth are naturally resilient, but transphobia, lack of acceptance, bullying, and barriers to accessing needed services take their toll. We know that trans youth are at higher risk for depression, homelessness, and suicide (Trans PULSE Project, 2013). Alexander describes the challenge of coming out to family, asking for support and getting abuse instead. "I wish I had had someone to tell me that it isn't your fault if your parents or family members aren't accepting." They self-advocated for themselves to parents and to medical professionals who did not listen. Alexander's survival is a testament to their resilience.

Asa's painting, titled *Isolation*, shows a vast distance from where they came from, and where they have arrived on their journey to their affirmed gender. While the figure in Asa's picture seems peaceful and contemplative, they are also literally a world away from where they started. Distance and disconnect with family of origin is all too common in the narratives of trans youth, and can lead to reduced support and greater vulnerability.

It does not need to be this way: we know that the single greatest protective factor for trans youth against depression, suicidality, and other negative outcomes is parental support of their gender (Trans PULSE Project, 2012). Some parents fear that encouraging their children to explore gender diversity may cause harm. After all, we live in a transphobic world, and there is always the fear that the child may change their mind. In reality, it is fine to support children and youth in expressing their gender. Some children may play with gender expression and put that play aside as they get older, but others do not. Regardless, allowing a child free range to dress and act the way they want is healthy and affirming. This may come with teaching them in age-appropriate ways about gender roles, social behaviour, and transphobia. Trans children who are able to successfully live as their affirmed gender show better mental health outcomes than trans children who have not transitioned (Olson et al., 2016). Affirming a child's chosen name is an important part of this process: research shows that youth who are called by their chosen name in different contexts are at a significantly lower risk for depression, suicidal ideation, and suicidal behaviour (Russell et al., 2018). It is far less harmful to trust youth when they tell us who they are, rather than trying to talk them out of their ideas about gender identity.

Many families' stances on trans youth have moral and religious origins. These beliefs are often bolstered by other social forces, including social values rooted in colonialism (Driskill, 2010), and dated and/or faulty scientific literature (Erlick, 2016). In either case, there is a key issue: the voices of adult authorities are the ones being listened to and centred rather than the voices and stories of trans youth. Both Ask and Tor speak to the hurtful ways that religion has been wielded by family members. In "Whose Whore," Ask recalls his parents' stinging response to him asserting his trans identity: "Do you want to go to hell? Stop this! This is sinning! Sinners go to hell!" Tor recounts a letter his grandparents wrote to him, writing that they "tell me where I'm headed in the afterlife / *Hell*."

There are an increasing number of faiths that are openly welcoming and affirming of trans people, which is a deeply meaningful cultural shift that will surely improve the lives of trans people of all ages. The near future, however, is not guaranteed to be a universally welcoming place for trans youth in either medicine, faith communities, or other important social spheres. What we are encouraging is that caregivers decentre the voices of the adults in these spaces and, instead, focus on the needs and voices of the trans youth in their lives.

FROM SELF TO COMMUNITY CARE

While the word "resistance" may conjure images of protesters with signs—and this is certainly one form of resistance—in this chapter we saw youth discuss and demonstrate many subtler forms of resistance. If we think of the essence of resistance as a way of pushing back against something that is trying to hold us down, then we can see how A.J.'s suggestion in "Words and Lists" of saying a few favourite words to help one feel "like less of a dumpster fire" is a kind of resistance. Earlier, we talked about self-care and, while the act of caring for yourself is a kind of resistance, the way we are thinking about resistance here goes beyond acts of self-care and extends into *community* care.

In a world where 22 to 43 per cent of trans people have made a suicide attempt (Bauer et al., 2015), simply remaining alive is a radical act. The youth in this section have shown us how their acts of self-care are transformed into acts of resistance when they shine their labours of survival outwards by helping other trans youth through familiar challenges and by changing the hearts and minds of the people in their communities. In "Whose Whore," Ask poignantly chronicles how he has used substances and sex work to stay alive when he could no longer live with his family. Jaxon describes fighting through the darkness of panic attacks and depression, sparring with dysphoria, and still being afraid. Alexander tells us about their trial-filled journey of seeking family acceptance and medical care. All of these stories are stories of survival, and in each one the author goes on to reach out to other trans youth, alchemizing their survival into an act of resistance and community care. Ask puts forward that he is fighting for a world that "celebrates all people for the good that we do and are." Jaxon writes: "Maybe my purpose is to help others realize that suicide is not an option. / Maybe I'm here to tell them to write a life letter instead," and Alexander offers the reader a promise that if they are sharing these struggles, that they too will be able to make it through.

Other writers in this chapter provided words of guidance as well. Maisie's piece, "Poem for Your Troubles," reminds us of the power of loving yourself and of reaching out to caring people for support. In "Self-Care," A.J. shares what they learned while at their lowest point and offers a message of hopefulness to others, including a reminder that "[j]ust because today sucked, doesn't mean tomorrow is gonna be just as awful." Those youth who did not speak explicitly to other trans youth are still engaging in acts of resistance because the act of labouring over these works so that they can be read and held by families, doctors, teachers, counsellors, other youth, and other young trans people is a brave and radical act of community care.

CLOSING CONSIDERATIONS FOR BETTER SUPPORTING TRANS YOUTH MENTAL HEALTH

✓ **Ask questions and *listen*.** Be cautious with "diagnosing" trans, non-binary, and Two-Spirit youths' experiences. While gender dysphoria and feelings of being in the "wrong body" are very real experiences for many trans youth, they are not the only ways trans people do or can experience their bodies. Rather than relying on medical diagnoses or popularized narratives to explain trans youths' experiences, talk to trans youth, *ask questions*, and most importantly, *listen* to what they have to say.

✓ **Remember the big, intersectional picture.** Rather than assuming a causal link between being trans and having poor health outcomes, consider the minority stress model as a way of making sense of the disproportionate challenges faced by young trans, non-binary, and Two-Spirit people. The minority stress model asks us to think about how systemic and interpersonal transphobia create the conditions under which poor mental health, self-harm, suicide, substance use, and underage sex work are more likely to occur.

✓ **Rethink language around "healthy" and "sick."** The current healthcare system is organized in ways that may privilege healthcare providers' desires to avoid liability rather than providing optimal care for trans, non-binary, and Two Spirit youth. We need to consider how we can uphold the dignity and right of trans youth to see themselves as whole and healthy (rather than positioning them as sick) while still ensuring they receive prompt, quality healthcare to support their gender identities. Offering trans youth the ability to speak their truth in their families and in healthcare settings is necessary for healing and health.

✓ **Have a contextual understanding of self-care.** Trans youth are offering themselves self-care in the best ways they know how and/or are available to them. It is important for clinicians not to take away higher-risk self-care behaviours (such as substance use) without first introducing more helpful self-care measures that are viable within an individual youth's circumstances. The greatest protective factor for trans youth against depression, suicidality, and other negative health outcomes is parental support of their gender. Actions like making space for gender diverse play and using a youth's chosen name and self-identified pronouns are simple and profoundly meaningful ways of improving trans, non-binary, and Two Spirit youths' mental health.

✓ **Encourage community.** Trans, non-binary, and Two-Spirit youth demonstrate a remarkable capacity not only to care for themselves, but also to care for others. Offering them opportunities to meet one another, elevating their voices, and centering their stories are powerful ways of creating networks of care among young trans, non-binary, and Two-Spirit people.

REFERENCES

American Psychiatric Association. (2013). *Diagnostic and Statistical Manual of Mental Disorders: DSM-5* (5th ed.). Washington: American Psychiatric Association.

Bauer, G. R., Scheim, A. I., Pyne, J., Travers, R., & Hammond, R. (2015). Intervenable factors associated with suicide risk in transgender persons: A respondent driven sampling study in Ontario, Canada. *BMC Public Health, 15*, 525.

Castañeda, C. (2015). Developing gender: The medical treatment of transgender young people. *Social Science & Medicine, 143*, 262–270.

Driskill, Q. (2010). Doubleweaving Two-Spirit critiques: Building alliances between Native and queer studies. *GLQ, 16*(1–2), 69–92.

Douglas, M. (1992). *Risk and blame: Essays in cultural theory.* London: Routledge.

Erlick, E. (2016). Depathologizing trans. In Z. Sharman (Ed.), *The remedy: Queer and trans voices on health and heathcare* (pp. 217–227). Vancouver: Aresenal Pulp Press.

Frost, D. M., & Meyer, I. H. (2017). Minority stress. In K. L. Nadal (Ed.), *The SAGE encyclopedia of psychology and gender* (pp. 1196–1198). Thousand Oakes, CA: SAGE Publications.

Halberstam, J. (1998). *Female masculinity.* Durham, NC: Duke University Press.

Long Chu, A. (2017). The wrong wrong body: Notes on trans phenomenology. *Trans Studies Quarterly, 4*(1), 141–152.

Madigan, S. (2011). *Narrative therapy.* Washington: American Psychological Association.

Nichols, M. (2008). Dreger on the Bailey controversy: Lost in the drama, missing the big picture. *Archives of Sexual Behaviour, 37*, 476–480.

Olson, K., Durwood, L., DeMeules, M., & McLaughlin, K. (2016). Mental health of transgender children who are supported in their identities. *Pediatrics, 137*(3), 1–10.

Reisner, S. L., Greytal, E. A., Parsons, J. T., & Ybarra, M. L. (2015). Minority social stress in adolescence: Disparities in adolescent bullying and substance use by gender identity. *Journal of Sex Research, 52*(3), 243–256.

Russell, S., Politt, A., Li, G., & Grossman, A. (2018). Chosen name use is linked to reduced depressive symptoms, suicidal ideation, and suicidal behavior among transgender youth. *Journal of Adolescent Health, 63*(4), 503–505.

Scheim, A. I., Bauer, G. R., & Shokoohi, M. (2017). Drug use among transgender people in Ontario, Canada: Disparities and associations with social exclusion. *Addictive Behaviors, 72*, 151–158.

Trans PULSE Project. (2012). *Impacts of strong parental support for trans youth.* Retrieved from http://transpulseproject.ca/wp-content/uploads/2012/10/Impacts-of-Strong-Parental-Support-for-Trans-Youth-vFINAL.pdf.

Trans PULSE Project. (2013). *Suicidality among trans people in Ontario.* Retrieved from http://transpulseproject.ca/research/suicidality-among-trans-people-in-ontario-la-suicidabilite-parmi-les-personnes-trans-en-ontario/.

Veale, J., Frohard-Dourlent, H., Dobson, S., Clark, B., & Canadian Trans Youth Health Survey Research Group. (2015). *Being safe, being me: Results of the Canadian trans youth health survey.* Vancouver: Stigma and Resilience Among Vulnerable Youth Centre, School of Nursing, University of British Columbia. Retrieved from https://saravyc.sites.olt.ubc.ca/files/2015/05/SARAVYC_Trans-Youth-Health-Report_EN_Final_Web2.pdf.

White, J. (2015). An ethos for the times: Difference, imagination, and the unknown future in child and youth care. *International Journal of Child, Youth and Family Studies, 6*(4), 498–515.

World Professional Association for Transgender Health (WPATH). (2011). *Standards of care for the health of transsexual, transgender, and gender nonconforming people* (7th ed.). Retrieved from https://s3.amazonaws.com/amo_hub_content/Association140/files/Standards%20of%20 Care%20V7%20-%202011%20WPATH%20(2)(1).pdf.

CHAPTER SEVEN

Acceptance

KEY THEMES

- Internal and external acceptance
- Gender transition as personal growth
- Language as affirmation

CRITICAL QUESTIONS

- Many of the youth in this chapter chose to write letters to or about themselves before they knew they were trans. If you could speak with your own younger self, what would you say? How might you be different from the person your younger self expected you to be?
- The chapter title, "Acceptance," brings to mind acceptance from parents and peers. However, most of the youth in this chapter chose to respond to the idea of self-acceptance. Why do you think that may be?
- How does tolerance differ from acceptance?

BOOKS WE LOVE

Picture Books

Genhart, M., & Passchier, A. (2019). *Rainbow: A first book of pride.* Washington: Magination Press.

Hall, M. (2015). *Red: A crayon's story.* New York: Greenwillow Books. *Also available in French*

Hirst, J., & Bardoff, N. (2018). *A house for everyone: A story to help children learn about gender identity and gender expression.* London: Jessica Kingsley Publishers.

Jackson, A. (2017). *It's okay to sparkle!* Kansas City, MO: Debi Jackson.

Lukoff, K. (2019). *Call me Max.* New York: Reycraft Books.

YA and Graphic Novels

Boteju, T. (2019). *Kings, queens, and in-betweens.* New York: Simon Pulse.

Garvin, J. (2016). *Symptoms of being human.* New York: Balzer & Bray.

Rose, S. (2020). *Our work is everywhere: An illustrated oral history of queer and trans resistance*. Vancouver: Arsenal Pulp Press.

Stevenson, R. (2019). *Pride: The celebration and the struggle*. Victoria: Orca Books.

Testa, R. J., Coolhart, D., & Peta, J. (2016). *The gender quest workbook: A guide for teens and young adults exploring gender identity*. Oakland, CA: Instant Help Books.

General Audience

Gonzàles, K., & Rayne, K. (2020). *Trans+: Love, sex, romance, and being you*. Washington: Magination Press.

Jenkins, A. (2015). *The T is not silent: New and selected poems*. Minneapolis: Trio Bookworks.

Kuklin, S. (2015). *Beyond magenta: Transgender teens speak out*. Somerville, MA: Candlewick Press.

Stryker, S. (2017). *Transgender history: The roots of today's revolution* (2nd ed.). Boulder, CO: Seal Press.

Thom, K. C. (2019). *I hope we choose love: A trans girl's notes from the end of the world*. Vancouver: Arsenal Pulp Press.

Memoirs/First Person Narratives

Coyote, I. (2019). *Rebent sinner*. Vancouver: Arsenal Pulp Press.

Dugan, J. T. (2018). *To survive on this shore: Photographs and interviews with transgender and gender nonconforming older adults*. Heidelberg: Kehrer.

Schwenke, C. (2018). *SELF-ish: A transgender awakening*. Pasadena, CA: Ren Hen Press.

Spoon, R. (2012). *First spring grass fire*. Vancouver: Arsenal Pulp Press.

Tobia, J. (2020). *Sissy: A coming-of-gender story*. New York: G. P. Putnam's Sons.

Self-portrait

By Ajam, age 14

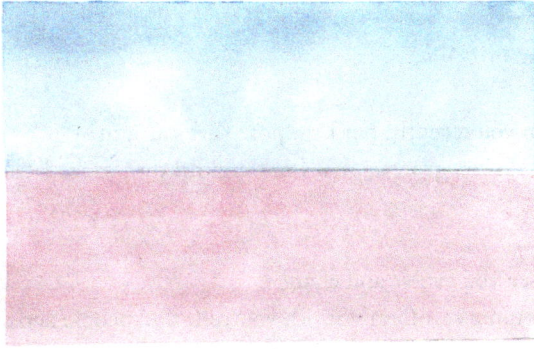

Dear Grace

By David Llewelyn, age 14

Dear Grace,

How have you been?

I haven't heard from you recently, but I suppose that's alright.
I'm glad I got to watch you grow up, but I'm thankful that you're letting me stand in the spotlight now.

It was inspiring to see you evolve and change.
I watched you grow more comfortable with yourself, find people and activities that made you happy.
You discovered things about yourself that you'd never dreamed of, and in doing that, you found me.
So thanks for doing that and bringing me to the light.

People miss you.
They miss seeing you in class or around town.
Sometimes people ask me what happened.
I simply tell them that your time was up.

I don't miss you at all.
Every time I hear your name, it hurts me.
But not a sad kind of hurt.
Not an "I miss you, please come back" kind of hurt.
It's a "Don't remind me of that person" kind of hurt.

Thank you for leaving so I could stay.
It really means a lot to me.

Sincerely,
David

PS: Even though it might have seemed like I did at times, I never hated you.

The Personal Dictionary of a Trans Semanticist

By Christopher, age 17

The word is *activist*. It's clunky, foreign; too big for my mouth to say, yet it follows me like a heavy debt. You won't see me with the picketers, but still they tell me every breath I take is something radical; every heartbeat, inexorably political. And so I, the activist, go to class in the mornings, take a seat in the back, and keep my head down until I get home.

The word is *boy*. I get addicted to it the summer I cut my hair short. I say it to myself in the mirror a thousand times. I say it to my friends as a joke that never lands. Again and again, I say it. In the sun, it seems like the perfect word, lit beautifully in the golden hues of killing time. But when the fall comes, I wonder if I dreamt it.

The word is *cowboy*. I remember it now: something I abandoned in the playground with the rest of my childhood wonders, laid to rest in a sandbox or a castle made of plastic. Dusting off old picture frames, I find it as it was—a declaration of make-believe identity that was endearingly misinformed then, questionably prophetic now. I shake it like an eight ball and beg it all my questions. No reply.

The word is *40 per cent*. It is our infamous number, our dancing death toll, ever-changing but never resolved. It is 40 per cent of us who nearly lose ourselves to the fray we've gotten caught in. It is 40 per cent of us who stop to wonder if this planet would be better off without us. And even that number, hanging overhead like the world's most precarious chandelier, can't stop me from putting the pieces together.

The word is *hormone replacement therapy*, written in the neon letters of a new headliner on Broadway. It is bright, electric, fantastic, and it arrives like an armistice amid chaos. It cures me of nothing, but teaches me, slowly, to do all the things I thought I couldn't: I speak to crowds, I shake strangers' hands, I look myself in the eyes. I breathe.

The word is *man*. For the longest time I don't know what it means. It is something made of stone when I am made of sand; it is something that burrows underground when I finally reach the mountaintop. They can call me a fool for trying, but I'll chase it all my life if it means catching up to it, just once.

The word is *strange*. I get used to it like I get used to shots in the leg and those real or imagined double-takes in the bathroom. At first, it stings like all words of its kind, all shots, all glances, but time erodes it into something oddly comforting. It is only a side effect of my freedom, and it won't be the last word I learn to stop hiding from.

The word is *trans*. For fourteen years I don't understand it. For two years I flinch when I hear it. For one year I scream it like I'm running out of breath. Now it sits easy in the concavity of a smile, comfortable on my tongue. I realize it is not a loaded weapon but an answer, finally, to a question that is not impossible anymore.

I AM ART

By Alexander McIntyre, age 16

After New Year 2018, I tattooed the words "I AM ART" on my right ankle. The words are for me. They are not for attention or recognition, they are a reminder.

Through the period of coming out and living as transgender, I have had to relearn who I am as a person. Not that being trans meant I lost who I was before coming out, but I came out during a period of growth that I would have gone through regardless. I had to have a clear understanding of my morals, beliefs, and identity to a point where I could defend them. Because in being trans, it's almost guaranteed that you will have to. I did, and still continue to.

With this being said, the words "I AM ART" are a reminder of validation. Validation of my gender, sexuality, and identity. A reminder that I am worthy of love, help, and self-care. A reminder that I, as a trans youth and valuable member of society, deserve to be listened to.

Although I still go through points of self-loathing, I am a work of art and I am allowed to love myself.

Victoria

By Tor Broughton, age 12

She wanted me dead
She was my lethal poison
She didn't want me looking ahead
She tried to keep my noise in
But Tor fought back
Showed her what was right
Now bravery he does not lack
He's fought the biggest fight
And now he leads the pack
I have such good friends and family
They help me carry all this weight
My best friend C is a real big ally
He helps me fight the hate
He always shows up at trans pride
Yet somehow he's still straight
Through all the needles and doctors
The poking and the pain
I still keep getting my hormone blockers
And I'd do it all again
I can see my future shining bright
Though sometimes it seems so far away
I can feel the sunshine; see the light
I'm so happy to live in today

A Letter to the Girl I Was Supposed to Be

By Jaxon Steele, age 16

I'm sorry.

I'm sorry that I used you as a mask for so long that you came to believe that you were a real person. I'm sorry that you will never get to be a mother. I'm sorry that you will never get to live a full life.

I'm sorry, but I couldn't hide behind you anymore. The life that you had set out for me wasn't a life that was worth living. I couldn't keep pretending to be someone that I was not.

You were a facade so broken in that it fit like a second skin, slipped tightly over my own. I wore this skin for so long that I didn't notice my already aching lungs were gasping for air. I didn't realize that you were constricting like a snake around my fragile glass heart, creating a constellation of cracks like the web of lies I had spun.

For a long time, I seriously considered succumbing to the encroaching tendrils of darkness. I couldn't tell why my skin didn't fit quite right, so I thought that I was a monster. I thought that my body would always look like broken clockwork; useless, never fulfilling its purpose.

I thought that I didn't deserve to live.

I didn't want to live.

Neither of us were happy.

It wasn't until I really looked in the mirror that I saw the pink paint of you chipping away—that I finally saw myself. Underneath all that pink, I saw blue. And I knew I had a fighting chance that you did not.

So I scrubbed and scrubbed until you finally peeled away from me and I saw myself for the first time, blue all over. I cut your hair. I erased your name and found a new one for myself.

And when I looked in the mirror, I finally saw me.

Flawed and warped and nowhere near perfect, but me.

I still can't breathe, but this time, it's by choice. Yes, my lungs ache, but it's worth it. Because imprisoning my ribs within a rigid binder means that my mind can finally be free.

Sarah: A Trans Girl's Story

By Alexander M-G, age 13

Author's note: This story is one I made up—it's not REAL.

Sarah walked down the street like always; scared and depressed.

"Hey loser," a guy walking down the street said to her. She ignored him. Sarah was trans and gay. She hated people bullying her. Her parents didn't support LGBTQ+ people. They still don't.

Her name is Sarah. It used to be Samuel, Sam for short. She was born a boy, but she goes by Sarah at school. Her parents don't know. Ever since she was four, she thought she was a girl. "Mama," she would say, "I'm a girl."

"No," her mum would say. "You're a little boy."

"That's right," her dad would say.

Ugh, she thought, thinking about that moment. She was running away from home because her parents didn't care about her. Ever since the day before when she told them she was trans and gay.

Sarah is only fourteen. She's in grade eight, in middle school. Her parents only cared about her older sister, Chloe, after she told them. Chloe is nineteen. She does not support Sarah either.

An old woman grabbed Sarah's arm. "Where are you running off to?"

"Why do you want to know?" said Sarah, trying to yank her arm back.

The woman wouldn't let go. "Answer me," she said.

"I'm running away from home," Sarah blurted out.

"Why?" said the woman.

"Because my family doesn't care about me anymore," Sarah said.

"Oh, why?" the woman said.

"Because I'm trans." It was hard for Sarah to tell that to a complete stranger.

"Oh," the woman said, and she loosened her grip while she thought about what Sarah said.

Sarah ran far away. She ran to a hotel close to her friend's house. Her friend Zoey and her family supports Sarah and the LGBTQ+ community. Sarah brought money, so she checked in and lay on her hotel bed. She fell asleep and dreamt of her own little world where everyone was supportive of the LGBTQ+ community. She would live in the perfect world for her. She woke up and realized it was morning. She went to her friend Zoey's house and asked if she could live there forever. They understood her story and let her stay.

Genderfluid

By Hope, age 15

How I saw myself
I hated how my hair
Was down and long
I thought it would be better
Short and up

Ponytail, bun, beanie
My hair tucked away
It looked better
I looked better

I felt more masculine
Not so feminine
I began to love it
More and more

Though questions had to be asked
"Why do you keep your hair up so much?"
"Why do you wear that beanie so much?"
"It looks nice down."

For years I wore that beanie
My hair hidden away
It was two years later
Someone told me what
I had been feeling
An actual term, definition
For what I had
Been feeling

In my own body
What it meant to me
In my heart

I knew the feeling was true
I am genderfluid
I feel masculine at times
Then feminine too

I get good days
I get bad days
And days I don't know
How I feel

But I make it through
In my hard times

She. Her
They. Them.
He. Him.

I find it hard at times
What can feel right with
My gender

What makes me happy
Is how I feel at the end of the day

Knowing I went out
Out in the world
As myself and not someone else

I am genderfluid
And that is a wonderful
Thing.

Embroidery

By Tor Broughton, age 12

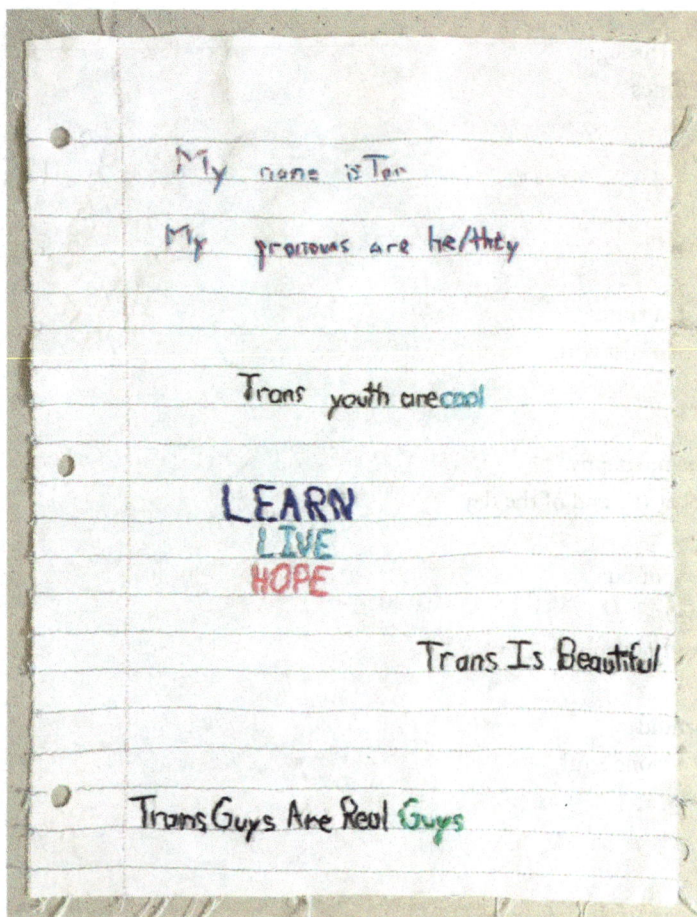

My name is Tor

My pronouns are he/they

Trans youth are cool

LEARN
LIVE
HOPE

Trans Is Beautiful

Trans Guys Are Real Guys

Enough. Acceptance

By Alyx MacAdams

"I am no longer accepting the things I cannot change. I am changing the things I cannot accept."
   – Angela Y. Davis

I have a confession: as a trans person, I find acceptance difficult to accept.

I know that when someone tells me "I accept you" they mean well, but the need for this statement is a painful reminder that trans acceptance, and the hopes for safety and belonging that accompany acceptance, is not automatic. Acceptance is like being handed an invitation to a future that promises rights, safety, love, and possibility, but having a gut feeling that lurking in the shadows of these promises is violence and harm. All the same, this invitation is alluring, and there is pressure to graciously accept it because, well, what if this *is* as good as it gets? The problem is that only the most privileged, those of us with the most potential to pass as "normal," will benefit from the invitation to acceptance. This is because when acceptance is tied to a settler-colonial nation it is complicit with racism, classism, ableism, ageism, heteronormativity, trans-misogyny, and cisnormativity, all of which fuels the belief that some trans people are too much, too difficult, too outsider (and I would argue too fabulous) to ever be acceptable. So I ask, what would happen if, individually and collectively, we refused acceptance; if we said, "Enough"?

The authors in this chapter, however, are clear: acceptance, both of oneself and from others, is life-giving for trans youth. Through Ajam, David, Christopher, Alexander M., Tor, Jaxon, Alexander M-G, and Hope's generous and thoughtful contributions, we witness acceptance as multi-dimensional, personal, and strong in its vulnerability. According to Jaxon, acceptance means standing in the mirror and seeing—really, truly *seeing, feeling,* and *believing in* oneself—for the first time. Acceptance is, as Alexander M. puts it, a bold statement: "I am a work of art and I am allowed to love myself." As David, Tor, Jaxon, and Hope all show in pieces about the "themselves of before" that lived in genders and bodies imposed on them, acceptance lives in the now but is grown from the soil of past strength, resilience, and survival. Knitting together the pieces in this section, a holistic understanding of acceptance emerges: acceptance as an affirmation and a validation that trans youth are deserving and worthy of love, safety, dignity, and joy. This is the acceptance that trans youth desire and are legitimately demanding from the adults and peers who surround them. When embodied, acceptance in this form is all at once an affirmation that trans people are worthy of love, a resistance to cis-as-better and cis-as-default, and an acknowledgement of the contributions that trans people and expansive gender embodiments offer to our families, communities, and society.

This book is about listening to trans youth, honouring their experiences, and uplifting their knowledge. Engaging with the pieces in this chapter has therefore been, for me, an experience of revisiting, reimagining, and reacquainting myself with acceptance. This is not to say that I am abandoning my critiques of acceptance, but rather that I am renewing my relationship to these critiques. Therefore, rather than shaping this response around the more commonly asked question, "How can acceptance of trans youth be increased?"—because this assumes acceptance is inherently good or beneficial to trans youth—I invite you along in my journey of considering what a politics of "abundant acceptance" could look like. I argue that abundant acceptance centres trans youth and their gender self-determination, while at the same time actively resists *unacceptable* forms of violence and exclusion that, masked as neutrality, are currently accepted. Unmasking neutrality extends far beyond addressing the pervasiveness of cisnormativity or binary ideas of gender. It requires an expansive approach, one that includes refusing to rest until the trans imaginary is decolonized (Aizura et al., 2014), disability politics is embraced by trans movements (Clare, 2013), and adults are displaced as the gatekeepers who determine what is "best" for young people (Lister, 2007).

I've structured this response around the question: What does a re-knowing of acceptance that comes from and is responsive to trans youth needs and desires look like? To answer this question, I lean into what the youth authors are saying by looking at acceptance through a *lack* and *abundance* framework. First, I discuss how mainstream understandings and enactments of acceptance fail marginalized trans youth by cultivating a sense that there is not enough acceptance to benefit all trans youth. In the following section, I propose that abundant acceptance of trans youth offers a source of possibility and systemic transformation. I conclude with a list of affirmations for allies, which I hope can offer guidance for readers about how to embody abundant acceptance in your own lives.

ENOUGH ACCEPTANCE?

In many ways, this is an unprecedented moment in history to be writing about trans youth and acceptance. Gains in legal recognition of gender identity and expression through amendments to provincial and federal human rights codes; government and non-profit agencies making efforts to be more inclusive of trans people, from changes on forms to improving service delivery; and in British Columbia, policy implementation and curriculum development focused on making schools more aware of and safer for young trans people—these are all examples of how acceptance, hard-earned through decades of trans activism (see Irving & Raj, 2014), has led to the recognition that trans people exist and the belief that we are deserving of protections and rights. Without dismissing the ongoing struggles and challenges of being a trans youth today, I am struck by how Tor, in "Victoria," is able to envision a future "shining bright," that he "can feel the sunshine; see the light," and is "so happy to live in today."

That (some) trans youth can imagine themselves into the future is monumental at a time when 67 per cent of trans people report that they fear they will die young (Bauer & Scheim, 2015). As a trans adult in their early thirties, I cannot help but look around at the community I love so dearly and wonder about how many of us will even make it through the next decade. Trans women of colour are dying at devastating and alarming rates; poverty keeps trans people hungry, cold, and unwell; trauma and precarious mental health make todays—let alone tomorrows—feel unbearable; and there is an underrepresentation of disabled people, young trans people, and trans families at events meant to bond and build our communities. In many ways it is a tender wonder that trans youth are envisioning gender-affirming futures. As Tor's poem demonstrates, while mainstream acceptance of trans people makes futures seem possible, the present day is still marked by internal struggles for self-acceptance and encounters with hatred both inside and outside of homes. Who, then, is actually benefiting from the trans acceptance that was supposed to flow out of the "trans tipping point"?

Even with acceptance, the future for trans youth is still precarious. It is devastating, but real, that the impact of a systemic lack of acceptance still threatens the lives of trans youth. In "The Personal Dictionary of a Trans Semanticist," Christopher makes mention of the 40 per cent of trans youth who have attempted suicide as the "infamous number, our dancing death toll, ever-changing but never resolved."[1] Personifying a statistic about death is quite a striking move on Christopher's part because it reminds readers that a number representing trans lives lost has a life of its own. In Jaxon's "A Letter to the Girl I Was Supposed to Be," he shares the isolation and heaviness of the internal struggle of not living as one's gender: "I seriously considered succumbing to the encroaching tendrils of darkness ... I thought that I was a monster ... I thought that I didn't deserve to live." Reverberating throughout Jaxon's piece is the painful process he experienced moving toward self-acceptance, and though there is relief in *recognizing* his gender in the mirror, as readers we are left with uncertainty about whether the freedom Jaxon concludes with is, indeed, self-acceptance.

Both Christopher and Jaxon's pieces are intimate insights into how lack of acceptance swirls and whirls around in the bodies, minds, and spirits of trans youth, and informs readers of how trans youth draw meaning about the worthiness of their lives. As the postscript in "Dear Grace" by David goes, "even though it might have seemed like I did at times, I never hated you." Similar to Jaxon's piece, whether David feels self-acceptance or not is unclear. What is clear is that David can hold a relationship with his past self that is not steeped in shame, anger, or disgust. He shows that acceptance can mean simply accepting what *is*. Indeed, "Genderfluid" by Hope is a terrific homage to how non-binary youth learn to exist and adapt to uncertainty and are able to let go of always needing to know who they are or how they will express their gender from day to day. This is not to say that acceptance balanced on uncertainty is easy, but I wonder what would happen if our communities learned to embrace the knowledge that trans and non-binary youth have about how to live with uncertainty instead of constantly fighting for it? These trans youth resist providing an equation for self-acceptance by instead sharing stories that transcend self-acceptance as an arrival point or a destination that ever has to be reached. This is not to say that trans youth should not be supported in exploring their gender, or in dismantling internalized shame, or in working toward any goal connected directly or peripherally to self-acceptance, but that this support should be offered on their terms and at their pace.

Additionally, explorations of trans self-acceptance are limited when sad, gruesome, and heart-wrenching statistics and stories about trans youth are used to shock (cis) audiences into acceptance. That these are the dominant representations available to trans youth, however, has the additional effect of shaping the ways trans youth understand themselves and what it means to be trans. To refuse this narrative, Alexander M. has had the words "I AM ART" tattooed on his ankle as "a reminder that I am worthy of love, help, and self-care. A reminder that I, as a trans youth and valuable member of society, deserve to be listened to."

One approach to countering the negative consequences of a ceaseless focus on the lack of acceptance of trans youth could be to highlight statistics about the positive outcomes of acceptance. Take, for example, how the *Canadian Trans Youth Health Survey* (Veale et al., 2015) reported that trans youth who were able to live as their felt gender were more likely to report having excellent physical and mental health (p. 68), and that trans youth who have an adult they can go to for support are four times more likely to report good or excellent mental health, and four times less likely to have considered suicide (p. 63). Although this is positive, it also risks oversimplifying acceptance within a binary of some youth being accepted while others are not. Therefore, it is also necessary to provide trans youth with a range of trans stories that are complicated and uncomfortable, and to encourage them to write, create, and share their own stories, as the Gender Generations Project (GGP) has done so beautifully. Thankfully, we do not have to look far to find exemplary work by trans writers, particularly Two-Spirit and trans-feminine people of colour, whose work can deepen awareness of how acceptance is more of a series of encounters than something that can be quantified, and make tangible the ways in which these encounters are shaped by privilege and context.[2]

As an example of the power of stories, I turn to "Sarah: A Trans Girl's Story," in which Alexander brings to life the wrenching reality that family rejection is a leading reason for why so many trans youth end up in precarious housing situations and thrust into poverty; couch surfing, sleeping in shelters, and living on the streets (Abramovich, 2012). While Sarah is able to stay at her friend's family's house (a beautiful nod on Alexander's part to the many families who stretch their own resources to keep trans youth housed and safe), this is not the case for many trans youth. Lack of acceptance not only keeps individual trans youth from safe shelter, it perpetuates a culture of cisnormativity that institutionalizes erasure of trans existence and trans bodies (Namaste, 2000; Pyne, 2011). Services segregate sleeping spaces and bathrooms based on gender, ask for gender (and rarely pronouns) on forms, and fail to provide adequate training to staff (Mottet & Ohle, 2006; Pyne, 2011).

Through erasure it is possible to understand how lack of acceptance is not individualized as an internal process that trans youth struggle to overcome, or one relegated to the private sphere of families or intimate relationships, because a lack of trans acceptance has seeped into the physical, administrative, and social structures that make up the landscape of our day-to-day lives. Cisnormativity creates a lack of acceptance that is so pervasive that it is invisible, or at least invisible until trans youth and adults encounter this lack through barriers to belonging and then demand change. Unfortunately, trans youth often have to fight to be accepted, even when they do not want to. In "The Personal Dictionary of a Trans Semanticist," Christopher talks about how even *existing* as a trans person means having to be, or at least be seen as, an activist. He says: "You won't see me with the picketers, but still they tell me every breath I take is something radical; every heartbeat, inexorably political. And so I, the activist, go to class in the mornings, take a seat in the back, and keep my head down until I go home." This description shows how "trans existence as resistance" may be a powerful message, but it is not necessarily a badge trans youth choose or want to wear. At the same time, it challenges dominant notions of activism and resistance as occurring on the frontlines of grassroots organizing by recognizing the ways our bodies, our day-to-day, and our relationships are spaces of trans resistance, even if what we are resisting is the very idea that being trans is, in itself, something radical. To be on the margins of society is to be constantly discovering the limitations, and the contingencies, of acceptance.

A helpful way to frame this discussion is to consider how *lack* has come to define acceptance. *Lack* refers to the scarcity of a resource; it gives a hollow sense that there is not enough of something. A lack of acceptance gives the impression that acceptance has to be earned, which raises the questions of who gets to be accepted, who doesn't, and why? As Dean Spade (2011) argues in *Normal Life*, legal and social recognition of trans people—for example, through the expansion of human rights legislation—stands to benefit those with privilege, those who are seen as "normal." While it appears that recognition will benefit all trans people equally, laws, policies, and practices that put this recognition into action often do not address and can even perpetuate the marginalization of some trans people by not also addressing how racism, classism, ableism, and heteronormativity are embedded into how the state functions and who it seeks to protect. In other words, the trans people who are most likely to find acceptance, at least in the sense of being protected under law, are those who are privileged, those who fit within a white, middle-class, non-disabled, heterosexual, masculine, and binary (or at least binary-read) norm (Spade, 2011). Lack produces the idea that it is too much of a burden on society to accept all trans people, and therefore puts the onus onto trans people to fit within the pre-established boundaries for what and who is deemed acceptable.

In Canada, these boundaries of acceptability operate on racial-gender lines. As Leanne Simpson (2017), a brilliant Michi Saagiig Nishnaabeg scholar, writer, and artist, describes:

> [T]he heteropatriarchy of settler colonialism has regulated the bodies of Indigenous women and 2SQ [Two-Spirit, Queer], and trans people particularly, to death. We live in a vat of heteropatriarchal violence. In this reality, gendered practices that once existed in a different context no longer generate the same intimate relationships in a settler colonial context, at the very least, not for everyone. (p. 141)

While policies and legislation seem to progressively benefit trans people, the notion of progress reinscribes the settler-colonial nation-state as benevolent and renders unseen the multitude of ways the gender binary was violently imposed on Indigenous communities (Simpson, 2017, pp. 127–128). For those of us who are white and of settler ancestries, it is our responsibility to grapple with how celebrating formal recognition of trans people in law and policy also means legitimizing the governance of a nation-state founded on racism, land-theft, and genocide. At the crux of trans acceptance, therefore, is the question of whether we are willing to accept social change on an incremental basis of accepting the most normative among us and hoping this acceptance reverberates outward, or whether we will dream of and embody an acceptance that encompasses all trans people, and the differences between us, by refusing to comply with and uncritically celebrate a system that has failed us and our siblings for too long.

ENOUGH. ACCEPTANCE (NOW).

In my work with parents and primary caregivers of young trans people, I am constantly encountering parents who cannot fathom how a family could choose to not accept their trans child. For these parents, acceptance is unconditional, whereas for families who only somewhat support their trans children, their acceptance has limitations and parameters, and as research shows, this has dire consequences for the health and well-being of trans youth (Travers et al., 2012). As all of the contributions from Tor, Hope, Alexander M., Jaxon, Alexander M-G, Christopher, David, and Ajam demonstrate, there is an urgent need for boundaries constraining individual acceptance to be shattered. So urgent is the need that, in "A Letter to the Girl I Was Supposed to Be," Jaxon compares the feeling of living a façade to "gasping for air." This suffocation of self demonstrates the necessity of abundant acceptance that allows for the entirety of a young trans person to exist and that trusts the twisting path of gender self-determination.

Abundance conjures a comfortable sensation of bountifulness, a feeling that there is enough, for everyone, of everything necessary for *more* than just survival, but for a life well lived. Thankfully, trans youth are increasingly experiencing abundant acceptance through caring relationships with friends, family, animals, and others who love them and are willing to risk their own privilege and safety to support trans justice. In "Victoria," Tor relates the importance of allies as those who "help me to fight the hate." As Tor reminds us, acceptance is not only action-oriented, it resists the notion that it is sufficient to accept within private spheres of the home and family only, because acceptance is a decidedly public act. This is especially important given how some trans children and youth are only allowed to express their gender expansiveness inside the so-called "private sphere" of their homes. While this is a decision parents and caregivers sometimes make out of a desire to keep their children safe, when conditions are put on acceptance, an opening is made for shame to fester and grow. Hope states the importance of public gender expression in "Genderfluid" by describing how, even though they find it hard sometimes, it makes them happy: "Knowing I went out / Out in the world / As myself and not someone else." While decisions to not allow children to express their trans and nonconforming genders may feel as though they are coming from a place of wanting to ensure safety, this conveys a sense that the reality of the continued lack of acceptance of trans youth is a burden that should be carried by trans youth themselves. Abundant acceptance would instead honour gender self-determination and agency, and focus on what needs to change so that trans youth can flourish.

While some trans youth feel sparks of abundant acceptance, continuous encounters with lack of acceptance elsewhere (at school, with extended family, in health and mental health care settings, in faith communities, on social media, etc.) dampen the protective power of this acceptance. Lack surrounds trans youth to the heart-shattering point that trans youth are put into positions of having to defend themselves because not only their identity, but their moral character and *value*, is put into question. As Alexander M. puts it in "I AM ART," he needs to have a clear understanding of his morals, beliefs, and identity "[b]ecause in being trans, it's almost guaranteed that you will have to [defend them]." Abundant acceptance, therefore, must exist both in and within relationships and be willing to hold society, professionals, and government accountable so that it is no longer a resource granted on the basis of worthiness. Abundant acceptance is as peaceful and warm as the world that Sarah, from Alexander M-G's story "Sarah: A Trans Girl's Story," dreams of, "where everyone was supportive of the LGBTQ+ community." By embracing all of the aspects that make trans youth wonderfully, complicatedly, and challengingly who they are, we can ensure that "Trans is Beautiful" is embroidered not only on paper, as Tor has done, but on our hearts.

ABUNDANT ACCEPTANCE: AN ANTIDOTE

Reframing acceptance around abundance means being guided by and honouring the gender self-determination of trans youth in such a way that who belongs within acceptance is expanded, and what is made unacceptable are systems and beliefs that threaten to reduce the creativity and possibility trans youth embody. This is acceptance as relational. Acceptance as political. Acceptance as action. Acceptance as resistance, refusal, and solidarity. Abundant acceptance is an antidote to forms of acceptance that lack the bravery to question a system grounded on principles that are so exclusionary and divisive that acceptance, as a concept, would be necessary to begin with.

In the illustration *Self-Portrait* by Ajam at the beginning of this section, we only see the top half of a face. Perhaps we would assume acceptance to look like this face being seen in full, proud and visible, and in turn read this image as hiding away due to a lack of acceptance. However, abundant acceptance makes room for this partial view. Abundant acceptance gently arrives at where an individual is at while simultaneously working for change so that a full view is safe and possible. This is part of re-knowing acceptance. The authors and artists have shown that acceptance can mean "feeling the sunshine, feeling the light" (Tor); knowing oneself as a work of art (Jaxon); seeing trans not as a "loaded weapon but an answer" (Christopher); being free (Alexander M.); being understood, safe, and housed (Alexander M-G); affirming identity as "a wonderful thing" (Hope); being themselves (Ajam); and being brought to the light (David).

I began this response with a quote by Angela Davis, a brilliant Black feminist scholar, political activist, and prison abolitionist: "I am no longer accepting the things I cannot change. I am changing the things I cannot accept." Inspired by how these words can be spoken as an affirmation, I conclude with affirmations for allies that I hope offer a reframing of acceptance as an inward practice that can reverberate outward. Affirmations are validations that we can carry with us, that we can use to set intentions for our days, that we can turn to in moments of need. For example, Hope offers a wonderful affirmation in their poem when they say: "I am genderfluid / And that is a wonderful / Thing." The purpose of providing a list of affirmations is to offer ideas about what those of us who wish to be allies (and yes, queer, trans, non-binary, and Two-Spirit adults, this applies to us, too) can accept about what it means to struggle in solidarity with trans youth. I invite you to use these affirmations however feels good for you, but some ideas, especially if you are newer to affirmations, include: copying these down and having them available for when you are in need of some inspiration or need to stay grounded; drawing an affirmation when you wake up and noticing when it comes up for you throughout your day; or using these as conversation starters with trans youth, family members, friends, and/or colleagues. Make it a creative and crafty endeavour by writing the affirmations out and making them look fancy and spectacular. Most important? Accept the journey these affirmations take you on.

AFFIRMATIONS FOR ABUNDANT ACCEPTANCE

✓ **I accept that I have a role to play in resisting discrimination against trans youth because all inequity and injustice are unacceptable.** I acknowledge that systems of violence are rooted in settler colonialism and disproportionately target Two-Spirit, trans, and non-binary Black, Indigenous, and people of colour, and people with disabilities. I accept my responsibility to learn about and resist all structures of violence and oppression, even if I am not directly affected.

✓ **I accept trans youth as the experts of their own lives.** I accept that honouring gender self-determination will likely challenge what I think is best for trans youth. I can best support by listening and allowing my actions to be guided by trans youth.

✓ **I accept that I will have to unlearn some of my beliefs about gender.** I have learned some beliefs and stereotypes that are harmful to trans people. I accept that any lack of knowledge about gender diversity is an occasion for personal growth, that my learning will not be linear, that I will make mistakes, and that much of my growing will happen through feeling challenged and uncomfortable.

✓ **I accept that struggling for social change can be difficult and exhausting, and I will be gentle with myself in this work.** I accept that learning more about and witnessing trans youth experience erasure and violence, and barriers to care and rejection from those who should love them, will make my mind, heart, and body ache. I will remember that I am not alone; this is a collective heartache that can bring me closer to those I am fighting for.

✓ **I accept that I will be transformed by the magic of having young trans people in my life. I celebrate this, and I celebrate them.**

NOTES

1. The often-cited statistic that 40 per cent of trans people have attempted suicide comes from an extensive national survey done by the National Survey for Transgender Equality, and reflects the US context. According to the Ontario-based Trans PULSE Project survey, 47 per cent of trans youth have considered suicide, and 19 per cent have attempted suicide (Scanlon et al. 2010).
2. As an incomplete list to get you started, see the works of Arielle Twist, jia qing wilson-yang, Kai Cheng Thom, and Vivek Shraya.

REFERENCES

Abramovich, I. A. (2012). No safe place to go—LGBTQ youth homelessness in canada: reviewing the literature. *Canadian Journal of Family and Youth / Le Journal Canadien de Famille et de La Jeunesse, 4*(1), 29–51.

Aizura, A., Cotton, T., Carsten/LaGata, C. B., Ochoa, M., & Vidal-Ortiz, S. (2014). Introduction. *Transgender Studies Quarterly, 1*(3), 308–319.

Bauer G., & Scheim, A. (2015). *Transgender people in Ontario, Canada: Statistics to inform human rights policy.* Trans PULSE Project. Retrieved from http://transpulseproject.ca/wp-content/uploads/2015/06/Trans-PULSE-Statistics-Relevant-for-Human-Rights-Policy-June-2015.pdf.

Clare, E. (2013). Body shame, body pride: Lessons from the disability rights movement. In S. Stryker & A. Z. Aizura (Eds.), *The Transgender Studies Reader 2* (pp. 261–265). New York: Routledge.

Irving, D., & Raj, R. (2014). *Trans Activism in Canada: A reader.* Toronto: Canadian Scholars Press Inc.

Lister, R. (2007). Why citizenship: Where, when, and how children? *Theoretical Inquiries in Law, 8*(2), 693–718.

Mottet, L., & Ohle, J. (2006). Transitioning our shelters: Making homeless shelters safe for transgender people. *Journal of Poverty, 10*(2), 77–101.

Namaste, V. K. (2000). *Invisible lives: The erasure of transsexual and transgendered people.* Chicago: University of Chicago Press.

Pyne, J. (2011). Unsuitable bodies: Trans people and cisnormativity in shelter services. *Canadian Social Work Review / Revue Canadienne de Service Social, 28*(1), 129–137.

Scanlon, K., Travers, R., Coleman, T., Bauer, G., & Boyce, M. (2010). Ontario's trans communities and suicide: Transphobia is bad for our health. *Trans PULSE E-Bulletin 1* (2). Retrieved from http://www.transpulseproject.ca/public_downloads.html.

Simpson, L. (2017). *As we have always done: Indigenous freedom through radical resistance.* Minnneapolis: University of Minnesota Press.

Spade, D. (2011). *Normal life: Administrative violence, critical trans politics, and the limits of the law.* Brooklyn, NY: South End Press.

Travers, R., Bauer, G., Pyne, J., Bradley, K., Gale, L., & Papadimitriou, M. (2012). *Impacts of strong parental support for trans youth.* Retrieved from http://transpulseproject.ca/wp-content/uploads/2012/10/Impacts-of-Strong-Parental-Support-for-Trans-Youth-vFINAL.pdf.

Veale, J., Saewyc, E., Frohard-Dourlent, H., Dobson, S., Clark, B., and the Canadian Trans Youth Health Survey Research Group. (2015). *Being safe, being me: Results of the Canadian trans youth health survey.* Vancouver: Stigma and Resilience Among Vulnerable Youth Centre, School of Nursing, University of British Columbia.

Afterword

By Glynne Evans, age 74

Ditch The Straights' Jacket

Mother was scared of the neighbours
Dad rolled his eyes far away
The Principal said, "Just a phase, I suppose"
Most kids just thought I was gay

Well, the neighbours felt sorry for mother
Or wanted to know all the "dirt"
Dad was "sure we aren't Scottish"
So I "shouldn't be wearing a skirt"

One kid thinks I'm a really great rebel
And my bravery's really cool too
My Teach says, "It's gone far enough now"
—She's afraid we'll meet in the the loo

Though I've known I am trans for years now
My parents I never dared tell
When I did, they said I am selfish!
And surely I'd go straight to Hell

I told them I'd not go anywhere straight, thanks
And what hell they were making for me
Stop treating me, please, like merely a chattel
And refer to me, kindly, as "she"

The shrink said, "Nothing will work here"
To make me "normal as most"
So my parents must learn to accept me
Or I must accept that I'm toast

A trans friend who is old, and a rock of support
And cheerful in spite of it all
Has told me to grow a very thick skin
But if needed, show flashes of gall

She's had her "phase" now for decades
And it certainly isn't a sham
So "passing" is not what the "phase" did
Passing will affirm who I am

Now, Trans are musicians and singers
Politicians and athletes, and it's true!
Even bosses are beginning to hire us!
Will that give my parents a clue?

A Binary Binder

My brother wears a frilly dress
An Auntie goes by "he"
I can be gender neutral
- Until I have to pee.

Process and Methodology

By Dr. Lindsay Herriot and Kate Fry

ORIGINS

The roots of *Trans Youth Stories* and the Trans Tipping Point (TTP) Project, now called the Gender Generations Project (GGP), stretch back to Lindsay Herriot's doctoral field-work in 2014 when she was conducting narrative inquiry with Gay–Straight Alliances in coastal British Columbia. Kate Fry, then a tenth grader, was a participant in her dissertation research, and the two kept in touch through community organizing and activism. Years later, we stopped for coffee in front of the Vancouver SkyTrain after an LGBT-related community action and chatted about the seemingly binary representation of young trans life (triumph/tragedy) in the mainstream, wondering if and how that "single story" could be changed (Adichie, 2009).

Furthermore, Lindsay and Kate had both seen how the cis-LGB people in LGBT spaces habitually and often unwittingly absorbed and assimilated trans issues into their own. We wondered how we, as cis, queer women, could contribute to more robust trans-centred spaces and were curious about how we could use our privilege to amplify trans work without centring ourselves. On one hand, we knew that trans folks should not have to carry the burden of doing the emotionally draining and usually unpaid work of teaching cis people about transphobia and its associated prejudices. On the other hand, allies who join in this work need to prioritize those with lived experience and not take up all of the space themselves. How, we wondered, could we navigate these tensions?

The eventual result of these ongoing conversations was the Trans Tipping Point, named in response to the *Time* magazine cover proclaiming that 2014 was the "Transgender Tipping Point." Adapting this title was meant to provoke questions about what it might be like to grow up as trans right after this alleged watershed moment, and the alliteration in "Transgender Tipping Point" seemed eye-catching and trendy enough to use on funding applications. Even then, however, the idea of a "tipping point" for trans rights was being met with criticism (see Fisher, Phillips, & Katri, 2017; Moore O., 2017). We always expected that the youth would want to retitle the project, but despite encouragement, they chose to keep it until just before this book went to press, at which point they'd renamed it the Gender Generations Project (GGP). For consistency in the rest of this chapter, we will refer to it as the GGP.

With Kate and Lindsay later relocating to the University of Victoria (Kate to begin her undergraduate degree; Lindsay to start work as a sessional/adjunct lecturer), the GGP had a geographic and institutional home. Through longtime involvement with the Canadian Association for the Study of Women and Education (CASWE), Lindsay reconnected with Faculty of Education associate professor Dr. Kathy Sanford, who generously agreed to serve as a faculty collaborator on the project. The Gender Generations Project had officially begun.

RECRUITMENT AND DEMOGRAPHICS

Consistent with our core value of keeping cis folks to the margins and centring trans voices, we are choosing to tell the remainder of the GGP "story" in collaboration and dialogue with three of the founding mentors. As adult mentor Tash McAdam explains, "over the course of the [Gender Generations Project], mentors have been an integral part of the program. Mentors ran workshops, worked with the youth on their pieces, edited, and provided a safe space for the youth participants to create and explore their art." Three of the founding and longest serving mentors, Serena Lukas Bhandar, H. Kori Doty, and Tash McAdam, sat down together for a chat about the experience. You'll find some highlights of the conversation throughout the rest of this chapter.

After securing permission from the University of Victoria's Research Ethics Board, recruitment of participants began in earnest through snowballing, social media, emailing service providers, including all of the local Gay–Straight Alliances, etc. Interested youth and mentors alike had to identify as non-cisgender, submit an application, and sign a consent form. Youth needed to be under age eighteen,[1] have their parents also sign a consent form,[2] and submit a writing sample; adult mentors needed to explain their background working with youth, and submit a workshop proposal.

The writing sample component of the youth application added a level of seriousness to the programming as we were cultivating a community of writers with the aim of being published. Further, as any writer knows, writing is filled with the onerous and sometimes overwhelming process of submitting proposals, and we wanted our potential youth to experience success in what for many was their very first writing application. All of the youth who applied received a professional response on university letterhead, congratulating them on their application and reflecting on the specific strengths of their writing sample. This meant that participants would walk into the program with the pride and confidence of having already accomplished something simply by being accepted into it.

To increase accessibility, all bus tickets, writing materials, programming, meals, and snacks were free, and the program provided billets for out-of-town youth and mentors alike. In later years, when the GGP moved from being a university research study to a community organization, fundraising covered the travel costs for all participating British Columbia youth. We were also able to open the program to youth without requiring parental permission.

Recruitment was ongoing throughout the school year. Both new to Victoria, Lindsay and Kate built relationships with other queer and trans youth organizations not only to recruit for GGP, but to spotlight and uplift all the great local work being done by and for queer and trans youth.[3] Mindful of how we were white settlers arriving on new land and leading a new project, we intentionally did lots of quiet, unglamorous, and behind the scenes work with, and for, other groups, such as setting up, stacking chairs, cleaning up, providing childcare, handing out flyers, promoting events, and giving rides. These connections with other organizations were crucial to the GGP ethos. At its core, the project was designed as an exercise in community building, and we wanted to mitigate the ways in which we were cis, white settlers starting a new project in a new city.

Despite our best efforts, white, transmasculine, able-bodied folks were overrepresented among mentors and more so among youth. This lack of diversity is partly a reflection of the realities of structural privilege and oppression, and partly due to Lindsay and Kate's own shortcomings. The GGP, especially in that first year, was imbued with the worldviews of white, able-bodied, cisgender, and formally educated women. Although we reached out specifically to potential BIPOC and femme/girl/women-identifying youth and mentors alike, and several did join, such participants were still disappointingly underrepresented. The communities and connections that were made while recruiting for GGP were disproportionately white, and the retreats themselves were also held in predominantly white, middle-class neighbourhoods in Victoria, including at the University of Victoria itself.

Beyond the limitations of recruiting for this program as cis, white women, we speculate there were additional barriers to trans girls' participation. Founding mentor Serena explains: "It's just not safe for trans girls to be out, and therefore trans girls just often don't realize that they're trans or don't come out. Having trans girls and trans folks of colour underrepresented in [the GGP] is really hard." It is also possible that the UVic ethics requirement that participants seek parental consent proved to be an additional barrier for trans girls, in addition to all youth who needed to be closeted at home. Tash lamented, "We have this project that's elevating trans youth and we're missing a huge portion of the most vulnerable trans youth."

Seeing dominant identities overrepresented among youth, mentors took it upon themselves to disrupt and intervene. Founding mentor Kori explains:

As a trans masculine person, I've witnessed a lot of young trans guys replicate the most toxic masculinity because they're insecure and they want to pass. They have extraordinary amounts of privilege that they need to get their heads around. They need to get right about and find ways to be responsible with the fact that they're growing into white men in a time where they're accessing a whole bunch of power that they've never been trained to use. It would be really irresponsible not to address that.

Tash adds:

They can get caught up in their identity as trans people and fail to recognize that white privilege still exists and trans masculine privilege and being perceived as masculine comes with its own set of privileges whether or not you're perceived as trans. We have to recognize and engage with that.

Kori and Tash's leadership speaks to the possibilities of a mindful and responsible intergenerational community. Understanding what it means to live as an individual whose identity is caught at the intersections of power and oppression, as many of our white transmasculine youth do, is a complicated process. Kori and Tash have grappled with that process themselves and were therefore able to offer some much-needed guidance on it. Before we went out to the world to talk about inclusion and identity, we looked inwards and tried to address dynamics of power and privilege and how we were complicit in them in our own created community. As Serena rightly points out, "there's still so much room for it to grow and change and evolve and become more things for more people in the community."

While recognizing and taking ownership of these shortcomings, we caution readers not to assume that the author biographies at the end of this volume capture all of our participants' intersectional identities. More than a few chose not to include their minoritized racial, religious, ethnocultural, physical abilities, neurological differences, or other identity labels, for reasons unknown to us. Perhaps they didn't feel them relevant to their story, or maybe they either deliberately or unintentionally excluded them. A not insignificant minority wrote under a pen name and omitted a host of identifying characteristics, some of which indicated a minority status, from their bios. Whatever the case, many identity markers are unnamed in this book.

Furthermore, the author bios are not an accurate count of how many youth attended the retreats. Several youth participants who created writing during the retreats chose not to have their pieces included in this volume. One author and one artist declined to submit bios, while still another published under the name Anonymous with no accompanying bio. These inconsistencies can prove vexing when trying to make declarative claims about how many youth we worked with, and who was and was not represented. The best numerical statement that we can offer is that there are twenty-six young authors and artists featured in this book, and both the mean and median age of participating youth was fourteen.

VALUING MENTORSHIP AND MENTORING VALUES

From the start, relationship, mentorship, and intergenerational community were the guiding values of the GGP. Lindsay continues to enjoy more than a decade of professional, personal, and spiritual mentorship from Dr. Alan Sears in the Faculty of Education at the University of New Brunswick, and Kate, in turn, considers Lindsay a great friend and mentor. As we circled back again and again to ideas of care and mentoring we realized that if this was indeed a "tipping point" for the current generation of trans youth, one distinguishing feature was surely that there were now out, visible trans adults and elderly folks. Our job as organizers would be to facilitate in-person intergenerational connection.

As stated in our first successful seed grant application,[4] the guiding goals or measures of success for the GGP have always been "based on the following criteria, with each component foundational to the one that follows it:

1. That each youth feels welcome, valued, and that they share control and leadership over the project as a whole.
2. That each youth becomes friends with at least one peer and establishes a positive mentoring relationship with at least one of the adults.
3. That each youth learns something new about trans history, culture, and writing, and that they produce at least one piece of writing of which they feel proud.
4. That we submit a book-length manuscript of [our work] at the end of the project.

5. That each youth is supported in assuming a leadership role in some aspect of the knowledge translation.

Concurrent with these measures, each adult mentor needs to feel valued and be compensated in some form for this project to be considered a success."

Relationship and community building were intentionally positioned as more foundational and of greater importance than any published writing that might come out of this project. We were particularly attuned to how we could nurture long-lasting intergenerational friendships and solidarity. Drawing from Indigenous worldviews,[5] we viewed these relationships as a circle, embodying mutual connection and equality, rather than a line, which denotes hierarchy or a binary. Tash, who is also a practising secondary school teacher, elaborates on this: "Change has to happen in two directions at once. … Working with the [GGP] has really influenced my pedagogy, working with young people instead of making them work for you, or making them work, and just being a collective force, a team." Serena agrees, noting how age differences between youth and mentors simultaneously mattered and didn't matter. "We do straddle that line between being adults in their minds, but we're also peers. We're also on the same level as them which I think is very different from a lot of the adults in their lives."

This shared experience of being trans, and for some youth and mentors alike just beginning their gender transition, created space for less hierarchical and more equitable connections between adults and youth. Kori reflects on the responsibilities of mentors in this new type of relationship:

> It's our responsibility to share the perspectives that we have that they don't have. And it's also our responsibility to take a step back and recognize that we don't have any grounds to be authorities in their lives. We have grounds to be *resources* in their lives; if anything, we have a responsibility to be resources in their lives.

Taken together, Tash, Serena, and Kori's comments capture the idiosyncrasies of the equality and mutuality in mentors' relationships with youth while also noting mentors' age-based obligations. It is Kate and Lindsay's view that the rich, high-quality writing in this volume was only possible because the writing itself always took a backseat to relationship and connection. The most important outcome of the GGP was the creation of a simultaneously intergenerational and youth-centred trans community. Any potential publications were seen as a bonus, not a requirement. This ordering of values paradoxically produced writing of the highest calibre, not only in this volume but in the stories, poems, essays, and other youth-created writing from the GGP that were shared and published elsewhere.

THE RETREATS

Our three weekend-long retreats, one each in October, February, and May, followed essentially the same format, with a Friday night pizza party, workshops all day Saturday, and refinement and planning on Sunday (see sample program). "Paladins" is Tash's creative non-fiction description of the energy on the Friday nights:

> The elders are full of excitement and joy as the young knights gather. They've travelled far and wide to join this worthy quest. Some are already famed across the land, their brave deeds echoing between settlements, tales spreading like wildfire; like resilience. Some are untried in battle, determined to test their mettle. They train together, sharpen their weapons, and hone their skills. They name the demons they will slay: hate, ignorance, intolerance. Dysphoria, self-destruction, bitterness. Together, they build a shield that other young warriors will use to fight their own monsters. These truth wielders, word warriors, bold boys, gallant girls and undauntable enbys band together. Between them, they make magic, forge weapons so strong they'll never be broken. Each must go back to their own homestead, but they'll take with them the strength of the family they've built, the bonds they've fashioned. A network of unvanquishable goodness, shining light into the darkest corners of the nation. Around them, monsters tremble.
>
> These giants come to slay.

TRANS TIPPING POINT
FEBRUARY 2-4 RETREAT

FRI

Fairfield Gonzales Community Association, 1330 Fairfield Road

6:30pm - Pizza and Snacks
7pm - Welcome, Introduction of Project and Mentors
7:30pm - Trans Embroidery, Hang Out
9pm - Bedtime :)

SAT

Fairfield Gonzales Community Association, 1330 Fairfield Road

9:00am - Coffee & Conversation
9:15am - WORKSHOP 1
A) Costume poetry (Rose) B) Writing Trans/enby Characters 2.0 (Chris)
10:30am - Introvert Time
10:45am - WORKSHOP 2
A) Scene Writing in Plays/ Screenplays (Kat)
B) Writing to Read Aloud (Al)
12pm - Lunch
1pm - Keynote w/ Dr Lee Airton
2pm - Choose your own adventure!
A) Politician Prep- Speaking Truth to Power B) Trans Embroidery
C) Introvert Time
3pm - WORKSHOP 3
A) Comics/Graphic Novels (Sabrina) B) Writing Queer Speculative Fiction (Ziggy)
4:15pm - Introvert Time
4:30pm - WORKSHOP 4
A) Narrative Voice As Spirit (Chase) B) Poetry 101 (Serena)
5:45pm - Supper & Quiet Time
7:30pm - 9:00pm - Trans Hirstory in 99 Objects (Legacy Art Gallery)

SUN

Artemis Place, 3020 Richmond Road

9:00am - Coffee & Conversation
9:15am - WORKSHOP 5
A) Painting with Words (Tirian)   B) Visionary Activism (Kori)
10:45am - Planning Part 1
11:45am - Lunch
12:45pm - Planning Part 2
1:45pm - Clean Up
2:00pm - Goodbyes :(

WE LOVE OUR FRIENDS & SUPPORTERS!

FACEBOOK: @ TRANSTIPPINGPOINTPROJECT
CONTACT: LINDSAYHERRIOT@UVIC.CA

Over the course of that first year we had over thirty youth and more than twenty mentors. While the trans participants, ranging from age ten to seventy-four, "slayed" in workshops, open mics, icebreaker games, and scheduled introvert time, Lindsay, Kate, and a small but dedicated team of cisgender volunteers attended to the logistics. On a laughably small budget,[6] we ordered pizza and cooked all the other meals, kept the spaces clean, organized the travel and billeting for the out-of-towners, maintained records and paperwork, paid the bills, and coordinated the volunteers. Although we all shared meals and downtime together, the workshops themselves were strictly trans-only spaces: neither Kate, Lindsay, nor any of the cis volunteers attended or set foot in a GGP workshop. In so doing, trans youth and their mentors were physically centred while their allies worked quietly on the sidelines. We were deliberate in choosing this centre/margin physicality to communicate how allies could support a vulnerable group without taking up all the space. This experience of trans-only spaces is captured in the following vignette:

Tash: You can't be the token trans if everyone's trans. That reminds me of another really special moment at the first retreat. We were in one of UVic's lecture halls doing a check-in. One of the youth put their hand up and said, "This is the first time I've ever been in a room with only trans people." It was one of the youngest youth who pointed this out, and none of us had realized. When we looked around and registered that truth, I swear about half of us burst into tears; it was a spontaneously shared wave of emotion, acknowledging that we have never had this experience before. It was incredible. It's one of the moments that I look back on and recognize as a defining moment for me as a person. To realize that I've never been in a space that was solely trans people. Aside from, obviously, small groups of my friends, which is very different from being in a room of 30 people, most of whom I don't know.

Serena: Honestly, it was really empowering.

Kori: There's this extra sparkle when they get to come and they get to be these creative powerhouses where also their transness isn't a defining factor of who they are. It's like a defining factor of how they belong. But like, they're not "the trans kid."

Participation in all programming was voluntary, and youth could come and go as they pleased. We always had a dedicated "introvert room" stocked with puzzles, Legos, and books where youth and mentors alike could escape for some downtime. Youth especially were encouraged to take care of their whole selves, and prioritize their own mental, emotional, physical, and spiritual well-being during the jam-packed weekends. Breaks and self-care were repeatedly encouraged. We also had a table full of cards and contact info for local service providers that cater to LGBTQ youth and frequently encouraged youth to check them out.

As Kate and Lindsay never attended any of the workshops, we turn now to Serena and Tash's conversation about them:

Serena: We [myself and another mentor] were jaded about queer organizing in general, and we didn't really have an experience of trans organizing ... walking in on the [GGP] was a really pleasant surprise. To see that there could be so much more than what you could imagine ... I had no idea what I was getting into. I walked in on the first day of workshops with a whole lesson plan and texts for youth to read, and then threw out most of it when I realized what talented and strong and creative writers the youth already were. It was incredible.

Tash: I've never experienced anything like the passion for creation, for art, for each other, and for the world that came out of the workshops at the [GGP]. ... I loved the way the youth chose their workshops. We did a brief intro to what we would be working on, and the youth signed up for the workshop they wanted. This meant popular workshops could run multiple times, and that we ensured that the focus was on what the *youth* wanted to work on and learn.

These observations circle back to Lindsay and Kate's original conversation about how trans youth are already capable and creative people who know what they do and don't want to learn. Mentors clearly shared that value and adapted on the fly to be continually responsive to the directions that youth chose. In doing so, learning and programming were continually circular and collaborative rather than a hierarchy of adult "knowers" and youth "learners." Four of the eight scholarly respondents served as mentors or volunteers at the retreats, and youth knew that their work in the eventual book publication would reflect that circular, intergenerational dialogue, with the adult scholars theorizing and asking questions about the youth's writing.

Sunday mornings were an important decision-making time. Each planning session began with an open review of the budget. Stored in a shared, password-protected spreadsheet, Kate and Lindsay displayed the numbers with an overhead projector and facilitated youth conversations about where the money was coming from and how it was being spent. We explained how we saw ourselves as stewards of what was really the youth's money, and this demanded line-by-line budget transparency. Based on these meetings, several youth volunteered to co-write funding applications with Lindsay and Kate and were successful in securing grants from groups like the Vancouver City Savings Credit Union (VanCity), the Victoria Foundation, the Tegan and Sara Foundation, and TransCare BC. Mentors were then excused for a coffee break, and the youth debriefed with Kate and Lindsay about the mentors themselves. Youth were free to raise any concerns about each mentor, and through democratic dialogues decided which mentors should be invited back. As the retreats progressed throughout the school year, some youth volunteered to screen incoming mentor applications and decided whether or not to accept them into the program.

THE FUTURE

Originally designed to run for a single school year, Kate and Lindsay realized that the final retreat in May was actually the beginning of a new kind of community. While the youth and their mentors drafted and edited the pitch to the publishers, we charted a course for the future. Thanks to continual fundraising,[7] there were just enough financial resources to hire interested youth and mentors to assume paid leadership positions so we could fade further into the background. The GGP is therefore ongoing, entirely under trans leadership, and until COVID-19 lockdowns hit, had hosted three retreats per year. It is Lindsay and Kate's position that, despite its flaws, the GGP embodies resilience simply by existing. Kori elaborates: "There's lots and lots of money and resources poured into us hating ourselves and us being horrible to each other. The idea that we will grow up, and we will exist, and we will thrive and we'll create valuable cultural resources. That is resistance." There is much to be proud of, and still so much room to grow.

Though not a mentor running workshops, 74-year-old Glynne Evans was a founding volunteer and author of the book's Afterword. More important than her running errands and giving rides (although these tasks were a godsend!), Glynne listened with and cared for our trans youth participants and adult mentors. In being physically present, she modelled that life as an out trans woman was not only possible, but filled with joy, connections, and purpose. She later wrote:

> Attending the [formerly named] Trans Tipping Point events was very rewarding due to the energy and often precocious thoughts and political awareness of many of the kids. It was also heartening and affirming when one participant confided that their attendance "might have saved my life." As the anointed "Team Grandma" it was so evident how much progress their generation has made hereabouts compared with my own. I waited from age three to my late sixties to act on my gender dysphoria.

Glynne's analysis should give us all pause. Although imperfect, and continued progress is not guaranteed, perhaps we're at more of a tipping point than we recognize. Serena agrees: "Knowing that trans youth could have happy, wonderful childhoods despite the crappy world we live in helped me discard my fears and jaded feelings that trans and Two-Spirit and non-binary folks will always be oppressed. The youth are so clever and determined. There's nothing their generation can't achieve if they set their hearts and minds to it." Certainly regarding family and kin networks, the GGP invited imaginative space for new types of arrangements. Serena further notes:

> We're modelling, through our intergenerational relationships, families that don't fit the nuclear mould, multi-family and multi-generational kinds of networks. Collective networks that reject the heteropatriarchy. I realized I wanted to be a parent because of the [GGP], and that I *could* be a parent. It's not something I had thought I was capable of before.

Perhaps one of the most exciting outcomes of the Gender Generations Project is this potential for a greater reimagining of chosen families and intergenerational kin networks. While queer and trans folks have a well-established history of creating and popularizing chosen families, these families are often excluded from popular narratives of trans life that focus on rejection by families of origin.[8] Although some GGP youth were alienated from immediate and/or extended original family members, many were not. Indeed, a number of the participants' cisgender parents and siblings formed the backbone of the GGP volunteer team, and our project would not have existed without their emotional support and unpaid labour. A project like the GGP shows everyone involved, youth and adults, trans and cis people, multiple examples of a loving familial community that can include both biological and chosen members.

In thinking about the changes from that first retreat to the present, we'll conclude with Kori and Tash's observations, which strike a hopeful tone for our future.

Kori: I think of youth who spent the majority of the first night in the hallway cloakroom with the person they came with. A couple years later, they're in leadership positions in their college and they're really stepping into confidence and leadership that we need.

Tash: We repeatedly have youth who are new to the program, who maybe came alone or with an adult, who are so shy and don't know how to integrate ... who then, at the next retreat are an old hand helping out the new kids. They know where everything is, and what's up, and know everybody's names, and you can tell that they're really feeling confident and welcome and part of the community. In just one weekend, that's happened to them. The relationship depth is astounding. The openness that these young people come with [and] the willingness to make those connections, it's magic.

It's indeed been magic, and we, Lindsay and Kate, are humbled to have contributed to it.

NOTES

1. One youth celebrated their nineteenth birthday between submitting their application and attending a retreat; however, they were still a secondary school student during their participation.

2. This is a continuing challenge for research with trans youth as only those with parental support are eligible for participation in in-depth, qualitative studies.

3. Between the two of us, we volunteered and/or promoted the work of Gender Spectacular, Queer Peers, Queer Youth Open Mic, Stashes and Lashes Collective (Runs in the Family), UVic Pride, Queer Quills Writer's Collective, and Victoria Pride Society Youth Initiatives. Readers, especially those on Vancouver Island, are encouraged to check them out, volunteer, and donate to them.

4. Written by Kate, and generously awarded by the Vancouver Island Public Interest Research Group.

5. Reconceptualizing relationship from a line to a circle has been a long process and is a book unto itself. Lindsay first learned this way of thinking from Wolastoqi scholar David Perley of the Tobique First Nation in his roles as her professor and Director of the Mi'kmaq-Wolastoqey Centre at the University of New Brunswick in 2008. At the risk of pan-Indigenizing the

worldviews of the original nations of Turtle Island, Kate and Lindsay's ongoing learning of relationality as a circle is informed by the teachings of the following nations and writers: Métis, Cree, and Anishinaabe (Anderson, 2011); Lakota/Sioux (Brendtro, Brokenleg, & Van Bockern, 2002); Ojibwe (Child, 2012); Blackfoot (Little Bear, 2000); Mi'kmaw (Moore S., 2017); Anishinaabe (Kimmerer, 2015); and the incredible picture book grounded in Tap Pilam Coahuiltecan Nation's teachings (Gonzàlez & Garcia 2017).

6. The GGP budget never included remuneration for Kate or Lindsay. We had so few resources to begin with that it didn't feel right for financial support to go to cis folks like us. A grant received midway through was contingent on there being a small work–study stipend for Kate; otherwise, all of her work was unpaid. Lindsay's GGP work was unpaid; as a sessional/adjunct, she was only compensated for university courses taught, not for research or organizing.

7. Lindsay's grant applications had a steep rejection rate, Kate's were mostly successful, and those written with or by the youth themselves were funded 100% of the time.

8. For recent literature on the relationships between trans youth and original/chosen families, see Weinhardt et al., 2019; Hailey, Burton, & Arscott, 2020; Ward, 2019; and Hull & Ortyl, 2019.

REFERENCES

Adichie, C. N., Films for the Humanities and Sciences (Firm), & Films Media Group. (2009). *TED Talks: Chimamanda Adichie—The danger of a single story* [TED Talk]. New York: Films Media Group.

Anderson, K. (2011). *Life stages and native women: Memory, teachings, and story medicine.* Winnipeg, MB: University of Manitoba Press.

Brendtro, L. K., Brokenleg, M., & Van Bockern, S. (2002). *Reclaiming youth at risk: Our hope for the future* (Revised ed.). Mission, BC: Solution Tree.

Child, B. J. (2012). *Holding our world together: Ojibwe women and the survival of community.* New York: Penguin Books.

Fisher, S. D. E., Phillips, R., & Katri, I. H. (2017). Trans temporalities. *Somatechnic, 7*(1), 1–15.

Gonzàlez, X., & Garcia, A. M. (2017). *All around us.* El Paso, TX: Cinco Puntos Press.

Hailey, J., Burton, W., & Arscott, J. (2020). We are family: Chosen and created families as a protective factor against racialized trauma and anti-LGBTQ oppression among African American sexual and gender minority youth. *Journal of GLBT Family Studies, 16*(2) 176–191.

Hull, K. E., & Ortyl, T. A. (2019). Conventional and cutting-edge: Definitions of family in LGBT communities. *Sexuality Research and Social Policy, 16*(1), 31–43.

Kimmerer, R. W. (2015). *Braiding sweetgrass: Indigenous wisdom, scientific knowledge and the teachings of plants.* Minneapolis: Milkweed Editions.

Little Bear, L. (2000). Jagged worldviews colliding. In M. Battiste (Ed.), *Reclaiming Indigenous voice and vision* (pp. 77–85). Vancouver: UBC Press.

Moore, O. (2017). The importance of a forward-looking trans poetics. *Philament 23*, 31–54.

Moore, S. (2017). *Trickster chases the tale of education.* Montréal: McGill-Queen's University Press.

Ward, M. (2019). *Transitional perspectives on family: Impact of coming out on the personal meaning of family for transgender individuals* (MA Thesis, University of Cincinnati, Cincinnati, OH). Retrieved from https://etd.ohiolink.edu/.

Weinhardt, L. S., Xie, H., Wesp, L. M., Murray, J. R., Apchemengich, I., Kioko, D., Weinhardt, C. B., & Cook-Daniels, L. (2019). The role of family, friend, and significant other support in well-being among transgender and non-binary youth. *Journal of GLBT Family Studies, 15*(4), 311–325.

Author Bios

Editors' note: There is no one "right" way to write an author bio. Just like the trans youth themselves and the stories they shared in this book, there's lots of diversity. Some authors wrote a lot about themself, others wrote very little. A few chose not to write a bio at all.

A.J. Gabriel is a 17-year-old writer who goes by he/him/his pronouns, and strongly dislikes writing in the third person. Unfortunately, he also enjoys fuelling his inner rage, so he will continue to write this as though he were someone else. A.J. identifies as male, and lives his life as a regular dude, despite his doctor sending him on a different path at birth. He could go on and on about how he decided to turn his assigned identity on its head, but that is not why we are here at the moment. You picked up this book, and we are so very grateful that you are taking time to take a look at the works of a bunch of queer teens. Of course, A.J. is not a professional anything—he could be considered a professional procrastinator, though—and is not here to tell you what you can and can't do. He simply wishes to express his passion for how important self-love and self-care are. Loving yourself and caring for yourself are so important, and A.J. hopes to reach out to those who come across his work, and encourage people to remain curious.

Ajam (any pronouns) is a genderqueer artist living in Victoria, BC. From a very young age the story of Peter Pan has been a major influence on their art and their gender experience. As part of the Gender Generations Project, they are working with politicians to help create better policies for BC's trans youth. Peace out!

Alexander M-G is a trans male, he is thirteen years old, he lives in Victoria, British Columbia, and he likes reading, writing, fencing, swimming, and horseback riding. His favourite book is *The Darkness Rising* series.

Alexander McIntyre is a 16-year-old transgender boy living in the Slocan Valley, British Columbia. He is an experienced creative writer and multimedia artist who is also very involved in the theatre community. He is fairly new to the transgender community, but has worked hard to spread awareness about LGBTQ+ acceptance in his rural location.

Alyx MacAdams is a white settler of Gaelic Scottish, Irish, and English ancestry living in Lekwungen territories. Their Master of Social Work thesis centred a critical analysis of how trans children's experiences of care are shaped by and resist normative citizenship, transnormativity, and neoliberalism. An Aquarius through-and-through (sun and ascendent), Alyx has always been interested in issues of justice and organizing for social change. This has taken them on a wandering path of organizing and working as a facilitator, youth worker, outdoor educator, and anti-violence worker. These days they can be found facilitating programs for trans children and their parents/primary caregivers, doting on their plants, and filling their heart with the joyous wonders of co-parenting a young child.

Asa O'Connor-Jaeckel is a 13-year-old, carbon-based life form living with their parents and potted plants in Victoria, British Columbia. They enjoy reading, writing, acting, drawing, running around open fields like an insane chicken, jumping off of high things, contemplating the existence of everything, and—of course—consuming pickles. They are often found singing as loud as they can, and rummaging through recycling bins for makeshift bookmarks.

Ask Spirest is an 18-year-old feminine presenting trans guy from St. John's, Newfoundland. A second-generation youth, his life bridges experiences of Chinese cultural standards and Canadian socialization. He spends his time writing in between (and during!) activism work, leading his high school's GSA, and fighting queer homelessness on the Youth Advisory Council with Choices for Youth. Ask co-founded the LGBTQ2S+ Youth Advisory Council with the AIDS Committee of Newfoundland, and knows how essential it is for trans and queer youth to feel that we're in this together.

Astri Jack is a queer, cisgender woman and white settler living on the traditional lands of the Kosampson family of Lekwungen speaking peoples (Victoria, British Columbia). Astri works in child and youth mental health and is passionate about play, arts, and narrative based therapies. She is also a qualitative researcher in the fields of mental health, queer identity, and children, youth, and families. She is committed to anti-oppressive, intersectional approaches in her practice and believes that social justice work that upholds the inherent dignity of all beings is our most powerful tool for creating lasting and meaningful change.

Christopher is a 17-year-old high school student from Nanaimo, British Columbia. He is passionate about creative writing and working with youth, and in his spare time he is (very, very slowly) teaching himself to play the guitar. He hopes his writing will help to reassure young trans kids while also humanizing the trans experience for those who struggle to understand it.

Christopher Wolff (he/him/they/them pronouns) is a trans writer, facilitator, and educator living and working on Coast Salish territory as an immigrant from Western Europe. Besides having had the pleasure of being an adult mentor for the Gender Generations Project, Christopher has also been involved with several community organizations in Vancouver, where they have worked to improve access and services for queer and trans folks. Christopher is currently doing research on the cultural and social history of transgender artists. In his spare time, they attempt to finish the various novels he has started writing.

Danny Charles is a young, Indigenous, female to male guy who uses he/him pronouns. He is from Victoria, British Columbia, is seventeen years old, and loves painting, working with kids, dad jokes, and puns.

David Llewelyn is a 14-year-old trans guy who uses he/him pronouns. He was born and raised in Victoria, British Columbia, and writes anything from short stories to emotionally charged persuasive essays about the failings of DC movies. In his spare time, David enjoys playing guitar, working with chain mail, and making sarcastic comments at the back of his classes. He also enjoys memorizing useless information, such as the serial number on the Starship Enterprise (which, in case you were wondering, is NCC-1701).

Dylan Ariawan is an 18-year-old artist from Nanaimo, British Columbia. He is currently studying clinical psychology and visual arts at university for his passion. His artworks are a combination of abstract realism and minimalism, and are conceptual as well as personal. He aspires to one day be able to help people in their emotional challenges through works of art.

Finn Lewis is thirteen years old. He lives in the Greater Vancouver area of British Columbia, Canada. He is passionate about art, and spends his time creating comic style, hand-drawn characters. Nearly all of Finn's characters and storylines centre around LGBTQ themes. His hope is that one day these stories might help to "normalize" LGBTQ people and eliminate the stigma attached to them.

Glynne Evans uses female pronouns but will respond to any if food is offered. She is a 74-year-old white settler who is somewhat embarrassed by her white privilege and by her delaying from the age of three until the age of sixty-six to act on her gender self-knowledge. She is heartened by the remarkably kind reception she has had from her pre- and post-transition friends and acquaintances. She is so fortunate to have had such a good reception for her own transition, especially in the context of being a privileged white settler among poorly treated Indigenous folks and other disadvantaged groups. Her main preoccupations are doing her tiny bit to mitigate climate change and helping reduce exposure to the pandemic among the most endangered. Glynne's verses in the afterword are not in the least bit autobiographical, except in the direction of the gender change.

Hope is fifteen years old and goes with the pronouns they/them/theirs. They are from Victoria, British Columbia. Hope got into writing when they were fourteen and poetry when they were fifteen. Hope has always enjoyed writing as a break from stress and anxiety. Writing has helped them through much of their life and through their high school experience.

Isaiah Hagerman is a 19-year-old man with trans experience from St. John's, Newfoundland who uses he/him pronouns. He is an avid writer and poet, and an advocate for youth. As an active and enthusiastic member of the Youth Leadership Council with Choices for Youth, he works alongside his team to break down barriers for youth. His focus is on intersectionality, and love is his work.

J. Matsui De Roo is a registered clinical counsellor, clinical supervisor, and consultant in private practice. A mixed race Japanese-Canadian, queer, non-binary settler, Matsui lives and works on the ancestral, unceded lands of the Musqueam, Squamish, and Tsleil-Waututh First Nations. Matsui's work is grounded in anti-oppression theory and practice. Areas of focus include resilience and healing from trauma, abuse and oppression; honouring intersectional queer, trans, and gender diverse identities; resisting ableism when living with chronic pain, disability, and illness; and celebrating sexual health, wellness, and pleasure.

Dr. Jake Pyne is an Assistant Professor in the School of Social Work at York University. As an advocate in Toronto's trans community for many years, Jake worked on projects to improve access to health care, housing and emergency shelter, family law justice, and support for gender independent children and trans youth. His doctoral research explored thinkable futures for trans youth and brought together transgender studies, critical disability studies, critical autism studies, fat studies, and queer of colour critiques. Jake's current research (Dis/Human Others) explores the intersection of autistic and trans life.

Jasper Ledgerwood is a 14-year-old trans writer living in Windsor, Ontario and trying his best in life. He goes by he/him pronouns, and really loves cats. He hopes that this book will raise awareness for the trans community and make the lives of trans youth a little easier.

Jaxon Steele is a 16-year-old raised in the Okanagan Valley of British Columbia. He enjoys long hikes with his dog, exploring new places, and spending time with his group of ultra queer friends. Through his writing, he hopes to reassure and affirm other trans youth while they are navigating the treacherous waters of growing up in a binary, cis-centred world.

Kate Fry is a writer and editor currently living as a white settler on the unceded lands of the Lekwungen speaking people. Her writing has appeared in several publications, including *Prism International, This Side of West, Bad Dog Review,* and *The Albatross.* She recently completed a BA with honors in English Literature from the University of Victoria. Kate co-founded the now-called Gender Generations Project in 2017 with her great friend and mentor, Lindsay Herriot.

Kyle Shaughnessy is a Two-Spirit, trans person of mixed Indigenous (Dene) and European ancestry. He is a social worker and writer originally from all over the Northwest Territories and small-town British Columbia and has been supporting trans and Two-Spirit youth and their families since the early 2000s. He has worked in the public healthcare system as a trans health advocate, LGBT2Q+ youth program coordinator, and an educator on trans and Two-Spirit wellness. Kyle has an ever-increasing appreciation for the experiences he has witnessed and history he holds as a now middle-aged member of Vancouver's trans community and feels a deep honour in working alongside youth on intergenerational community projects.

Dr. Lee Airton is an Assistant Professor of Gender and Sexuality Studies in Education at Queen's University, which is situated on traditional Anishinaabe and Haudenosaunee territory in Katarokwi-Kingston, Ontario. As a teacher educator and non-binary person with they/them pronouns, Lee is proud and delighted to know the youth who are part of the GGP Project, and hopes to see some of them in teachers' college someday. From 2012–2019, Lee ran They Is My Pronoun, a Q&A-based blog about gender-neutral pronoun usage and user support with over 30,000 unique visitors in 2017 alone. Lee is also the founder of the No Big Deal Campaign, a national social media initiative that helps people show support for transgender people's right to have their pronouns used. In recognition of their advocacy work, Lee received a 2017 Youth Role Model of the Year Award from the Canadian Centre for Gender and Sexual Diversity. Lee's first book, *Gender—Your Guide: A Gender-Friendly Primer on What to Know, What to Say and What to Do in the New Gender Culture*, offers practical steps for welcoming gender diversity in all areas of everyday life, and is available from Adams Media. With Dr. Susan Woolley, they are also the editor of *Teaching About Gender Diversity: Teacher-Tested Lesson Plans for K–12 Classrooms* (Canadian Scholars' Press).

Lindsay Cavanaugh is a full-time PhD student at the Ontario Institute for Studies in Education (OISE) at the University of Toronto. She studies queer and decolonial ways of teaching and learning. Lindsay is a white settler, cisgender, and queer educator with Irish, French, and British ancestry. She taught high school learners on Lekwungen territory in (Victoria, British Columbia) and Anishinaabe territory (in a remote Oji-Cree community called North Spirit Lake First Nation, Ontario). She is passionate about supporting trans, non-binary, two-spirit, and queer educators and youth navigating K–12 schools and changing schooling systems so they are more affirming places. Lindsay volunteers with the Queering Schools Network, which is a local collective of LGBTQIA2S+ educators and youth in Victoria that emerged from her participatory master's project.

Dr. Lindsay Herriot is a full-time inclusion/special education teacher in the Greater Victoria School District. She also works at the University of Victoria in several capacities, including as an adjunct/sessional professor in the Faculty of Education and School of Child and Youth Care and as a fellow at the Centre for Studies in Religion and Society. A cisgender, bisexual, white settler, Lindsay is originally from unceded Mik'maq territory near Moncton, New Brunswick and is of Acadian, Scottish, and Anglo heritage. She now lives on unceded Lekwungen-speaking lands in Victoria, British Columbia, with her spouse and two young children.

Luna Orion. From the depths of the Fraser Valley in British Columbia, Luna Orion is a flourishing non-binary writer who is fourteen years old and goes by they/them pronouns. They love all things queer, nerdy, and musical. They hope their contributions to the GGP help to create more understanding of non-binary identities.

Lupus is a 14-year-old, trans, non-binary individual who goes by they/them pronouns. Born and raised in Alberta, Canada, they write stories in many different genres and styles; specifically, comics, short stories, fantasy, and fiction. As a young author, they have no lack of creative inspiration, and write every week. Lupus hopes this anthology of writing helps change the perspectives of other young, queer individuals, and helps them discover more about themselves.

Maisie Bodrug lives in Victoria, British Columbia. She goes by she, her, and hers. She won the Victoria Pride Society's Outwrite Ezine competition and read her winning poems at the Pride in the Word event in 2018. She has also read her poetry at the Outstages event for the Fringe festival, and her art was displayed at the UVIC Legacy art gallery for the second GGP event. She wants to study anthropology in university one day and travel to Japan.

Max is a 13-year-old transgender student, writer, and artist from Squamish, British Columbia. He has very strong views about the fact that Pluto is a planet, even if some people say it isn't [*Editor's note: it isn't* ☺]. Max advocates for transgender rights and hopes to be able to do more in the future.

Owen Miller is a 16-year-old STEM student in Victoria, British Columbia. As an openly transgender male, he works toward gender variance awareness within schools and through British Columbia legislation. He loves his family and is especially enthusiastic about chemistry. He hopes to develop and improve treatment for people in transition.☺

Samuel Busch is a 17-year-old artist of all kinds who lives in the very Western part of Canada. He/they love(s) to write poetry, stream-of-consciousness works, and multimedia art journals.

Tash McAdam is a Welsh-Canadian educator, activist, and author. They write fast-paced, plot-focused young adult fiction centring marginalized identities. More about their writing can be found at www.tashmcadam.com. They were the first mentor on board with the Gender Generations Project and it has been a life-changing and affirming experience for them. They're usually found lost in a book or their own head.

Tor Broughton is an advocate for transgender youth in the Okanagan. He is a TedX presenter, public speaker, and trans rights activist. He loves football, music, writing, and flipping. Tor is twelve years old and has been out and proud for three of those years. He loves his supportive friends and family and has always had a passion for storytelling.

Yakusinn DeBoer is a nonbinary person from Kelowna, BC, who loves to view and experience others' art. They are 18 years old and like spending their time honing their artistic skills in every medium, including digital painting, music, and writing.

Glossary

By Tash McAdam

Agender
(adj) a person who does not identify with any **gender.**

Bigender
(adj) a person who moves between "woman" and "man" gender-based behavior and
identities.

Binder
(noun) a tight-fitting item of clothing worn on the torso to give the appearance of a flat/
flatter chest.

Biological sex
(noun) a socially constructed, unfixed medical term used to refer to hormonal, chromo-
somal, and anatomical characteristics that are often used to classify a person as female
or male or **intersex.** Alternate terms include: sex, physical sex, anatomical sex, or sex
assigned/designated at birth (AFAB—assigned female at birth; AMAB—assigned
male at birth).

Cis / cisgender
(prefix / adj) *cis* is a latinate prefix meaning "on this side of." In the context of gender, it
denotes that one's sex assigned at birth and one's gender identity are aligned. The
opposite of **trans.** Pronounced /sɪs/.

Cisnormative / cisnormativity
(noun) the assumption that everyone is cisgender, and that cisgender identities and people
are therefore superior to trans identities and people.

Feminine of centre / masculine of centre
(adj) a range of terms of gender identity and gender presentation for folks who present,
understand themselves, and/or relate to others in a more feminine/masculine way.

Feminine presenting / masculine presenting
(adj) someone who expresses gender in a more feminine or masculine way; for example, in
their hairstyle, fashion, demeanour, clothing choice, or overall style.

Gender binary

(noun) the construction of gender as an either/or state. The gender binary imposes a rigid set of rules and expectations upon society, demanding that people identify solely as a "man" or "woman." The gender binary ignores the nuances of gender identity that many people experience.

Gender creative / gender expansive / gender nonconforming

(adj) people, often children, who do not conform to traditional, stereotypical, or socially expected gender roles.

Gender dysphoria

(noun) feeling that one's internal gender identity does not match one's sex assigned at birth and experiencing a range of psychological symptoms.

Gender expression

(noun) how an individual presents their gender through appearance, dress, behaviour, and/or other indicators.

Genderfluid

(adj) someone who experiences their gender dynamically. Genderfluid people may experience their gender as a mix of boy and girl, man and woman, with movement between and around these points.

Gender identity

(noun) one's internal sense of identity as masculine, feminine, both, or neither.

Genderqueer

(adj) people who do not identify with the binary of man/woman, or an umbrella term for many gender nonconforming or non-binary identities.

Genderqueer people may think of themselves as one or more of the following, and they may define these terms differently:

- combining aspects of man and woman and other identities (bigender, pangender);
- without gender or identification with a gender (genderless, agender);
- moving between and around genders (genderfluid)

Heteropatriarchy

(noun) a socio-political system of dominance in which cisgender heterosexual men are afforded privilege, favoured, and remunerated for presenting masculine traits. Women or people who display traits deemed feminine receive less societal privilege in a heteropatriarchal society.

Hormone blockers / puberty blockers

(noun) medical intervention that postpones "biological" puberty in order to alleviate the intense dysphoria that can be a result of the body going through a puberty that does not match the gender identity of the person. Hormone blockers are prescribed to pubescent youth who may or may not choose to pursue hormone replacement therapy (**HRT**) later in life. The effects of hormone blockers are temporary and reversible.

HRT / hormone replacement therapy

(noun) hormone treatment to align secondary sexual characteristics (e.g., fat distribution, hair growth) more closely with one's **gender identity**.

Intersex

(noun) someone whose hormones, chromosomes, or anatomy differ from the two expected patterns of male or female.

Non-binary

(adj) umbrella term for all genders other than female/male or woman/man. Not every non-binary person identifies as trans and not all trans people identify as non-binary.

Queer

(adj) an umbrella term used to describe **LGBTQ2S+** people and/or their community. This term originated in academia but was later utilized as hate speech. *Queer* has been reclaimed from its earlier negative use, and the term is valued for its defiance and because it can be inclusive of the entire community. Traditionally a pejorative term for people who are gay, *queer* is still disliked in some parts of the LGBTQ2S+ community. Because of its complex history, this word should only be used for self-identification or with consent (i.e., "My cousin identifies as **genderqueer.**")

Trans / transgender

(adj) *trans* is a latinate prefix meaning *across* or *changing thoroughly*. In the context of gender it denotes the lack of alignment of one's sex assigned at birth and one's gender identity. The opposite of **cis**. Although now trans/transgender is commonly used and considered most respectful, some identify with and use the term transsexual.

Transfeminine

(adj) someone assigned a male sex at birth who identifies as feminine but may not identify wholly as a woman.

Transition

(noun) the process of moving or changing from one state to another. In regards to gender identity, transition usually denotes social changes (one's name, expression, appearance) and/or medical intervention such as **HRT** or gender-affirming surgery.

Transmasculine

(adj) someone assigned a female sex at birth who identifies as masculine but may not identify wholly as a man.

Transphobia / trans-antagonism

(noun) fear, hatred, or dislike of transgender people, and/or prejudice and discrimination against them by individuals or institutions.

Two-Spirit

(adj) *Two-Spirit* (also two spirit or, occasionally, twospirited) is a modern umbrella term used by some Indigenous North Americans to describe Native people who identify as having both a masculine and a feminine spirit. The term was coined in 1990 at the Indigenous lesbian and gay international gathering in Winnipeg, and was designed to distance Indigenous people from non-Native peoples. While the word has been generally accepted, there are many traditional communities who reject the term because of its binary implications.

Resources We Love

RESOURCES AND SERVICES FOR TRANS YOUTH AND THE ADULTS WHO LOVE THEM

Believe Out Loud - Exists to represent and advocate for a belief system that unequivocally embraces, affirms and celebrates lesbian, gay, bisexual and transgender people – ultimately leading to a world without discrimination, violence and abandonment. Services, resources, and community to reconcile faith and identity available for trans youth and all who love them.
www.believeoutloud.com

Gegi.ca – A comprehensive toolkit helping you or a loved one advocate for your gender expression and gender identity human rights at school, with info specific to each Ontario school board. Relevant to other provinces and territories as well.
www.gegi.ca

Gender Creative Kids – Evidence-based resources for gender creative kids and their families, schools, and communities. All materials also available in French.
http://www.gendercreativekids.ca/

Gender Spectrum – Information to create gender-sensitive and inclusive environments for all children and teens.
http://www.genderspectrum.org/

InterACT – Advocacy, resources, and services for intersex youth and those who love them.
https://interactadvocates.org/

It Gets Better Project – Aims to uplift, empower and connect lesbian, gay, bisexual, transgender, and queer (LGBTQ+) youth around the globe. itgetsbetter.org

MOSAIC – Trans Newcomers Hub – Online community, resources, and peer support for trans newcomers to Canada.
https://www.mosaicbc.org/resources/trans/

Native Youth Sexual Health Network – Online resources and services for Two-Spirit youth and their families and caregivers.
http://www.nativeyouthsexualhealth.com/index.html

PFLAG Canada – National organization that offers peer-to-peer support striving to help all Canadians with issues of sexual orientation, gender identity and gender expression. Chapters all across Turtle Island in Canada and the United States.
https://pflagcanada.ca/

Q Chat Space – Digital LGBTQ+ centre where teens join live-chat, professionally facilitated, online support groups.
www.qchatspace.org

QMUNITY – BC's Queer, Trans and Two Spirit Resource Centre – located in Coast Salish territory in Vancouver, British Columbia.
www.qmunity.ca

Rainbow Health Ontario – Information about LGBTQ health and links to LGBTQ-friendly physical and mental health services in Ontario.
http://www.rainbowhealthontario.ca/

Sex & U – Run by the Society of Obstetricians and Gynaecologists of Canada; provides accurate, credible, and up-to-date information and education on topics related to sexual and reproductive health.
https://www.sexandu.ca/

SOGI 123 – Helps educators and parents make schools inclusive and safe for students of all sexual orientations and gender identities (SOGI).
https://www.sogieducation.org/

Trans Lifeline – Crisis line for trans and questioning people, staffed by trans-identified volunteers, 24 hours a day. 1-877-330-6366.
https://www.translifeline.org/

Trans Care BC – British Columbia-wide hub providing information about gender-affirming care and support.
http://www.phsa.ca/our-services/programs-services/trans-care-bc

Transforming Hearts Collective - Intersectional supports and resources for faith communities looking to become more LGB and trans welcoming, inclusive, and affirming. transformingheartscollective.org

Urban Native Youth Association – 2 Spirit Collective – Provides support, resources, and programming for Indigenous youth, ages fifteen to thirty, who identify as two-spirit or LGBTQ+ (lesbian, gay, bisexual, transgender, queer, gender nonconforming, along with many other identities), and for those who are questioning their sexual or gender identities.
https://unya.bc.ca/programs/2-spirit-collective/

RESEARCH INSTITUTES ABOUT TRANS YOUTH

Canada Research Chair on Transgender Children and their Families – Multidisciplinary research program rooted in trans-affirmative approaches, with children and their families. All materials and services also available in French.
jeunestransyouth.ca

Family Acceptance Project – Strength-based research about trans youth and their families, schools, religious groups, and other institutions.
http://familyproject.sfsu.edu/

Stigma and Resilience Among Vulnerable Youth Centre – Rigorous, award-winning research on how stigma, discrimination, violence, and trauma affect the health of young Canadians; identifies factors that foster youth resilience in spite of stigma.
https://www.saravyc.ubc.ca/

Trans PULSE – A community-based research project investigating the impact of social exclusion and discrimination on the health of trans people in Ontario, Canada. Findings relevant for other provinces and territories.
http://transpulseproject.ca/

Trans Youth CAN! – Multidisciplinary team of academic, clinical, service provider, and knowledge user partners studying healthcare for trans youth and effects on their families across Canada.
https://transyouthcan.ca/

PRONOUN-SPECIFIC RESOURCES

My Pronouns – Everything you ever wanted to know about pronouns.
https://www.mypronouns.org/

No Big Deal Campaign – Free posters and printables to get comfortable with pronouns.
https://www.nbdcampaign.ca/

They Is My Pronoun – Interactive guide to incorporating all-gender pronouns in everyday life.
http://www.theyismypronoun.com/

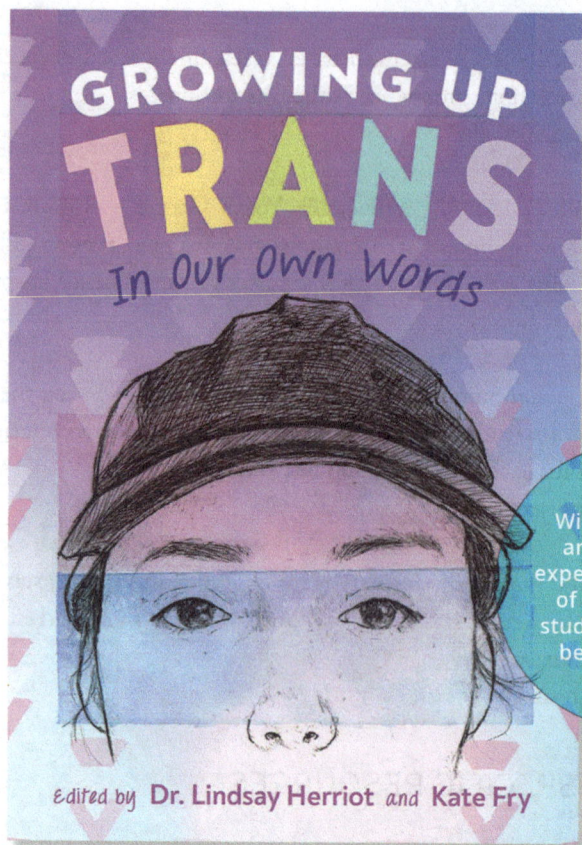